Sustainability Management
Certified Professional (SMCP)
The First Professional Accreditation

Angela Casler
California State University, Chico

Rose Luke
University of Johannesburg, South Africa

Kendall Hunt
publishing company

This edition has been printed on FSC certified post-consumer recycled paper.

Dedicated to the many pioneers who have committed their careers and livelihoods to establishing the field of sustainability management.

To our future leaders, lead with your values and enduring hope for the future.

Contents

Preface   vii

About the Authors   xi

Introduction   xiii

Chapter 1: Strategic Sustainability Management   **1**
    1.1 Introduction   1
    1.2 What Is Strategic Management?   1
    1.3 What Is Sustainability Management?   2
    1.4 Embedding Sustainability Management into Strategy   4
    1.5 Why Pursue Sustainability Management?   5
    1.6 What Is a Sustainable Organization?   7
    1.7 Holistic Management Decision Making   9
    1.8 Sustainability Management System (SMS) Policy   9
    1.9 Sustainability Terminology and Frameworks   18
    1.10 Engineering Approaches   24
    1.11 ISO 26000—Social Responsibility   26
    1.12 Summary   35
    1.13 Experiential Exercise   37

Chapter 2: Systems Thinking Approaches and Environmental Metrics   **43**
    2.1 Systems Thinking Approaches   43
    2.2 Systems Thinking and System Dynamics Approaches   46
    2.3 Achieving and Measuring Efficiency   53
    2.4 Environmental Management Metrics   54
    2.5 Emissions Management and Metrics—Carbon Footprint   70
    2.6 Summary   74
    2.7 Experiential Exercises   77

Chapter 3: Policies for Decision Making and Change Management   **91**
    3.1 Introduction   91
    3.2 Chapter Overview   92
    3.3 Sustainability Management System (SMS) Policy   93
    3.4 Environmental Management System (EMS) Policy   95
    3.5 Environmental Preferable Purchasing (EPP) Policy   100
    3.6 Summary   104
    3.7 Experiential Exercises   105

Chapter 4: Aligning Business Systems to Achieve Systemic Change   **111**
    4.1 Introduction   111
    4.2 Aligning Business Systems   111

4.3   Change Management   112
4.4   The Role of Senior Management   114
4.5   The Role of Middle-Level Management—Tactics   124
4.6   The Role of Operations Management   129
4.7   Aligning Business Systems—How Each Department Plays a Role   132
4.8   The Role of Human Resource Management   132
4.9   The Role of Equipment, Health, and Safety (EHS)   137
4.10 The Role of Facilities Management   140
4.11 The Role of Information Technology   146
4.12 The Role of Accounting and Finance   150
4.13 The Role of Marketing   152
4.14 Aligning Business Systems—Putting the Pieces Together   155
4.15 Experiential Exercises   157

Chapter 5: Supply Chain Management   **165**
5.1   Part I: Strategic Approaches   165
5.2   Part II: Operations and Terminology   173
5.3   Part III: Sourcing and Purchasing   186
5.4   Part IV: Sustainable Supply Chain Metrics   191
5.5   Summary   192
5.6   Experiential Exercises   193

Chapter 6: Certifications—Built Environment and Products   **199**
6.1   LEED/USGBC Green Associate   200
6.2   Energy Star Certification   209
6.3   WaterSense   214
6.4   NSF International   217
6.5   Green Seal   219

Chapter 7: Certifications—Triple Bottom Line Focus   **229**
7.1   Fair Trade USA   229
7.2   USDA Organic   232
7.3   Marine Stewardship Council   234
7.4   Forest Stewardship Council   243
7.5   Summary   249

Chapter 8: Communications and Sustainability Reporting   **257**
8.1   Sustainability Management Metrics—Triple Bottom Line Focus   257
8.2   Internal Communication   261
8.3   Informal External Communication   261
8.4   Formal External Communication   262
8.5   Global Reporting Initiative   263
8.6   Summary   270
8.7   Experiential Exercises   271

Conclusion   **277**

Preface

Professional certification in sustainability management is available to both experts in the field, as well as to professionals and students who would like to learn how to manage for sustainability. This study guide compiles well-respected concepts and methodologies on how to manage for sustainability. The study guide is the preparatory guide to prepare for the examination.

The certification examination questions are derived directly from this study guide. This study guide organizes key management principles and concepts to strategically position organizations to achieve long-term success. The standards and body of knowledge for the certification examination have been formed with the collaborative efforts of many respected business, government, and non-profit leaders. The vision behind creating the certification is to enable the wide dissemination of the knowledge, skills, and abilities of professionals in sustainability management so that these become management norms. Any professional, in any type of workplace setting, can strategically manage for economic performance, social responsibility, and environmental stewardship simultaneously. Professionals in any role or department can manage for sustainability. Participation from every department is essential to aligning business systems around the organization's strategy. Therefore, this certification is intended for professionals in human resource management, operations management, engineering, production, procurement, equipment, health and safety, fleet and facility management, information technology, accounting, finance, marketing, and of course sustainability and environmental management. Change management throughout the workplace can be achieved through aligning business systems to meet organizational strategies. Thereby, senior, middle-level, and front line managers align tactics to achieve long-term strategic priorities as a single system. The certification examination is written for professionals in any job role, in any workplace setting, to perfect a key skillset that enhances decision-making and process improvement.

Certification will attest to professional experience and education in the field of sustainability management and is awarded by the Sustainability Management Association (www .sustainabilityma.org) in two levels of distinction:

1. **Sustainability Management Certified Professional (SMCP)**—the premier designation reserved for professionals with significant work experience and exposure to a body of knowledge

2. **Sustainability Management Certified Associate (SMCA)**—the designation for students or professionals who wish to certify their general knowledge of sustainability management frameworks and methodologies

Background

The Sustainability Management Certified Professional (SMCP), project was forged in 2010, by a talented cross-sector group of professionals. The executives and managers from these organizations began serving as the "Design Team" to collaborate on the body of knowledge that should be tested regarding the methodologies and frameworks that were consistent across industries and sectors. Since 2010, the Design Team members have provided feedback, case study material, and peer review of the study guide.

There are many people to thank for all of their hard work. The deepest debt of gratitude belongs to the Design Team. Thank you to the Design Team members that have been heavily engaged in the founding ideas to create the Sustainability Management Certified Professional (SMCP) accreditation: Jeff Miller and Jack Harris from Pacific Living Properties, Amanda Fairley from Waste Management, Peter Perrault and Chad Lew from NetApp, Steve Rodowick from the Butte Country Recycling Facility, Jeff Trailer, Chair of the Department of Management – CSU, Chico, Ray Boykin, previous Associate Dean and Professor Emeritus College of Business – CSU, Chico, Jessica Lundberg and Tim Schultz from Lundberg Family Farms, Cheri Shastain and Mandi McKay from Sierra Nevada Brewing Company, Mike Pembroke and Pete Bonacich from California Water Services Company, Cathy Rodgers from IBM, Ann Adams from Holistic Management, Carl Peters and Jill Ortega from Recology, Michelle Visentin from Roebbelen Contracting, Linda Hermann from the City of Chico, Matt Madison from REUp Power, Julia Sabin and Bob Wagner from Smucker's Quality Beverages, Jerry Hart from CA EPA, Ryan Rogers from GreenTraks, Mike Burns from Shaw Contract Group, Jim Wagoner from Butte County Air Quality Management District, Nigel Topping from Carbon Disclosure Project, Cheryl Baldwin from GreenSeal, Robert Hrubes from Scientific Certification Systems, Dick Braak from Quadco Printing, Jenna Larson from Fair Trade USA, Mike DeCasare from Marine Stewardship Council, Mark Starik from San Francisco State University Center for Ethical and Sustainable Business, and a host of highly intelligent professors from CSU, Chico – Ray Boykin, Lee Altier, Hyunjung Kim, Jeff Trailer, Daren Otten, and Joe Greene.

Thank you for your support, encouragement, feedback, and most of all, for your great ideas!

The SMCP project is only funded by the hard work of many individuals. This project was not funded by grants or sponsorships. With the deepest gratitude, thank you to the executives who peer reviewed chapters while travelling on planes and trains, to the PhDs who worked tirelessly to provide content, to the patience of an international co-author, to dedicated and passionate student interns, and to the countless executives who listened and offered feedback and support. In particular, recognition goes to these professionals who went above and beyond:

Amanda Fairley	Jim Wagoner
Ann Adams	Joe Greene, PhD
Cathy Rodgers	Lee Altier, PhD
Cheryl Baldwin	Mark Starik, PhD
Devin Middlebrook	Michael Rehg, PhD
Greg Holman	Michelle Visentin
Hyunjung Kim, PhD	Peter Perrault
Jeff Miller	Ray Boykin, PhD
Jeff Trailer, PhD	Reka Lassu
Jenna Larson	Steve Rodowick
Michael Rehg, PhD	Wendy Brooke

Acknowledgments

The generous sponsorship of student interns from Waste Management and Pacific Living Properties made the research, project management, and event planning possible. Sponsorship enabled students to learn valuable skills in project management, research, writing, and event planning through internships. Thank you to each student intern for your dedication and passion. You have been an immense asset and your hard work is very much appreciated.

Devin Middlebrook
Shasta Chambers
Amanda Leonis
Jill Loewen
Sara Hopes
Alex Biery
Nolan Tatro
Colleen Cole
Kevin Foley
Brittany Marino
Nicholas Tedrow
Katherine Barbin

A very special thank you and debt of gratitude is owed to all of the supporters who serve on the Design Team and the organizations that support the certification.

All-Points Petroleum	Lee Altier—CSU, Chico Department of Agriculture
Butte County Air Quality Management District	Lundberg Family Farms
CA Environmental Protection Agency	Marine Stewardship Council
CA Water Services Company	Michael Rehg, CSU, Chico Department of Management
Carbon Disclosure Project	Neal Road Recycling and Waste Facility
Chabin Concepts	NetApp
CSU, Chico's Institute of Sustainable Development	Northgate Petroleum
CSU, Chico's College of Business	Pacific Living Properties, Inc.
Dennis Gawlik—U of WA Emeritus	Pepsi Co.
Evergreen 6, A PG&E Solar School	Peterson Power Systems
FAFCO	Proctor and Gamble
Fair Trade USA	Ray Boykin—CSU, Chico Department of MIS
Frito Lay	Recology
Green Hotel Association	REUp Power, Inc.
Green Seal	Roebbelen Contracting Inc.
GreenTraks	Rose Luke—University of Johannesburg
Helen Cox—CSU, Northridge	SAP
Hewlett Packard	Scientific Certification Systems
Holistic Management International	Shaw Contract Group
Hyunjung Kim—CSU, Chico Dept. of Management	Sherwin Williams
IBM	Sierra Nevada Brewing Co.
IBM Global Business	Sierra Pacific Packaging Inc.

J.M. Smucker	Smurfit Stone
Jeff Trailer—CSU, Chico Department of Management	U.S. Department of Agriculture
Joe Greene—CSU, Chico—Sustainable Manufacturing	Upper Crust Bakery
Kimpton Hotels	Waste Management
Klean Kanteen	Wendy Brooke—U of Wisconsin, Platteville

There are many organizations highlighted throughout the study guide. Thank you for your leadership, your transparent approach to public relations, and your dedication to making a difference.

On a more personal note, this project could not have been completed without the loving support of our families. This journey is one that we all walked together. We appreciate your own personal sacrifices, but more importantly, we appreciate all of the encouragement and patience.

Thank you to the Kendall Hunt Publishing, Inc. team for your enduring support and guidance.

Finally, thank you to the pioneers around the world who have shaped the field of sustainability management. Because of you, tomorrow is more important than today.

Angela Casler and Rose Luke
www.sustainabilityma.org

About the Authors

Angela Casler has a wealth of senior and middle-level management experience within industries spanning banking, international banking, heavy highway trucking, restaurant, business development, training, and sustainability management consulting. Angela is the owner of Sustainability Management Consulting, which designs strategic management plans for organizations by conducting assessments. She is also an instructor for the California State University, Chico, College of Business Department of Management. Her primary focus is on sustainability management, management, global business, and business communications. She also has the opportunity to interact with students as a faculty advisor for several student organizations. In addition, she is the Minor in Managing for Sustainability Coordinator and the Sustainable Business Partnership Director. She obtained her MBA from Cameron University and her BS in Management from the University of Maryland.

Rose Luke obtained her Business Commerce, Business Commerce Honors, and Masters of Commerce degrees at the University of Stellenbosch and the Rand Afrikaans University respectively. She is a senior researcher at the Institute of Transport and Logistics Studies (Africa) at the University of Johannesburg in South Africa. She teaches logistics and supply chain management at a postgraduate level and has been involved in the development of various courses for the logistics and supply chain industry in South and Southern Africa. Her research interests are transport, logistics, and supply chain management from a sustainability perspective.

Angela and Rose met in London, England at an Ethical Corp. conference.

Introduction

The evolution of the management discipline is well-underway. Trends in management are transforming leadership. The management discipline's evolution has progressed from governance to going beyond compliance, social responsibility to values-based leadership, the quality movement to sustainable manufacturing, and onward to the current evolution of understanding how organizations impact the environment and how actions impact society and the economy. Sustainability management is the next step in the evolution of the management discipline. It incorporates economic performance, social responsibility, and environmental stewardship—to include all three in strategy, decisions, function, and process.

Looming Trends Make the Case for Sustainability Management

It is simple—we can always do better as macro, socio, political, and economic trends loom. Generation Y and the millennial generations hold very high expectations for today's retailers and expect these retailers to be socially and economically responsible in addition to being environmental stewards. The next generation expects retailers to take responsibility for all activities that occur throughout the entire supply chain. The next generation expects the government to solve societal problems. The "green" trend is in the forefront spanning the media to the stock market. Weather patterns are shifting, ocean temperatures are rising, major storms have wreaked havoc and displaced people and ruined croplands. Commodity prices have reached record highs from rice to corn to gold, creating ripple effects across many value chains. Emerging markets want to lead Western lifestyles by driving cars, turning on the lights, and pumping water. Population growth in Asia and Africa is exponentially rising. In 2011, global population reached seven billion people on the planet, which placed an immense strain on the natural environment. Economic conditions are fragile—interest rates have been low for extended periods of time to ward off inflation; global super powers are laden with debt. Protestors are calling for the rich to pay for the poor—calling for social justice. Many consumers are living beyond their financial means. Politicians are more worried about getting re-elected than listening to their constituents; campaign funding has reached record highs—wherein mass amounts of political fundraising could easily solve many social or environmental problems. The cost of utilities will continue to grow as municipalities update antiquated infrastructure and the world searches for more sources to provide energy to meet growing demand.

Each generation faces major hurdles, yet optimism and ingenuity will always break down barriers. At this juncture, we can reimagine how we live the modern-day lifestyle. Education and commitment to long-term responsibility and integrity are the answers to sustainable growth. In combination with innovation and designing products for the environment, an exciting rejuvenation of ingenuity is being formed. Entrepreneurship is the solution to jump-start the economy. The journey is well underway and pioneers are already making the difference.

How to Become Certified

The Sustainability Management Association (SMA), invites you to collaborate with the best in class of certified sustainability managers. SMA's mission is to widely disseminate the knowledge and skillset of managing for sustainability in any type of organization as well as in any job role. The vision is to widely disseminate accepted sustainability management principles and methodologies as management norms. Join SMA in the quest to evolve the field of management with strategic alliances to achieve economic, social, and environmental performance.

Best in class professionals are already managing for economic responsibility by going above compliance, while embracing social responsibility. The next step in the evolution of management is to systemically embed environmental management into strategies. Simultaneously managing all three is well-known as Triple Bottom Line. The bottom line is that sustainability management reduces cost and risk, and creates opportunities for innovation and revenues to develop a strong brand reputation. Best in class organizations are quantifying metrics, both intrinsically and extrinsically, to report performance to stakeholders as values-based leaders. Sustainability management absolutely creates long-term value for stakeholders.

The Sustainability Management Association is the accrediting body of the Sustainability Management Certified Professional. The purpose of the certification is to award accreditation to professionals who holistically manage for economic performance, social responsibility, and environmental stewardship.

Professional certification will be designated in two separate tiers:

1. **Sustainability Management Certified Professional (SMCP)**—the premier designation reserved for professionals with significant experience and exposure to a body of knowledge
2. **Sustainability Management Certified Associate (SMCA)**—the designation for students or professionals who wish to certify their general knowledge of sustainability management frameworks and methodologies

The core competency of a SMCP is to efficiently and effectively manage human and natural resources to exceed stakeholder expectations. Certification validates a professional's knowledge, skills, and abilities in sustainability management.

Aligning business systems to achieve strategic priorities takes time and effort. Most organizations refer to sustainability management as a journey. It is a long-term journey. It is a long-term imperative. To achieve a workplace culture that manages for the Triple Bottom Line, every department must be aligned to actively participate, and this can be achieved through training and development. The SMCP study guide is an excellent "how-to" training guide to develop the skillset of managers.

The Sustainability Management Certified Professional accreditation will be similar to other managerial certifications that exist today, such as the ones in the fields of project management, supply chain management, management consulting, accounting, and the built environment.

Benefits of Certification

The SMCP certifies your understanding and retention of a body of knowledge. Education and experience will be two requirements to apply for the exam. Certification is best suited for business owners, governmental and nonprofit managers, and of course sustainability coordinators. Every employee plays a role in the journey to sustainability! Many organizations choose to certify their entire management team—from the human resources department to facilities management.

The core knowledge and skills of certified professionals are to:

- Understand and apply key sustainability methodologies, such as: Triple Bottom Line, closed loop management, life cycle assessment, life cycle costing, social responsibility, and sustainable manufacturing
- Align business systems around the organization's values
- Create policies that communicate the long-term vision of the organization
- Plan, execute, and evaluate program management to achieve desired results
- Communicate sustainable strategies to internal and external stakeholders
- Have knowledge of third-party certifications for environmentally preferable purchasing

The SMCP is the certification of a body of knowledge, such that if you are receiving accreditation, you understand major concepts such as triple bottom line, life cycle assessment, and life cycle costing as well as how to implement a sustainability strategy and how to conduct program management by measuring, tracking, evaluating, and improving processes. The certification will also attest to your knowledge of change management techniques as well as to your knowledge of building a culture of responsibility and environmental stewardship.

Certified professionals will have a competitive advantage in a field that is quickly expanding since more and more organizations are hiring formal positions of authority from entry-level to the C-suite. Therefore, with the certification, you will be a step ahead of your peers. Certification validates your knowledge and skills, so employers will also understand your skill set and abilities during the hiring process.

For employers, the SMCP can provide many benefits as well. Many design team members stated they would use it as a hiring criterion for formal positions of authority. Certified professionals can also be informal change agents within the organization to help build a culture and mindset. The number of certified managers on staff will also open new markets by differentiating your companies from the competition. The number of staff can also be another metric for sustainability reporting and a public relations tool as well. Finally, the organization could place the standard on job postings, requests for proposals, or require a SMCP in contract agreements.

Organizations can benefit in many ways by certifying the entire management team:

- Reduce risk and cost, while improving brand reputation and creating new revenue opportunities
- Establish a team that manages for sustainability as a management norm
- Establish SMCPs who can act as competent change agents
- Change management tactics to build a workplace culture
- Attract and retain the best talent
- Differentiator to recruit new hires who share similar values
- Meet continuous employee training and development requirements
- Report the number of certified professionals in financial and/or sustainability reports
- Open new markets and opportunities
- Obtain a competitive advantage

Whether the study guide is used as a how-to guide or a study tool to pass the exam, it will certainly bring value to the organization to build a culture of awareness. The competitive advantages of managing for sustainability will be reduced cost and risk, revenue growth, and brand recognition.

Please visit the Sustainability Management Association's webpage www.sustainabilityma .org for more details and information.

Chapter 1

Strategic Sustainability Management

1.1 Introduction

This chapter will define sustainability management, how it applies to strategic management, and the widely accepted frameworks and methodologies organizations use to manage for sustainability. As the certification examination is designed for frontline managers and above, many of the strategic approaches outlined in Chapter 1, may not be a function of your job description or may just be a simple review. The purpose of this chapter will focus on the strategic viewpoint to position your organization for the future. The chapter will also define how senior managers approach strategic transformation of the workplace. This chapter will be applicable to senior managers, small business owners, and will prepare middle-level and operational managers for the exam.

The role of senior management will be discussed in detail in Chapter 4—Aligning Business Systems to Achieve Systemic Change. Aligning business systems devises tactical and operational procedures and functions to meet the goals and objectives of the strategic plan and policy. Chapter 4 will also discuss change management, which designs tactics for middle-level managers and targets goals for frontline managers and departments. The chapter will also include how senior managers can be efficient and effective in transforming the organization toward sustainability management.

Chapter 1—Strategic Sustainability Management, will focus on how the organization can prepare for its future longevity as well as the valuable tools and concepts to manage for sustainability.

1.2 What Is Strategic Management?

The definition of strategic management is the function of planning, organizing, implementing, controlling, and evaluating long-term decision making for an organization. The process of strategic management creates a vision and mission, based on the organization's purpose, which can then be defined and communicated through a policy. The policy clearly communicates the purpose, vision, mission, objectives, and goals based on the values of the organization. The policy can then be achieved by devising tactics that align operational business units to meet those goals. Strategic managers play an integral role by creating an organizational culture or

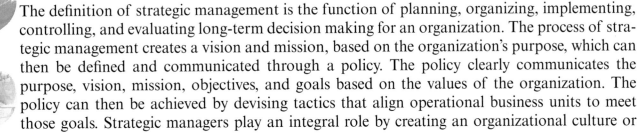

mindset based on the values, purpose, and vision of the organization and how it fits into the larger industry. Strategic management also considers the internal and external environment to position the organization for the future by planning for innovation and change. This is done by evaluating societal trends and needs, technological advances, global economies, governmental regulations, competitive environment, accessibility of raw materials, growth, and market conditions.

1.3 What Is Sustainability Management?

A widely accepted definition of sustainability management does not exist as of today. For the purpose of the exam, this section will discuss several commonly accepted definitions that will be referred to throughout the study guide:

- The word "sustainability" in the private sector means longevity.
- The term "sustainable development" refers to satisfying needs in the present without imperiling the needs of generations in the future.[1]

Organizations in both the private and public sector can devise models and systems to live in the present without jeopardizing the future. A system or process that is sustainable can be repeatedly carried out without negative environmental effects or high costs to anyone in the value chain.[2]

Another common definition of sustainability management is that it's a strategic management approach that considers an organization's impacts on the natural environment, human resources and external stakeholders, while achieving profitable results that ensure longevity. Moreover, the Triple Bottom Line (TBL), coined by John Elkington, defines sustainability management based on accounting terminology as the ability to manage for society, environment, and the economy.[3] Organizations manage profit as the bottom line. TBL ensures that strategies integrate profit not as the sole measure of success, but also resource efficiency for people and the planet. Strategies encompass considerations based on long-term outcomes that strive for positive impacts on people, planet, and profit, which are commonly known as the three Ps (people, planet, and profit) or the three Es (social equity, environment, and economy). A healthy environment is the basis of all life on the planet. Therefore, without a healthy natural environment, neither society nor the economy can be healthy or prosperous.

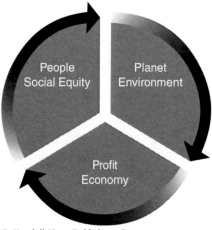

© Kendall Hunt Publishing Company

Figure 1: Triple Bottom Line

Throughout the book, when an internal organizational approach is being discussed, the three Ps of people, planet, and profit will be used. While discussing the external environment, the three Es will be widely used to discuss the impacts on the macro scale of social equity, economy, and environment.

It is important to understand the following terminology that will be referred to throughout the study guide.

1. Stakeholders
   Stakeholders are persons or entities that have a vested interest in the success of an organization. Stakeholders can be either internal or external throughout the value chain.

Internal Stakeholders	External Stakeholders
Board of Directors	Investors, creditors, and stockholders
Managers	Customers
Employees	Society
Internal auditors	Ecosystems
	Suppliers
	Regulators, auditors, and inspectors

2. Resource Efficiency
   Organizational efficiency can be achieved by minimizing wasted resources. Wasted resources include environmental aspects such as energy consumption, solid waste management, water consumption, and pollutants to air, land, or water. Wasted resources also include costs associated with paying for products twice, once as an input and again as an output. Oftentimes, organizations pay several costs for one product, for instance packaging. Packaging costs can be thought of as paying manufacturers and suppliers to ship goods to meet quality standards; the goods are separated for delivery, and the packaging is oftentimes thrown away. Thus, the second price paid is the cost for waste removal and hauling. Finally, human resources can also be a waste that is inefficient, such as spending time on inefficient processes or not having talented professionals in the right positions. Resource efficiency is a key managerial function. Organizations that are already managing for social responsibility and economic integrity, now have one more step to manage for environmental efficiency. Minimizing wasted resources is a step in the right direction. It is more important to reinvent processes that conserve inputs to ensure the organization is striving to be sustainable instead of merely less unsustainable.

3. Organizations
   Sustainability management applies to the public sector, private sector, as well as to non-profits or nongovernmental entities. Therefore, the term "organizations" will be used throughout to encompass both sectors.

Another definition of sustainability management is an organization that strives to reduce negative impacts and enhance societal benefits by creating methodologies and metrics to achieve positive contributions.[4] Measuring organizational performance is a key indicator of success. Sustainability managers measure progress and outcomes to evaluate if goals have been reached. Common metrics will be discussed in detail in Chapter 2.

The term "sustainability management" throughout the duration of the study guide will focus on managerial strategies, functions, and processes holistically encompassing people, planet, and profit (3 Ps), as well as the external environment of social equity, environment, and economy (3 Es).

1.4 Embedding Sustainability Management into Strategy

Combining the Purpose and Strategic Vision

Evaluating the organization's positive and negative impacts on social equity, environment, and economy is so important to creating a roadmap for the organization's strategy to include sustainability management as a purpose. Therefore, identifying positive impacts can be a good place to start toward understanding of the core purpose of the organization. A vision statement that clearly defines the values and purpose of the organization will help stakeholders clearly understand the future direction of the organization.

Examples of Strategic Vision Statements
A clear vision statement represents the purpose and values of an organization that communicates a clear roadmap to stakeholders.

NetApp, headquartered in Sunnyvale, CA, creates innovative products—storage systems and software that help customers around the world store, manage, protect, and retain one of their most precious corporate assets: their data. NetApp's vision statement defines a clear objective for managing environmental impacts internally and externally.

> We share in the global responsibility for protecting and preserving our environment today and for future generations by not only creating energy efficient products, but also by practicing sound environmental stewardship in all aspects of our business. Our Sustainability Program seeks to identify, drive, and raise awareness of improvements and changes in our processes, products, and operations that minimize our environmental impact; benefiting our business, our environment, and our community. Striving to be a model company in all facets of our business, we drive improved data center efficiency globally with our expertise and innovations in storage and data management solutions. We're also committed to free sharing of best practices in not only the data center and IT space, but all aspects our sustainability efforts throughout the company.[5]

Printed with permission from Peter Perrault, Green Giant, NetApp.

Another example is Waste Management, the largest waste service company in North America that is headquartered in Houston, TX. Their sustainability vision also encompasses an internal objective for employees to follow and for stakeholders to understand their core values.

> The path to a more sustainable future is about all of us who stand at the intersection of business and the environment. At Waste Management, our charge is clear. We will strive to find new and better ways to provide our customers with valued environmental solutions. We will extract more value from the materials we manage. And we

will continue to challenge ourselves to minimize our own operational footprint and improve the environment, even as we help our customers do the same.[6]

Printed with permission from Amanda Fairley, Sustainability Coordinator, Waste Management.

Pacific Living Properties, Inc. is a property management company headquartered in San Diego, CA. They have properties throughout the West Coast region of America. The company's vision statement is simply:

"We Care. Through a commitment to eco-friendly practices, our communities are committed to our BE GREEN program which actively pursues healthier environments while reducing our environmental impact."[7]

Printed with permission from Jeff Miller, CEO, Pacific Living Properties.

Agricultural leadership in healthy foods and choices for consumers has long led the path to sustainable management. Lundberg Family Farms is the largest organic rice farmer in America, which is still family owned, and is located in Richvale, CA. They are committed to stewardship and their mission statement is simple: "Lundberg Family Farms® is a mission-driven company that holds itself to a high standard in business, environmental stewardship, and the relationships it has with employees and business partners." Their core values of "integrity, respect, continuous improvement, and teamwork in the natural organic rice industry" ensure they meet stakeholder needs and respond to challenges in agriculture and soil integrity.[8] The vision statement is a pathway to creating an organizational culture. It can then be used to create a policy around the purpose, values, commitment, stewardship, and governance that the organization commits to.

Printed with permission from Tim Schultz, VP of Administration, Lundberg Family Farms.

1.5 Why Pursue Sustainability Management?

Why should sustainability become a strategic imperative to pursue? Both the social pressure from stakeholder expectations being extremely high and hard to meet, as well as the limits of finite resources, are driving the need to manage for sustainability. The carrying capacity of the planet is finite. Many resources are being consumed faster than they can be replenished. Managing natural resources makes perfect sense as does continuing to drive social responsibility. The challenge in today's environment is to meet stakeholder demands that retailers should be held accountable and responsible for all actions that occur throughout the supply chain. Emerging social trends of high expectations of business will continue to increase pressure to integrate sustainability management into strategy.

Continuous improvement of the management discipline is another important reason to pursue sustainability management. The evolution of modern day management has embraced going above compliance, integrating quality management, ethics and values, and social responsibility. The natural evolution, or next step, is to master environmental impacts and redesign the organization to meet the needs of the future.

© *Kendall Hunt Publishing Company*

Benefits of Sustainability Management

There are many benefits of pursuing sustainability management as well as risks of not being proactive.

Some of the benefits of engaging in sustainable management are as follows:

1. Reduce costs by reducing waste, energy, water, and pollution
2. Increase revenues through innovation and brand reputation
3. Proactively engaged beyond regulatory compliance
4. Opportunities to create new innovative products and services
5. Opens new markets
6. Retention of employees that have similar values
7. Protecting brand image and reputation
8. Public image enhanced
9. Reduce risks and insurance costs
10. Improve quality of life for stakeholders
11. Transform systems to respond to stakeholder pressure

Risks of Lagging

Many risks exist for organizations that do not pursue sustainability. Some risks of lagging and not leading are:

1. Risk management for pollutants
2. Obsolescent raw materials or increased expenses to operate as status quo
3. Attacks on brand image through the supply chain
4. Legal risks
5. Closed out of markets or loss of contracts
6. Reduced profits
7. Poor employee retention or recruitment
8. Delayed adaptation to change[9]

Evaluating Risk

The more hazards the organization is susceptible to, the higher the risk. To evaluate risk, it is beneficial to use a formula to guide decision making based on both current and future risk.

$$\textbf{Risk} = \textbf{Hazard} \times \textbf{Exposure}^{10}$$

The more hazards, the higher the risks. The susceptibility to exposure also increases risks. Fees and fines, public outcry, an attack on your brand image, or being closed out of markets have negative implications for organizations. Risks can be controllable or uncontrollable. Forecasting future risk will reduce exposure. Eliminating current and future hazards will reduce risk and exposure. Sustainability management reduces your risks. Period. Responsible organizations invest the funds they may have spent on fines or penalties into finding solutions or alternatives to risks.

Sustainability management is a journey. Change management does not happen overnight. Understanding the risks of not pursuing sustainability and the benefits of doing so are the reasons for change and will lead to a culture of continuous improvement. Change can then be possible once an organization understands its positive and negative impacts on society, economy, environment, and the external risks associated with the organization. (Change management will be covered in detail in Chapter 4.)

1.6 What Is a Sustainable Organization?

Sustainable organizations understand their positive and negative impacts on society, the natural environment, and the economy. They strive to optimize all three in decision making.

Sustainability managers position their organizations to optimize opportunities and defeat threats in the external environment, while implementing policies to internally manage for sustainability.

Sustainable organizations are profitable while reducing negative impacts to the natural environment and foster societal equity as an internal and external focus.

Sustainable organizations have clearly defined visions that reflect the values of environmental stewardship, social responsibility, and economic integrity. These values then pervade the organizational culture to create a mindset of sustainability that becomes systemic.

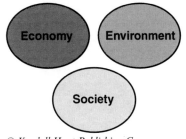

© *Kendall Hunt Publishing Company*

Sustainable organizations and managers understand that society and the economy both rely on a healthy natural environment. The three are not mutually exclusive. Without a healthy natural environment, neither society nor the economy can be sustained. Organizations in both sectors of government and business have a tremendous impact on the environment, the species that live within the ecosystem (to include humankind) and the economic impact of decisions. Therefore, the private and public sectors are not mutually exclusive as everything is interconnected.

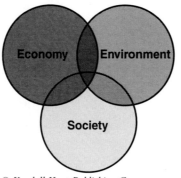

© *Kendall Hunt Publishing Company*

Senior managers can engage or partner with leaders within the government, nongovernmental agencies, and environmental leaders to work collaboratively to find solutions instead of making decisions that may have unintended consequences.

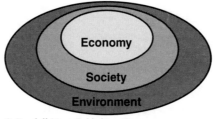

© *Kendall Hunt Publishing Company*

The existence of the human species will rely on all three entities working together to find solutions that are mutually beneficial. Neither society nor the economy can be sustained without a healthy environment.

The journey of sustainability management is not easy; it can be extremely daunting. Organizations understand that collaboration is imperative to attain strategic success. Collaborating with other sectors will achieve greater impacts than working alone, as neither sector can be successful without the other. Partnering with other companies, government, non-profits, and trade associations, all enhance the knowledge needed to envision the future.

Organizations pursue sustainability as values-based leaders. Therefore, sustainable organizations are careful not to greenwash, which is publicly touting achievements with few actions to back up claims. Sustainable organizations strive to exceed stakeholder expectations through actions and decisions within the organization.[11]

An example of government and business collaboration is the U.S. Department of Agriculture (USDA). In 2010, the California State Director of USDA Rural Development committed to an outreach program to help business succeed in rural communities through programs that would foster job creation and retention, as well as economic development, build sustainable communities, and infrastructure improvements. The outreach effort in 2010 consisted of the director personally holding consortiums to listen to local concerns from local cross-sector leaders. The USDA Rural Development responded by creating grant funding opportunities and easier access to lending programs. Tackling regional issues such as water, transportation, housing, workforce development, entrepreneurship seed funding, and green job training is complex, far-reaching, and assists many cross-industry professionals. The USDA is breaking down barriers for business and communicating well by welcoming conversations and fostering solutions.

1.7 Holistic Management Decision Making

Holistic management decision-making frameworks practice key sustainability values, principles, and initiatives directed by senior management. Having a holistic goal that articulates common ground for the Triple Bottom Line values of employers and employees then allows greater ability for each worker to contribute toward the sustainability of the company. Projects and tactics should be designed to meet the holistic values of the organization.

1.8 Sustainability Management System (SMS) Policy

Sustainability management is a journey and can be achieved by creating an organizational policy that establishes a strategic direction to manage for the future. A Sustainability Management Systems (SMS), policy also clearly communicates the organization's values, ethics and holistic management goals. An SMS policy establishes the following points.

Planning

- Vision statement that clearly communicates values and ethics to stakeholders
- Mission statement to establish organizational mindset of long-term value through Triple Bottom Line

Organizing and Tactics

- Understand external environment opportunities and threats, then develop strategies to gain competitive advantage through long-term planning
- Evaluate constraints on natural resources or raw materials facing obsolescence or future unaffordable costs
- Evaluate social responsibility impacts of all stakeholders throughout the value chain
- Evaluate industry's impact on economic responsibility
- Develop short-, medium-, and long-term goals for internal strengths and weaknesses
- Establish internal decision-making processes that focus on moving toward the Triple Bottom Line values articulated in the mission statement
- Establish partnerships within the value chain, to include suppliers, government entities, and nongovernmental agencies
- Create policies (see details in Chapter 3) to communicate strategic priorities.

Leading

- Create frameworks/terminology to talk about sustainability
- Training and development of policies and goals
- Change management techniques to benchmark progress and continuous improvement

- Create monitoring systems that measure for desired environmental, economic, and social outcomes and critical indicators for undesired or unintended outcomes
- Implement operational goals

Controlling

- Capital budget consideration for quick wins and long-term resource efficiency
- Financial expectations for long-term project management for return on investment, payback periods, and profit margins
- Define key metrics to benchmark and measure organizational TBL progress and outcomes
- Define how and when to report metrics across systems
- Establish how the organization will communicate achievements and challenges to stakeholders
- Take immediate corrective action
- Offer continuing education and development

Evaluating

- Key performance indicators to benchmark when the organization achieves a mindset of sustainability, as in evaluating when employees consider TBL as a job function while making decisions at all levels within the organizational structure
- Establish incentive and reward programs to celebrate success
- Empower employees to take action so change is driven top down as well as bottom up
- Revise policy as needed and seek continuous improvement
- Effectively communicate success and challenges to internal and external stakeholders, with a high priority focused on reporting the facts and metrics to show progress

It is important to understand that the journey will be difficult and oftentimes will delve into unknown areas outside your expertise. Partnerships between experts from academia, non-profits, or governmental agencies will be key relationships to learn more about environmental impacts in particular. For decades, businesses have already been responsibly managing social and economic responsibility; it is not unusual for a business to not understand its environmental impacts. To holistically manage the Triple Bottom Line, employee training will improve the ability to make effective decisions.

Sustainability Management System Policy

An SMS policy will provide employees with the tools to make decisions. For instance, front-line managers evaluate Materials Safety Data Sheets provided by manufacturers for hazardous materials or chemicals. The SMS will provide the information so that frontline managers not only understand the chemicals being handled by employees and customers, but will understand the environmental, health, and safety issues associated with the chemical. Employee education and training will assist managers in making procurement choices to evaluate which is a better TBL solution. Sherwin Williams' Eco Vision sustainability commitment focuses on the obligation to minimize or eliminate the impact of their products on the environment through a focus on zero liquid waste and solid waste. Since 1995, they have begun the journey to assist employees in understanding volatile organic compounds (VOC), and strive to manufacture and stock more products that are no or low VOC. Eliminating and reducing volatile chemicals has many benefits. First, low or no VOC product design provides safer working conditions for manufacturing employees. Manufacturers also discharge fewer chemicals in the waste stream. Second, it reduces exposure to customers who apply those paints or other products. When handling chemicals, exposure to chemicals can occur through contact as well as breathing off-gases released into the air. Third, low or no VOC products reduce chemical pollution to waste water treatment and landfills both in manufacturing and at end of life. The EcoVision strategy is an excellent way to communicate to external and internal stakeholders that Sherwin Williams is working toward finding solutions to high-quality products that will improve social, environmental, and economic impacts. EcoVision is a journey that creates awareness through offering customers better choices, which is a key competitive advantage for Sherwin Williams.

EcoVision strategy creates a strong brand image for stakeholders and establishes employee and consumer trust.[12] A policy and procedure crafted around a strong strategic vision clearly defines the goals and objectives of the organization.

Approach and Design of Sustainable Management System (SMS)

A sustainable strategy no longer envisions just a 5-year timeframe, but considers decisions for future generations 20+ years into the future. Many organizations use a strategic approach of backcasting, which envisions the industry's future, assesses the risks and opportunities, and then designs tactics to work toward reimaging and redesigning organizational change.[13] Backcasting is the opposite of projecting. Projections use past performance indicators to predict future outcomes. Backcasting imagines the future based on exponential growth of populations, material consumption, and technological demands on limited natural resources. Companies that backcast are able to imagine the challenges posed to society, the environment, and economic conditions. Backcasting can seem idealistic, because the future cannot be predicted precisely. It can also be difficult to convince investors to secure capital for 20+-year plans, which can hinder financing strategic goals. Therefore, it is important to ensure strategies are both feasible and viable to ensure success. Backcasting is risky and unprecise as the future is unpredictable. However, positioning the company for the future is always uncertain whether using projections or backcasting.

Sustainable strategies encompass managing for much more than profit, but managing an organization with limited resources. Sustainable strategies encompass decisions that will benefit the natural environment, stakeholders and society, and the longevity of the business and the economy. Strategic decisions should be based on solutions that encompass a balance between all three and are focused on long-term benefits. Senior management should effectively communicate future challenges to important stakeholders and support the strategic vision of the company.

Creating the SMS Policy is a process that begins with assessing what can be controlled internally plus working with partners to achieve results within the external environment to satisfy stakeholders. An organization begins by evaluating the positive and negative impacts of current and future states that it makes on the environment, economy, and society.

Phases can create roadmaps to ensure organizational success in sustainable management. Depending on organization structure and hierarchal staffing, the following phases can be implemented separately to create goals with feasible timelines:

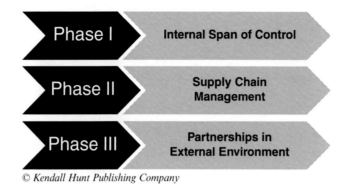

© *Kendall Hunt Publishing Company*

Or the three phases can be implemented simultaneously:

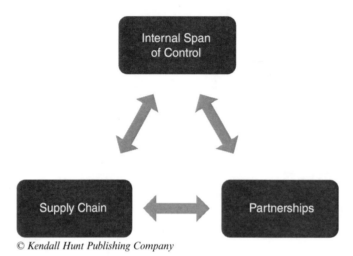

© *Kendall Hunt Publishing Company*

As a sustainability management system can be daunting, organizations should implement each phase either separately or simultaneously depending on strategic priorities.

Phase I: Internal Span of Control

Most organizations first assess factors of economic, societal, and environmental impacts that are both positive and negative to evaluate possible sustainable strategies. It is of the upmost importance to be able to identify and communicate how the organization is already managing for sustainability. Conducting an assessment of strategic priorities and operational processes on social impacts, environmental impacts, and investment into sustainability is a great place to start.

The next step would be to create a sustainable vision statement, which is a value statement that the organization can clearly communicate to stakeholders and motivate employees to exceed stakeholder expectations. Use the exercise in the back of the chapter to identify your personal values and then compare to the values of your organization. If the two match, the values you stated can be used to communicate a clear vision for what your company stands for. If they do not match, then this is a great starting point to develop a clear understanding of how the company can integrate values and morals into its vision.

Internal Managerial Control

Oftentimes sustainability management is easier to control when starting with an internal focus on process improvement. Let's use water management as an example. Water is such a precious resource that sustains all life on earth. How it is managed will be vital to the economy, environment, and all species including humankind. California Water Service Company, the third largest water company in America, is headquartered in San Jose, CA. The Chico District ensures they manage the facility by reducing energy consumption through lighting strategies, installing a solar array, using motion lighting in all areas that make sense, and ensuring ample daylighting brightly lights the facility. Sophisticated venting systems, dual-paned windows, building awnings, and shadings all continue to increase building integrity and reduce operational costs. Employee retention is high as the management team goes above and beyond to instill a sense of pride in the workforce and the employees are true stewards of water management. As you might expect from a water company, the best faucet aerators, low-flow shower heads, and low-flow toilets are installed in the building to reduce water usage. Management approaches sustainability in a manner so that employees do not have to think about their actions, as the appliances do the job for them.

External Managerial Control

Externally, California Water Service Company exceeds stakeholder expectations by assisting residential and commercial customers with water conservation. Regional water management issues are complex and require cross-sector collaboration plus responding to multiple nongovernmental agencies. Their end customers are these same stakeholders plus residential and commercial customers. Therefore, all partners have a vested interest in preserving this precious natural resource. California Water Service Company communicates to stakeholders that water conservation today will ensure water quality and abundance that withstands the population growth of tomorrow. The negative impacts of water shortages impact people, ecosystems, and businesses that rely on water. They combat negative impacts by planning 50-year projections of the water table to ensure water supply for future generations. Their strategic vision is simple: "Use Water Wisely. It's Essential."[14] As a company service, they offer educational programs for K–12 and universities, rebates for water-saving appliances, and plumbing fixtures to make conservation easy. Surprisingly, customers can have these fixtures delivered to the front door—free of charge. As the president of the company states: "Providing self-sustaining, finite natural resource, we are uniquely sensitive to the importance of protecting our environment. We are committed to being good stewards of our natural resources and are focused on 3 high-impact areas: conservation, water quality and reliability, and operational efficiency." The strategic focus on internal efficiencies and the macroeconomic and environmental impacts is a company culture at California Water Service Company.

Role of Senior Managers

It is imperative that sustainable strategies are supported by senior managers. Senior managers play an integral role in sustainability by empowering employees to clearly understand the organizational purpose and objectives that allow employees ownership of the strategy. Senior managers also play an integral role by evaluating capital budget requests to invest in short-, medium-, and long-term goals and objectives. Remember that sustainability management implementation must be feasible and viable, and oftentimes has a longer return on investment and payback periods. Pacific Living Properties standard is a payback period of seven years for expensive capital investments, such as the solar array on the headquarter buildings. Yet, other sustainable projects should be completed within three years to value and viability. Just like any other decision, sustainable investment must make business sense.

Managing and Quantifying Results

Sustainable Management Systems can be evaluated using the Triple Bottom Line (TBL) approach. Metrics and data can be collected to understand the investment already made into sustainable programs as well as to report organizational progress on target goals. Compiled data can then be communicated throughout business units to achieve systemic change and celebrate success. Tracking progress can also identify both intrinsic and extrinsic value.

In the table below, just a few examples are listed to understand some of the key metrics used for accounting TBL impacts. It is important to stress that tracking methodologies should evaluate quantifiable financial progress, such as reduced expenses and new revenue streams generation as well as measures of intrinsic value created. The following table shows some examples of TBL metrics.

Triple Bottom Line Measurement Examples

Economic Impact	Environmental Impact	Societal Impact
Healthy cash flows	Energy reduction	Create new jobs
Assets	Waste management	Employee retention rate
Debt management	Water management	Benefit packages
Expenses reduced via sustainability projects	Pollution abatement	Volunteer hours in community
New revenue streams	Urban expansion	Philanthropic contributions
Open new markets	Traffic congestion	Health and safety management
Environmental management system in place	Mass transit available	Risk management
Values-based leadership	Renewable energy produced	Compliance with employment law
Brand loyalty	Third-party certification	NGO partnerships
Exceed customer expectations	Labels and certifications	Vendor labor scorecard standards
Taxes generated for communities	Compliance with environmental law	Vendor code of ethics
Capital investment	Partnerships with government	Training and development
Research and development	NGO partnerships	New employee training
Technology investment	Distribution channels and models	Investment in green business
Data center management	Raw material reduction	Lifestyle management
Local sourcing	Recycling	Sustainable incentives

Metrics can create a clear snapshot of how the organization already manages for sustainability and how to position the organization for the future. TBL can be used as a tool for the following:

1. To identify positive impacts to TBL.
2. To establish target goals for new priorities and programs.

3. To establish key performance indicators to track progress and results.
4. To provide clear metrics to communicate to stakeholders.

The bottom line is sustainability management reduces expenses and oftentimes creates new revenue streams. As an example, to reduce pollution in fleet management, an organization invests in logistics software to manage employee travel. The impacts will reduce pollution in particulate matter and greenhouse gases (planet), reduce carbon footprint (planet), reduce fuel expense (profit), repair and maintenance on equipment (operational expense/profit), increase productivity and reduce stress for drivers (people). All of these impacts can also be quantified to track the total outcome of the sustainable management system. If logistics software reduces mileage by 10,000 miles per year for a car rental fleet using unleaded gasoline vehicles, the following metrics could be quantified for extrinsic and intrinsic value.

Annual TBL Impact of Logistics Improvement

Economic	Valuation	Environment	Valuation	Societal	Valuation
Reduced fuel	10,000 miles/23 mpg × \$3.03 = (\$1,317)	Carbon footprint	10000/23mpg × 19.56 lbs. CO_2E/1000 = 8.5 lbs. CO_2E	Travel expense reduced	10,000 × .55 per mile = (\$550)
Software expense	\$600			Increased productivity	10,000/60 mph = 166 hours × \$15 per hour = (\$2,500)
Repair and maintenance reduction	(\$600)	Less demand for gasoline	434 gallons reduced	Increased retention rate	+2.5%
Project outcome— reduced expenses	(\$4967) – \$600 = (\$4,367)	Recycled tires, safely disposed of auto fluids	Total pounds recycled	Increased motivation	Intrinsic

Overall, a \$600 investment yielded an annual \$4,367 reduction in expenses for the company.

When organizations reduce costs and resources, sustainability management will become business as usual. On a larger scale, Waste Management's fleet management goal is to reduce greenhouse gas emissions by 15% and increase fuel efficiency by 15% by 2020. This lofty goal will save the company approximately \$1 billion by saving 350 million gallons of fuel and 3.5 million metric tons of greenhouse gas emissions.[15]

Managers should calculate project management outcomes and report results company-wide. Each successful project should be celebrated to continue employee motivation and drive further suggestions.

NetApp recently built a Global Dynamic Lab (GDL). NetApp's goals for sustainability and reducing data center power consumption are reflected in the innovative design and construction of the GDL. Estimated power usage effectiveness (PUE) will be 1.2, or 80% more efficient than the average data center PUE of 2.0, resulting in cost savings of \$7.3 million a year. NetApp's energy efficiency improvements will also reduce greenhouse gas emissions by 93,000 metric tons a year, which is equivalent to removing 15,400 cars from the road. These efforts earned the GDL the EPA's first ever ENERGY STAR certification for Data Centers and achieved a near perfect mark by scoring a 99/100 on the EPA's performance scale. The environmental impact to reduce energy usage, the social aspect to improve storage capacity, and economic impact saved $7.3 million creating exceptional value to the company and stakeholders.

Communicating the Vision

As a next step in creating the SMS, senior management should communicate the organizational vision and why it matters to all employees. Transparency in communicating TBL impacts assist internal employees and external stakeholders to understand why the organization is implementing a sustainable management strategy. Next, organizations can clearly communicate positive and negative impacts to employees to enlist assistance immediately on improvement. Employees can continue to increase positive impacts and begin the journey to reduce negative impacts. Bottom up suggestions and empowerment will quickly allow employees to take ownership for the strategic objectives. Quick wins, or low-hanging fruit, can spark motivation in the workplace. When employees understand that something as simple as recycling affects them directly, they feel good about waste diversion and supporting recycling companies that are remanufacturing waste materials into new products.

Employee Empowerment and Engagement

Employees should also be involved in helping the organization achieve short-, medium-, and long-range goals and objectives. Clear organizational communication modes and frequent updates will generate workplace motivation and engagement. Celebrating success and recognizing achievements will continue to bolster systemic change and create a culture of sustainability.

Recology is an employee-owned waste service company headquartered in San Francisco, CA. Recology's strategic statement is "Waste Zero." Senior managers have challenged employees to not only help their customers manage solid waste resources, but to do so internally as well. Employees generously volunteer their time in the community; the company sponsors many non-profits and community projects, and also implements new ideas such as commercial and residential compost curbside pickup, electronic waste facilities, and customer education.[16]

Senior management support of sustainable initiatives is imperative to ensure employee empowerment and motivation. Clearly communicating expectations of financial ratios and capital investment limitations will also assist employees to meet organizational expectations.

Phase I focuses on the journey to create an organizational culture or mindset of sustainability. See Chapter 4 on how to implement organizational transformation and more details on the role of managers to drive the change.

Phase II: Supply Chain Strategy

Supply chain strategies are discussed in detail in Chapter 5, Supply Chain Management. The supply chain is an imperative area of collaboration to achieve sustainability strategies. There are two separate considerations for managing the supply chain. First, is the direct supply chain the organization currently does business with. Collaboration focuses on working with vendors both downstream and upstream to achieve sustainable initiatives. Second, is the external environment of all the industry's suppliers. External collaboration also includes sharing ideas with suppliers, competitors, government entities, and nongovernmental agencies. Collaboration through supply chain management will ensure that sustainable approaches are achievable, which will ensure faster results and exceed stakeholder expectations. No entity can achieve sustainability alone. Collaborating through industries and supply chains will ensure decisions are made to exceed partner expectations and open new markets.

The Electronics Industry Citizenship Coalition (EICC) is an excellent example of how the electronics industry collaborates with suppliers with a shared "code of conduct for global electronics supply chains to improve working and environmental conditions."[17] The five focus areas of the EICC are:

1. Labor;
2. Health and Safety;
3. Environment;
4. Management System; and
5. Ethics.

The coalition assists members on the journey of organizational change and enhanced performance using a standard scorecard methodology where suppliers have one set of standards to follow. This enables suppliers to ensure they are meeting the expectations of multiple stakeholders and eases adaptation of the code of conduct. Collaborating as an industry to improve performance creates an enormous impact.

Phase III: Collaboration

No individual or entity can achieve sustainability management systems alone. Therefore, sustainable strategies require collaborative efforts with external stakeholders. Many organizations design strategic management approaches with industry competitors, government regulatory bodies, nongovernmental agencies, and utility companies. Industries can work together to achieve sustainable strategies that will be far-reaching and achieve greater TBL benefits. To preserve industry or organizational trade secrets, organizations approach collaboration with a spirit of sharing that industries can achieve solutions together and create industry-specific standards. Industry collaboration also opens new markets and creates opportunities to compete in a global economy.

Businesses can be civically engaged with governmental leaders to create regulations or solutions for the economy, society, and environment. Sustainable communities devise regional solutions to local issues. Both the private and public sector have far-reaching implications on the communities in which they make an impact. Therefore, many organizations have begun the quest of responsibility to seek solutions that enhance performance by engaging with regulators and nongovernmental entities to create a system of solutions. Collaboration is the only way to reduce the stress on resources and to continuously improve resource material efficiency and life cycle assessment. The pressures on the limited capacity of the natural environment demand action from all sectors. Thus, working together will accomplish more than working against one another. Collaboration creates strategies for long-term solutions for society, environment, and the economy.

Examples of Cross-Industry Collaboration

Many exemplary examples exist of cross-sector collaboration. Smucker's Natural Foods, Inc., based in Chico, CA, consistently collaborates with government entities on key legislative action to protect the strict requirements of the organics industry. Through the support of a Senator from Vermont, the 1990 Farm Bill created consistent credible standards for organic farming practices to ensure consumer trust and understanding of standards that can be labeled as "organic." Today, the organic market is a fast-growing sector, which creates solutions for consumers by providing healthy choices due to reduced pesticides and herbicides, soil protection and longevity, and certification that organic farming standards are being adhered to. Strict requirements helped to create consistent standards that were acceptable to a broad set of stakeholders and are well known as the third-party certification of the USDA Organic label. The management team at Smucker's has also has been appointed by the Secretary of Agriculture to serve on the National Organic Standards Board (NOSB). The NOSB serves as the liaison between the industry and the U.S. Department of Agriculture (USDA). In addition, Smucker's vice president serves as the president of the Organic Trade Association (OTA), which was formed in 1985 and was formerly known as the Organic Foods Production Association of North America. The OTA is a business association with a mission to "protect organic trade to benefit the environment, farmers, the public, and the economy" in which organic foods can enhance quality of life and protect the environment.[18] Pioneering of the standards for organic farming was a long journey, and protecting the integrity of the organic market remains a challenge today. Yet to Smucker's management team, pioneering the effort of protecting soil longevity and ensuring a supply of quality organic products is essential to the ingredients in their products and also protects the Smucker's brands. Collaboration takes an enormous amount of time and effort, but Smucker's will tirelessly contribute as an advocate for organics as it is simply the right thing to do.

The business sector does not have all the solutions. Assessing an organization's impacts on the environment, society, and economy can be a daunting process. Many organizations need assistance understanding their positive and negative impacts. Seeking consultants or experts on societal issues, such as fair labor and wages, or working with nongovernmental agencies to understand biology or chemistry are key relationships to delve further into the impacts on people, planet, and profit. When an organization has a clear snapshot of its current impacts, it can then devise a strategic roadmap to reimagine the future and redesign tactics.[19]

To conclude this section of the chapter, the journey of sustainability is a learning process that is a long-term strategic approach. Be sure to understand that sustainable management is a process and entails both internal controls and external collaboration. Establishing a policy that encompasses both internal transformation and external collaboration will create a roadmap to success. Senior management must support and drive the transformation and offer tools to managers and employees to reimagine how work is processed to meet the strategic direction desired. Senior managers also collaborate with industry competitors, regulatory officials at local, state, and national levels, and nongovernmental agencies to expand the understanding of the impacts on the environment, economy, and society.

1.9 Sustainability Terminology and Frameworks

The following section will define the basic terminology and frameworks that are most prevalently accepted for sustainability management. These frameworks and methodologies are oftentimes used cross-industry and cross-sector.

Closed Loop Systems

The typical business process map is linear from materials extraction to disposal in the landfill. Raw materials are extracted and byproducts in production are not reused. This linear process is referred to as Cradle to Grave. The problem with Cradle to Grave is throughout the supply chain, the product creates waste streams that are not reused or recycled. Finally, the end user throws the product away in a landfill. Businesses that design for obsolescence to invoke repeat purchases are oftentimes creating cycles of waste streams and valuable resources are ending up in landfills. Cradle to Grave pays to bring the materials in and then pays again to move the materials out. Thus, paying twice for the same materials is just inefficient.

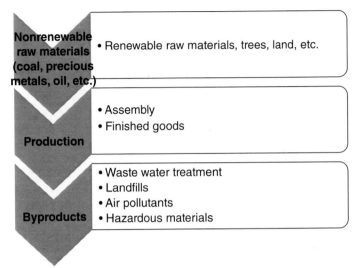

Nonrenewable raw materials (coal, precious metals, oil, etc.)
- Renewable raw materials, trees, land, etc.

Production
- Assembly
- Finished goods

Byproducts
- Waste water treatment
- Landfills
- Air pollutants
- Hazardous materials

© Kendall Hunt Publishing Company

End of life disposal to landfill wastes resources that can be reused and remanufactured into new products over and over again, such as glass, plastic, or precious metals.

Creating closed loop management systems, or Cradle to Cradle,[20] solves linear inefficiency. Closed loop management assesses wasted resources within an organization and creates new ways to reduce, reuse, remanufacture, or recycle waste in all facets of the product life cycle or supply chain. (Remember, resource efficiency means to manage all resources with minimal quantities at the lowest cost. The word "waste" does not mean garbage, but inefficiency of all resources.) Whether resources are reused internally or are to be used by another business will be unique to each industry. Closed loop systems maximize materials efficiency and resources are not wasted, organizations reduce costs, and other businesses benefit from new streams of raw materials that require fewer resources and energy to create finished goods.

An excellent closed loop system example is Lundberg Family Farms. During short grain brown rice production, whole kernels must pass strict quality control standards. The broken kernels become a byproduct. Instead of simply throwing the broken kernels away, they use the byproduct to design a new product: couscous. There are several benefits that will impact the Triple Bottom Line. First, they do not pay to have the waste hauled to landfills; instead they created a new revenue stream with a popular product. Not only that, the production of the couscous is highly efficient as it does not require the energy to process virgin kernels. In addition, the byproduct of the couscous can be made into another product of flour, thus reducing operating expenses even further. Social equity is the positive impact because couscous is a healthy food option that is organic or eco-farmed, and is gluten free. Another benefit is that consumers save time and reduce energy consumption as the couscous cooks faster than whole kernels. The positive environmental impact is that byproducts never reach the landfill, 100% of the kernels are reused to produce new products, which requires less energy in manufacturing. Thus, value is created by maximizing materials resource and enhancing environmental, societal, and economic impacts. A closed loop system manages inputs and outputs and reduces resource material waste, which saves money, creates new revenue streams, and eliminates waste streams.

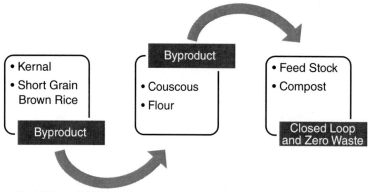

Another way to achieve closed loop management systems is to reimagine the current business process and only use what is needed in the first place to reduce byproducts in manufacturing and packaging waste. The waste generated in manufacturing, distribution, and retail inputs can be reduced to only use what is needed in the first place. Then the byproducts can be reused in production or sold to another organization as raw materials. Not only does this process create new revenue streams, it reduces landfill tipping fees, maintenance expense, pollutant cleanup or discharge, and even the risks of fees and lawsuits.

The next step is to redesign the old system toward sustainable outcomes. A product that is designed for longevity, disassembly, or repair can be used over and over again. Thus omitting the need to fill up landfills, waterways, and land with products that contain valuable resources, such as precious metals, electrical wiring, e-waste, glass, plastic, textiles, etc.

Sustainability managers use closed loop systems to identify how resources can be utilized to maximize efficiency and identify new uses for waste products. Managers then design metrics to track and record progress to measure outcomes of projects. The mantra of the three Rs to reduce, reuse, and recycle can immediately enhance organizational efficiency. First, it is important to reduce inputs to efficient levels or reduce hazardous materials with natural solutions. Second, reuse all byproducts or packaging or give materials to another company that needs it for raw materials. Finally, if all else fails, the last resort should be to recycle the material so it can be remanufactured and made into new products. Ideally, contracting with local suppliers reduces transportation pollution and costs, plus maximizes economic contributions to local companies. The goal of the three Rs is to strive toward zero waste to landfills, a framework mimicking the Total Quality Management movement's Zero Defect to the sustainability movement's Zero Waste.

An easy way to remember and implement closed loop management processes is use the six Rs:

1. Reimagine the current process
2. Redesign the process using alternative solutions
3. Reduce inputs to control outputs
4. Reuse everything to end of life
5. Rot any organic waste to compost or feed for animals
6. Recycle as a last resort

Smucker's Natural Foods boasts a 99.8% diversion rate from landfills. Since 2000, they have been the recipient of the Waste Reduction Award Program (WRAP), for exceptional sustainability management. They ensure closed loop management of all materials in the manufacturing process. They sell bailed materials for new revenue streams, such as 104 tons of cardboard, 199 tons of glass, 173 tons of metal, 40 tons of plastic, 3 tons of aluminum cans, 13 tons of office paper, and 2,680 tons of fruit pulp. They also have long-term contracts with recycling companies for hazardous materials, pallets, fruit, and tea.[21] Waste diversion is not only profitable by having systems in place to reduce waste inputs, but the system ensures output diversion as well. The outputs of recycling benefit recycling companies such as Smurfit Stone Recycling and all the buyers that purchase used materials including paper, cardboard, glass, plastics, metals, pallets, etc. When an individual or corporation decides to close the loop and recycle materials, the recycling industry creates jobs. The materials are sold to a buyer, and then transported to a remanufacturing company. Recycled materials will then be manufactured into a new finished good or packaging material. Remanufacturing goods significantly reduces energy and water to create a good from used materials rather than manufacturing virgin material.

Closed loop management systems just make good business sense. When you can create revenue streams, new jobs, and new resources for other organizations, as well as for your own, it creates a system of community economics that benefits all partners. Community economics is a methodology of collaborating to use resources efficiently. Closing the loop is not only good for your own organization, but can be a strategic imperative within a community.

Life Cycle Assessment

Life cycle assessment (LCA) measures the environmental impact of a product or service from extraction to end of life. Organizations assess inputs and outputs and design strategic, tactical, and operational goals to achieve efficiencies in energy, water, waste, and pollution management. Conservation and abatement techniques can reduce resource usage while restoring or protecting natural resources. LCA also leads to innovation and technological advances to find alternative approaches to achieve resource efficiency.

Images © 2012. Used under license from Shutterstock, Inc.

Figure 2: Life Cycle Thinking[22]

To conduct an LCA, organizations assess the products' or services' cost to the environment. The next stage is to quantify pollutants or contaminates to identify a "carbon footprint". Afterwards, data can be used to make decisions and prioritize organizational imperatives.

Once the organization knows how it impacts the environment, it can then devise strategic priorities based on the negative impacts on the natural environment. Inputs are evaluated from materials extraction, distribution, assembly, and then manufactured into finished goods. Outputs within the manufacturing process are measured and the byproducts of production are calculated as wasted or reused by the company or another company. Outputs are measured in pounds of carbon dioxide equivalents (CO_2e), including any nonrenewable energy sources used and consumed per unit. (See Chapter 2 for more on emissions metrics.)

Manufacturing companies oftentimes use the International Standards Organizations ISO 14001 for Environmental Management and ISO 14040 for Life Cycle Assessment. Organizations that are practicing these standards can also be certified by the ISO.

Triple Bottom Line Approaches

The Triple Bottom Line (TBL) framework, coined by John Elkington, manages for society, environment, and the economy (Elkington, 2000). Organizations manage profit as the bottom line. The Triple Bottom Line (TBL) ensures that strategies integrate profit not as the sole measure of success, but also resource efficiency for people and the planet.

Strategies encompass considerations based on long-term outcomes that strive for positive impacts on people, planet, and profit. Clear metrics to measure organizational outcomes will track progress and help develop goals and objectives. In accounting, professionals measure and manage outcomes on a regular basis. Sustainability management relies on quantifying capital investment, cost reductions, new revenue streams, and reduction of inputs and outputs to evaluate program outcomes. Sustainability management accounting for TBL also encompasses natural resource usage, such as megawatts of energy used, water input and discharge, solid waste weight and weight diverted, and pollutants to air, water, and land.

Managing Triple Bottom Line through Life Cycle Assessment

What gets measured gets managed. TBL is a tool that organizations use to focus strategy and also to quantify impacts. Whereas, LCA differs from TBL as it is a tool that identifies and quantifies the environmental impact of a product or process. Once those measurements have been determined through LCA, the data compiled can now be combined with social and economic metrics for TBL.

As a simple example, riding a bicycle to work will have the following fictitious TBL impacts based on LCA.

Environment	Economic	Equity
Emissions eliminated 1,038 tons of CO_2	Fuel savings per year $928	Daily exercise = healthy mind and body
Raw materials used for bike: aluminum, rubber, plastic, leather, precious metals, lightbulbs, etc.	Can be repaired and rubber tires can be recycled for $25	Use local repair shop
Further reduces driving to the gym reducing CO_2 by 538 tons	Reduce costs for gym membership	Ride bikes with friends
End of life: Zero waste—repair and reuse	Sell bike on online retail store	Give to charity at end of life

Life cycle assessment can be extended further by quantifying TBL metrics to quantify the ripple effects of a product's raw material to disposal.

Metrics and Accounting

Sustainable practices can be measured with key performance indicators. Clear metrics will assist organizations in measuring outcomes. Cost savings can immediately be attained by reducing, reusing, and recycling resources. Oftentimes, there are opportunities to create new revenue streams. Metrics are a clear indicator of organizational success and then can be used to communicate internally and externally with stakeholders to measure sustainable performance. Metrics are used to quantify LCA progress and then can be communicated with the Triple Bottom Line framework that satisfies the needs of people, planet, and profit and then determines opportunities that still exist for continuous improvement. (See Chapter 2 for sustainability metrics.)

As an example, if an organization were to use more natural daylighting within the facility, they could measure the TBL impacts with the following metrics:

Approach: Using natural daylight instead of artificial lighting for 3 hours per day.

- 3 hours x kWh = pounds of CO_2e (planet)
- 3 hours x kWh x Cost = Utility expense reduction (profit)
- 3 hours x intangible benefit = Increased productivity due to effects of natural light on workforce (people)

Continuous improvement of the lighting strategy will be considered, but daylighting was a no-cost, low-hanging fruit initiative that could be implemented quickly and have an immediate positive impact on all three realms of the TBL.

Managers that practice sustainability utilize conventional business tools and methodologies to evaluate results, such as cost benefit analysis, activity-based costing, return on investment, payback period, net present and future value, cost reductions, and new revenue generation. The finance and accounting methodologies remain the same, but some metrics have been devised to track environmental management approaches that are not yet recognized by Generally Accepted Accounting Principles (GAAP). For example, greenhouse gas (GHG) emissions and reductions are accounted for in a separate balance sheet. The reduction in GHG as a measure of carbon dioxide equivalent (CO_2e) is accounted for as an asset on the balance sheet. Emissions are accounted for as liabilities. Another example is LCA, which measures the true cost of a product through the entire life cycle. Environmental impacts are not accounted for in activity-based costing and are not currently recognized by GAAP.

Life Cycle Costing

Life Cycle Costing (LCC) is another metric tool to evaluate the cost of a product over its lifetime. Many organizations use LCC as a comparative analysis tool to make procurement and business processing decisions based on organizational values, a desire to meet stakeholder expectations, and assist employees on making decisions on inputs and outputs.

Purchasing decisions using LCC as a tool move well beyond price, quality, or warranty. LCC compares alternative products based on longevity, durability, volatile organic compounds, toxicity, locally sourced, labels and certifications by third-party auditors, social responsibility, societal impacts through the supply chain, consumer disposal, and energy and water reduction, etc.[23] Many organizations work with suppliers to reimagine the products and services that would enable them to be more sustainable. LCC is a tool that can be used to ensure inputs meet the values of the organization as well as outputs. In this case, everyone wins as innovation sparks new opportunities, the economy grows, organizations satisfy stakeholders, and solutions are created for customers.

Xerox is an excellent example of LCC. The copy machine manufacturer has created a business model that services the client by replacing parts with remanufactured parts. Innovative design in automation has now connected the copy machine to the desktop computer to enhance features such as fax, copy, scan, email, or print straight from your personal computer. Xerox then offers a service to the client to take back the old copier when a customer upgrades. They then remanufacture the parts for reuse. Thus, Xerox offers choices to customers with the option to lease or buy a product that can be repaired and then taken back at end of life. Thus, the business model offers customers an excellent LCC option by reducing negative impacts on the environment and waste to landfill, satisfying customers with a repair and service contract, creating jobs to repair parts, and creating long-term relationships with customers. Best of all, Xerox's business model is focused on creating closed loop solutions for both the company and their customers. Xerox is an excellent example of driving value through creating alternatives that reimagine business models instead of simply reducing impacts.

1.10 Engineering Approaches

Design for the Environment—Sustainable Manufacturing

Innovation is the key to sustainable manufacturing and design, which considers a healthy natural environment, society, and economy. In a global economy, global supply chains create new strains on organizational systems. Designing for the environment is a practice that will ensure longevity of raw materials and reduce waste to landfill. Engineers, managers at all levels, and entrepreneurs create products and services that reduce natural resource usage, remanufacture goods for new parts and products, and reuse byproducts from raw material extraction to finished goods. Cradle to grave, or raw material to landfill, can no longer sustain society for generations to come. Organizations pay for materials and then pay to throw them away, thus paying twice for the same material good. Designing for the environment uses every resource possible either internally or externally. Designing for the factor of X is the key to creating the solutions needed today for the future. X can simply be Zero Waste or anything that is an inefficient process or wastes resources. Designing for X is the key to sustainable manufacturing.

Engineers at Hewlett Packard (HP) frequently use Design for X as their mantra for Designing for the Environment. HP has collaborated with packaging companies to design cardboard to fit the materials and components inside a box to reduce using Styrofoam packaging or bubble wrap. This example has extraordinary ripple effects. Cardboard is oftentimes recycled by many end users. Cardboard can be remanufactured extensively and reused as new packaging materials. When packaging is designed to fit the components in a box to ensure quality control of products, the packaging now has an end of life solution for the end consumer. The challenge in redesigning packaging to fit each model of their equipment, from laptops to printers, was a large risk and investment for the company. Yet, the investment builds consumer loyalty by giving the end user the ability to make the choice to recycle. Designing for the environment is a solution for everyone in the value chain.

In the future, manufacturers will not design for recyclability or obsolescence, but instead for repair, reuse, longevity, and durability. Sustainable manufacturing will ensure a material's resource efficiency for future generations. Managing inputs and outputs will reduce expenses and also provide new revenue streams to create values-based leadership and competitive advantage.

Sustainable Manufacturing

Sustainable manufacturing is a discipline that incorporates principles of lean manufacturing with environmental stewardship. Lean manufacturing is a process that uses low-cost manufacturing techniques to produce parts with low-energy usage, just-in-time scheduling, low material usage, low scrap generation, and efficient processes. Sustainable manufacturing utilizes green materials and sustainable processes. Green materials are materials made from bio-based or recycled sources. Sustainable manufacturing processes reduce GHG emissions, waste generation, and pollution. Sustainable processes produce sustainable products with lower energy, lower greenhouse gas emissions, lower waste generation, and lower water usage more than conventional metal, plastic, and ceramic products. Sustainable manufacturing uses bio-based or recycled materials in its process. Therefore, features increase recycling of metal, plastic, paper, glass, and other materials. Sustainable manufacturing can help companies produce products with lower cost and lower environmental impact. Sustainable manufacturing incorporates LCA in the supply chain of its production operations.

California State University, Chico offers an undergraduate sustainable manufacturing major. The plastics lab is a hub of innovation for research and development. The faculty and students are researching biodegradable plastic bottles made from corn and bacteria, called polylactic acid (PLA), rather than petroleum based. At end-of-life the polylactic acid is sent to compost facilities where it is consumed by anaerobic digestion, soil bacteria, and then converts to water and CO_2.

Green chemistry minimizes the use of hazardous materials and toxic chemicals in products and processes. Pollutants are reduced or eliminated at their source. 3M designs products with little or no volatile organic compounds that are well-adapted and proven to meet customer expectations. Bioengineering is also another popular way to utilize natural systems, such as ladybugs to feast on other species of insects rather than using pesticides. Still another intriguing sustainable manufacturing methodology is called biomimicry.

Biomimicry

Nature does not foul its own nest. Designing for the environment also uses the practice of biomimicry, to learn how nature creates closed loop systems. Janinee Benyus is a leading biomimicry consultant.[24] Biomimics believe that biology has many answers for the man-made chemistry utilized prevalently today. Finding solutions existing in nature sparks innovation that can create new product design from living systems.

Innovation, inspired by nature can include smart business tactics that examine how nature finds a solution for all closed loop systems. When engineers study biology or the natural environment, such as photosynthesis, self-assembly, natural selection, or self-sustaining ecosystems, they can design a manufacturing process that mimics nature. These processes already exist in nature, such as a temperature-controlled termite mound instead of air conditioning and heating units that are less effective.[25]

Why should engineers design for biomimicry? The human species is also subject to ecology, just as every other species is. When resources are depleted faster than they can be replenished, the ecosystem will not support life. Humans can choose to live within the natural limits of the planet and thrive, or stretch the boundaries to irrevocable damage.[26] According to Benyus,[27] nature's laws and strategies include designs such as:

- Nature runs on sunlight;
- Nature uses only the energy it needs;
- Nature fits form to function;
- Nature recycles everything;
- Nature rewards cooperation
- Nature banks on diversity;
- Nature demands local expertise; and
- Nature curbs excesses from within and taps the power of limits.

Humankind can also design for closed loop systems that do not degrade natural resources but rejuvenate. Biomimics do not learn *about* nature, but learn *from* nature to understand how to live within the limits of the ecosystem.[28] Learning from nature can create inspirational new design parameters for engineers and organizations.[29]

Examples of biomimicry are prevalent in many industries. Reimagining the manufacturing process to mimic nature can create many positive TBL impacts. Eastman Kodak's research and development studied the peacock and how the pigments on the feathers reflect light to create light. Eastman Kodak then designed the organic light emitting diode (OLED) for external and internal lighting options. OLEDs do not require electricity or batteries and can be applied to backlight electronics such as cell phones, personal computer monitors, cameras, external street lighting, and indoor floor track lighting, etc. OLED lighting will eliminate battery usage and energy used from the grid for devices; thus, it eliminates volatile organic compounds and reduces greenhouse gas emissions.

Another prevalent example of biomimicry is the auto manufacturing industry. They have studied locust communication to understand infrared technology in order to develop software to detect blind spots or tailgating that improve customer safety. These are just a few examples of how manufacturers can study nature's design and mimic the process through technological advances that add value through safety and innovation to all stakeholders.

Biomimicry should not be confused with bioengineering. Biomimicry mimics how nature already solves design challenges. Bioengineering uses natural solutions to replace chemicals. A good example would be using chemically derived fertilizers vs. natural compost or worm castings.

These concepts focus on activities, processes, and reimagining the product. It is very important to remember that sustainability management captures the TBL of society, economy, and the environment. All three are interrelated and interconnected. The next section will provide more details on the major concepts of social responsibility to deepen knowledge and understanding of major frameworks and concerns regarding society.

1.11 ISO 26000—Social Responsibility

The International Organization for Standardization developed ISO 26000 to create a guide for social responsibility. Social responsibility is defined as ethical and transparent behavior of both decisions and activities that impact society and the environment.[30] Social responsibility encompasses four key points:

1. Sustainable development, which includes the health and welfare of society
2. Accounts for stakeholder expectations
3. Governance with applicable laws and international norms of behavior
4. Values and ethics are integrated systemically[31]

The basic concept of social responsibility is an organization's willingness to consider social and environmental impacts in decision making; as well as the willingness to be held accountable for those decisions.[32]

ISO 26000 is not a certification for social responsibility, but simply a guide for social responsibility.

ISO 26000 makes it clear that there is a difference between social responsibility and sustainable development. Sustainable development is defined as meeting the needs of today without sacrificing future generations' needs.[33] In contrast, the main focus of social responsibility is focused on the organization itself and its interactions with society and the environment.[34]

History of ISO

The International Organization for Standardization (ISO) is a nongovernmental organization (NGO) that produces international standards on a wide array of subjects:

- ISO 9000 Quality Management
- ISO 14040 Life Cycle Assessment
- ISO 14001 Environmental Management Standards
- ISO 146 Air Quality
- ISO 147 Water Quality
- ISO 190 Soil Quality
- ISO 22000 Food Safety and Management Systems

ISO is based in Geneva, Switzerland and has 163 international members.[35] 450 experts from 99 countries helped develop ISO 26000 over a period of five-years.[36]

Understanding Social Responsibility

Historical Background

The social responsibility movement called for treating human capital with equity or fairness. Social responsibility continues to evolve as societal trends continue to emerge. Businesses have been engaged in positively impacting employees and local communities for generations. However, ISO 26000 makes the clear distinction that social responsibility applies to all types of organizations, not just businesses.

In recent years, awareness of social responsibility has greatly increased around the world. Increasing pressure from consumers, owners, and investors is another trend calling for organizations to be more socially responsible. This is due to several trends: increased globalization, ease of mobility, and the technological advances because of the Internet.

Now more than ever, organizations and individuals can quickly see the impacts of decisions on both a local and global scale. Therefore, responding to growing pressures and expectations of behavior are more important than ever before.

Principles of Social Responsibility

Social responsibility is made up of seven general principles. The following sections of this chapter are excerpts from ISO 26000.[37]

1. Accountability
   Accountability for consequences to society, the economy, or the environment.

2. Transparency
   To be transparent an organization needs to disclose clear and sufficient information about its impacts on society and the environment. Organizations should be transparent in regards to where and why it is operating, its decision-making process, and any other operating aspects that directly relate to social responsibility. An organization does not need to publish material that is confidential or would violate a law.

3. Ethical Behavior
   Ethical Behavior dictates that an organization should behave ethically in conducting business. The activities should be based on the values of honesty, equity, and integrity.

4. Respect for Stakeholder Interests
   Organizations need to identify all stakeholders and discover their needs, and then attempt to meet those needs.

5. Respect for the Rule of Law
   No organization is above the law and every organization needs to respect and follow all laws in their area of operation.

6. Respect for International Norms of Behavior
   In some situations an organization may find a conflict between international norms and the rule of law. In these situations, the organization needs to find a balance between respect for the law while still adhering to the international norms.

7. Respect for Human Rights
   Organizations must respect human rights. Where they are not protected, they should not take advantage of them.

Recognizing Social Responsibility and Engaging Stakeholders

Recognizing Social Responsibility
There are three key relationships that an organization needs to identify in order to engage in social responsibility.

1. Relationships between the organization and society
2. Relationships between the organization and its stakeholders
3. Relationships between stakeholders and society

Clause 6 of ISO 26000[38] explains that an organization needs to be responsible for the impacts within its sphere of influence throughout the value chain. However, just because an organization has the ability to influence their value chain they do not have to do so.

Stakeholder Identification and Engagement
A critical step for an organization to implement a socially responsible policy is to identify stakeholders. In many cases, an organization may not be aware of all its stakeholders, but attempts to identify them should be made. To identify stakeholders, an organization should identify all parties that are, or could be, both positively and negatively affected by the organization's decisions. The next step is to engage those stakeholders. This can be done in a multitude of ways and has many benefits for the organization. These benefits include increased goodwill, performance review, gained knowledge of society's expectations, and improvements in an organization's social responsibility program.

Guidance on Social Responsibility: Core Subjects

The next section will provide an overview of common issues surrounding social responsibility.

Organizational Governance
This is the most critical core subject of social responsibility. Governance is a key factor in an organization's ability to achieve responsibility in regard to following the law. An organization should implement its governance structure based on the principles and core subjects of social responsibility. The governance structure will allow an organization to develop strategies, create a socially responsible environment, effectively use resources, create communication channels, and implement socially responsible practices.

Human Rights
The Universal Declaration of Human Rights was adopted by the General Assembly of the United Nations in 1948.[39] Every organization has the duty to respect human rights within its span of control or influence. Stakeholders may also express a desire for an organization to protect human rights in areas where it operates.
ISO 26000 lays out eight human rights issues:

1. Due Diligence
   An organization is responsible for identifying, addressing, and preventing any current or potential human rights impacts.

2. Human Rights Risk Situations
   An organization may be faced with situations that present greater risk in regards to human rights issues. For example some situations may involve political instability, poverty, child labor, and corruption.

3. Avoidance of Complicity
   Complicity is carrying out illegal or wrongful acts. The duty of an organization is to not do any business with another organization that violates human rights.

4. Resolving Grievances
   Even when an organization believes it is respecting all human rights, it should still have proper channels for people to report violations. An organization should do its best to fairly and quickly remedy any human rights abuses reported to them.

5. Discrimination and Vulnerable Groups
   An organization should not discriminate against anyone with whom it comes in contact with. Organizations also need to be careful when dealing with protected

classes of vulnerable groups, such as women, children, people with disabilities, migrants, or any other group of people discriminated against for any reason.

6. Civil and Political Rights
   Organizations should respect everyone's civil and political rights including the right to life, freedom, and owning property.

7. Economic, Social, and Cultural Rights—do not impede on inherent human rights. A socially responsible organization will take steps to guarantee all people have access to these rights.

8. Fundamental Principles and Rights at Work
   The International Labor Organization (ILO) laid out the basic rights people have while working, these include freedom of association, the elimination of forced or compulsory labor, the elimination of child labor, and the elimination of discrimination regarding employment and occupation.

Labor Practices

Labor practices are the policies an organization establishes regarding work norms. ISO 26000 presents five major issues regarding labor practices:

1. Employment and employment relationships

2. Conditions of work and social protection
   Organizations should provide good working conditions. This includes wages and compensation, scheduling time and breaks, holidays, disciplinary and dismissal policies, maternity leave, and welfare matters.

3. Social dialogue
   Social dialogue is the communication between government, workers, and organizations and should take into account the needs of both employers and workers.

4. Health and Safety at Work
   Organization should diligently keep workers safe and free from illness. By ensuring the health and safety of employees an organization can greatly reduce its burden on society.

5. Human Development and Training in the Workplace
   An organization should have programs, which improve the skills of its workers, in turn benefiting society as a whole.

The Environment

Every organization makes an impact on the environment. Environmental responsibility is a key factor for an organization attempting to be socially responsible. The four environmental principles of ISO 26000 are:

1. Environmental responsibility;
2. Precaution;
3. Environmental risk management; and
4. Polluter pays.

In addition, ISO 26000 identifies four key environmental issues:

1. Prevention of pollution
   Organizations need to strive to reduce pollution in all aspects of operation. This includes air, water, waste, toxic chemicals, and any other identifiable forms of pollution. To be effective an organization needs to identify, measure, record, and report sources and reduction of pollution.

2. Sustainable resource use
   Resource consumption should not exceed the rate of replenishment. Nonrenewable resources should be used at a rate lower than sustainable substitutes available. To be environmentally responsible an organization should focus on energy efficiency, water conservation, efficient use of materials, and minimizing resource of a product.

3. Climate change mitigation and adaptation
   The current state of our climate is changing and organizations should practice:
   a. Mitigation by reducing greenhouse gas emissions; and
   b. Adaptation to reduce the susceptibility of an organization to climate change.

4. Protection of the environment, biodiversity, and restoration of natural habitats
   In order to be environmentally and socially responsible organizations need to help protect the environment and restore natural habitats. In order to be successful, an organization should value and protect ecosystems and biodiversity, use land and resources in a sustainable manner, and use sound development practices.

Fair Operating Practices
Fair operating practices are ethical practices organizations use to interact with other organizations or stakeholders. ISO 26000 describes five issues relating to fair operating practices:

1. Anti-Corruption
   Corruption is the misuse of trust to make private gains. Corruption damages an organization's reputation and can result in criminal prosecution for those involved. An organization should put policies and practices in place that help to identify, eliminate, and prevent corruption.

2. Responsible political involvement
   Civic engagement is a key attribute to how organizations can positively impact public policies and society.

3. Fair Competition
   Organizations should not partake in anti-competitive practices such as price fixing or illegal activities. Fair competition is beneficial to both organizations and society. The benefits include innovation, quality, efficiency, growth, and improved processes.

4. Promoting social responsibility in the value chain
   An organization can make large impacts on society by promoting social responsibility throughout its value chain. Part of being socially responsible is having ethical procurement and distribution practices. This is made much easier if all of an organization's suppliers and buyers are socially responsible. This can be accomplished

by integrating social responsibility into the qualifications for purchasing and distribution.

5. Respect property rights
   The right to own property is an innate human right and no organization should do anything to take this away from anyone. This also includes intellectual property and knowledge of culture.

Consumer Issues

Organizations have the responsibility to its customers to give them accurate and truthful information about the products they are buying. Organizations also have the duty to make safe products and reduce the risk in using its products. Consumer issues should focus on these seven areas:

1. Fair marketing, factual and unbiased information, and fair contractual practices.
   Consumers need to be given enough factual information to make informed decisions. Organizations should not lie to or deceive consumers. Fair contractual practices should include clear language and terms, be fair, and contain sufficient information.

2. Protecting consumer's health and safety.
   Organizations have an ethical duty to design and produce products that are safe to use and clearly state how to use the product safely. It should also act quickly to remove any product on the market that is found to be dangerous.

3. Sustainable consumption.
   To promote sustainable consumption an organization needs to educate its consumers about the product, its life cycle, and environmental impact. The organization needs to design products that are meant to last and efficiently use resources. Product design should also minimize health risks and negative environmental impacts on society.

4. Consumer service, support, complaint, and dispute resolution.
   The duty of an organization to a consumer extends even after initial purchase. It is the duty of the organization to provide customer support. An efficient customer service system can increase customer satisfaction and reduce complaints.

5. Consumer data protection and privacy.
   In the digital age of the Internet, organizations need to pay special attention to how they collect, use, and protect user data. Failure to do so can tarnish an organization's reputation and expose customers to fraud and other risks. Organizations should limit data collection to critical information, let consumers know how their data will be used, and take measures to keep the data safe and secure (ISO 26000, 2010).

6. Access to essential services.
   In most cases the government is responsible for providing its people with access to essential services. However, in some situations the government is unable to do this. In these situations, organizations can fill the gaps. If an organization is involved in providing essential services they should do it justly and non-discriminately.

7. Education and awareness.
   Organizations should try to empower their customers to be well-informed through education.

Community Involvement and Development

Being involved in the community is a key aspect of both social responsibility and sustainable development. Community involvement and development builds relations within a community and then helps to improve it. Social investment is a critical tool in developing communities. This can greatly benefit an organization from improved goodwill, brand loyalty, to attracting a talented employment pool. ISO 26000 outlines seven key areas to consider enhancing community involvement:

1. Community Involvement
   A proactive approach is needed for community involvement. Organizations should strive to make their communities better off than before.

2. Education and Culture
   Education and culture are the backbone of a community. An organization should add to this by supporting continued educational programs, both formal and informal.

3. Employment creation and skills development
   Creating jobs positively contributes to society and reduces poverty. Organizations routinely also contribute to society by developing the skills of its employees.

4. Technology development and access
   The core competencies of an organization's technology knowledge can benefit local communities by promoting human resource development.

5. Wealth and income creation
   Investment in local entrepreneurship programs and development of local suppliers can contribute to wealth and income for a community. In return, an organization can directly benefit from the creation of community wealth and income by creating brand loyalty.

6. Health
   No organization should contribute to the peril of any person's health. Organizations should also contribute to health programs in communities and promote healthy lifestyles.

7. Social investment
   Investing in social causes and community needs can greatly improve the quality of life and provide volunteer activities for employees.

Guidance on Integrating Social Responsibility Throughout an Organization

Clause 7 of ISO 26000 provides organizations with guidance and key issues to help further understand and implement social responsibility. Not every issue discussed in ISO 26000 will be applicable for every organization. Therefore, it is important for an organization to determine which subjects of social responsibility are relevant.

ISO 26000 presents four ways of implementing social responsibility:

1. Due Diligence
   Due diligence is the identification of actual and potential negative social, environmental, and economic impacts of decisions and activities. The goal is to avoid

and mitigate impacts. In addition, organizations should also use due diligence to influence other organizations to be socially responsible.

2. Determining relevance and significance of core subjects and issues by analyzing activities of the current state and setting future state target goals.

3. Sphere of Influence
An organization's sphere of influence includes both internal and external relationships. These include political and economic relationships, legal authority, and influence of public opinion. Organizations should use their influence on others to encourage sustainable development and social responsibility in the external environment.

4. Establishing priorities for addressing issues
Prioritization will help organizations achieve goals much faster and solve the most pressing challenges first.

Integrating Social Responsibility

1. Raising awareness and building competency for social responsibility
To integrate social responsibility into an organization it takes commitment from everyone in the organization. This should be a top-down process with the organization's leadership creating a company culture to support social responsibility.

2. Setting direction of an organization for social responsibility
To be successful in implementing social responsibility an organization needs to create and train employees on policies and procedures based on sustainability management strategies.

3. Building into an organization's governance, systems, and procedures
Social responsibility should not be a separate priority, rather it should be integrated into the decision making process of each employee.

Enhancing Credibility Regarding Social Responsibility

Establishing and maintaining credibility is very important when it comes to social responsibility. Some ways credibility can be transparent to stakeholders are committing to stakeholder engagement, obtaining certification when applicable, and joining associations and peer organizations that promote social responsibility.

When communicating social responsibility, the more accurate and rigorous details are will enhance credibility with stakeholders.

An organization cannot control all the actions or activities outside its sphere of influence. Building relationships, partnerships, and communicating values to internal and external stakeholders will enable implementation and continuous improvement.

1.12 Summary

To review, important frameworks in sustainability management are the following:

1. Closed loop management
2. Life cycle assessment
3. Triple Bottom Line
4. Life cycle costing
5. Design for the environment
6. Sustainable manufacturing
7. Biomimicry
8. Green chemistry and bioengineering
9. ISO 26000 Social Responsibility Guide

Strategic management reimagines the organization and industry far into the future and positions the company for longevity. Considering risks and opportunities and devising strategies, structures, and programs to continuously improve economic, social, and environmental performance is just the beginning toward the journey of sustainability management.

1.13 Experiential Exercise

Values and Vision Statement

What are your personal values? To determine your vision statement based on values and ethics, it is important to understand your own values as well as the values of the organization.

Write down your personal values for each category.

Economy or Profitability	Environment	Human Resources and Community

What are the values of your organization?

Economic Impact	Environmental Impact	Societal Impact

In what ways do your personal values and the values of your organization coincide?

Formulating the Vision Statement

Brainstorm vision statements that reflect your values. Do your new ideas align with your existing vision and mission statements? If not, can you combine them or construct a new one that encompasses your values?

SAMPLE QUESTIONS

1. The definition of strategic management is the function of planning, organizing, implementing, controlling, and evaluating long-term decision making for an organization.

   A. True
   B. False

2. The term "sustainable development" refers to satisfying needs in the present without imperiling the needs of generations in the future.

   A. True
   B. False

3. Sustainable organizations and managers understand that society, the economy, and a healthy natural environment are mutually exclusive.

   A. True
   B. False

4. Sustainable organizations are careful not to greenwash, which is publicly touting achievements with little to back up claims.

   A. True
   B. False

5. Some examples of stakeholders are: customers, suppliers, society, and ecosystems.

   A. True
   B. False

6. To holistically manage the triple bottom line, it is the main responsibility of primarily top managers to know how to make decisions which will not negatively impact the environment.

   A. True
   B. False

7. No individual or entity can achieve sustainability management systems alone.

   A. True
   B. False

8. ISO 26000 is a certification for social responsibility, not simply a guide for social responsibility.

   A. True
   B. False

9. All of the following are sections of ISO 26000, except:

    A. Accountability
    B. Accessibility
    C. Transparency
    D. Ethical Behavior

10. Which of the following constitutes the set of ISO 26000 environmental principles:

    A. Polluter pays, precaution, environmental responsibility, and ethical management.
    B. Precaution, ethical management, environmental responsibility, and life cycle analysis.
    C. Environmental responsibility, social responsibility, polluter pays, and close loop systems.
    D. Environmental risk management, polluter pays, precaution, and environmental responsibility.

Answers: 1A, 2A, 3B, 4A, 5A, 6B, 7A, 8B, 9B, 10D

ENDNOTES

[1] *Our common future, Report of the world commission on environment and development.* (1987). Oxford: Oxford University Press.

[2] Senge, P, Smith, B, Kruschwitz, N, Laur, J, & Schley, S. (2008). *The necessary revolution: How individuals and organizations are working together to create a sustainable world.* New York:Doubleday Publishing Group. (p. 9).

[3] Elkington, J. (2000). *Cannibals with forks.* Oxford: Capstone Publishing.

[4] Nattrass, B. & Altomare, M. (1999). *The natural step for business: Wealth, ecology, and the evolutionary corporation.* B.C.: New Society Publishers. (p. 169).

[5] *Sustainability at NetApp.* Retrieved January 20, 2011 from: http://www.netapp.com/us/company/our-story/sustainability/

[6] *Waste management 2010 sustainability report.* (2010).Retrieved January 20, 2011 from: http://www.wm.com/sustainability/pdfs/2010_Sustainability_Report.pdf

[7] *Pacific living properties we care.* Retrieved January 20, 2011 from: http://www.pacificliving.com/green/index.php?id=1

[8] *Mission, values, and vision. Lundberg Family Farms.* Retrieved January 20, 2011 from: http://www.lundberg.com/Family/Values.aspx

[9] Hitchcock, D. & Willard, M. (2006). *The business guide to sustainability. Practical strategies and tools for organizations.* Virginia: Earthscan. (pp. 3–8).

[10] Hitchcock, D. & Willard, M. (2006). *The business guide to sustainability. Practical strategies and tools for organizations.* Virginia: Earthscan. (p. 65).

[11] Hitchcock, D. & Willard, M. (2006). *The business guide to sustainability. Practical strategies and tools for organizations.* Virginia: Earthscan. (pp. 3–8).

[12] *Caring in full color.* (2009). The Sherwin Williams 2009 Sustainability Report. Retrieved January 18, 2011 from: http://careers.sherwin-williams.com/pdf/csr/CorporateSustainability_English.pdf

[13] Nattrass, B. & Altomare, M. (1999). *The natural step for business: Wealth, ecology, and the evolutionary corporation.* B.C.: New Society Publishers. (p. 25).

[14] *Water conservation.* (2009). California Water Service Company. Retrieved January 20, 2011 from: http://www.calwater.com/conservation/index.php

[15] *Waste management 2010 sustainability report.* (2010).Retrieved January 20, 2011 from: http://www.wm.com/sustainability/pdfs/2010_Sustainability_Report.pdf

[16] *Recology. zero waste.* Retrieved on January 25, 2011 from: http://www.recology.com/index.htm

[17] *Electronics industry citizenship coalition code.* (2009). Retrieved February 8, 2011 from: http://www.eicc.info/EICC%20CODE.htm

[18] *Who we are.* (2010). Retrieved February 8, 2011 from: http://www.ota.com/about/accomplishments.html

[19] Esty, D. & Winston, A. (2009). *Green to gold: How smart companies use environmental strategy to innovate, create value, and build competitive advantage.* New Jersey: Yale University Press. (p. 127).

[20] McDonough, W. & Braungart, M. (2002). *Cradle to cradle.* New York: North Point Press.

[21] CalRecycle. (2011). Waste reduction awards program: Smucker Quality Beverages, Inc. Retrieved February 8, 2011 from:http://www.calrecycle.ca.gov/wrap/CaseStudies/Manufacture/Smucker

[22] The National Institute of Standards and Technology. (March 2, 2009). *Life cycle thinking.* Retrieved September 28, 2010 from:http://www.nist.gov/mel/msid/dpg/lifecycle.cfm

[23] Hitchcock, D. & Willard, M. (2006). *The business guide to sustainability. Practical strategies and tools for organizations.* Virginia: Earthscan. (p. 183).

[24] Benyus, J. (1997). *Biomimicry: Innovation inspired by nature.* New York: HarperCollins Publishers, Inc. (p. 2).

[25] Benyus, J. (1997). *Biomimicry: Innovation inspired by nature.* New York: HarperCollins Publishers, Inc. (p. 6).

[26] Benyus, J. (1997). *Biomimicry: Innovation inspired by nature.* New York: HarperCollins Publishers, Inc. (p. 5).

[27] Benyus, J. (1997). *Biomimicry: Innovation inspired by nature.* New York: HarperCollins Publishers, Inc. (p. 7).

[28] Benyus, J. (1997). *Biomimicry: Innovation inspired by nature.* New York: HarperCollins Publishers, Inc. (p. 9).

[29] Senge, P, Smith, B, Kruschwitz, N, Laur, J, & Schley, S. (2008). *The Necessary revolution: How individuals and organizations are working together to create a sustainable world.* New York: Doubleday Publishing Group. (p. 286).

[30] ISO 26000. *Guidance on social responsibility.* (2010). Nov. 1. ISO.org. Retrieved May 26, 2011 from: http://webstore.ansi.org/FindStandards.aspx?SearchString=26000&SearchOption=0&PageNum=0&SearchTermsArray=null%7c26000%7cnull

[31] ISO 26000. *Project overview.* (2011). ISO.org. Retrieved June 3, 2011 from: http://www.iso.org/iso/iso _catalogue/management_and_leadership_standards/social_responsibility/sr_iso26000_overview .htm#sr-7

[32] ISO 26000. *Guidance on social responsibility.* (2010). Nov. 1. ISO.org. Retrieved May 26, 2011 from: http:// webstore.ansi.org/FindStandards.aspx?SearchString=26000&SearchOption=0&PageNum=0&SearchTe rmsArray=null%7c26000%7cnull

[33] *Report of the world commission on environment and development.* (1987) Dec. 11. United Nations Department of Economic and Social Affairs. Retrieved June 5, 2011 from: http://www.un.org/documents/ga/res/42 /ares42-187.htm

[34] ISO 26000. *Guidance on social responsibility.* (2010). Nov. 1. ISO.org. Retrieved May 26, 2011 from: http:// webstore.ansi.org/FindStandards.aspx?SearchString=26000&SearchOption=0&PageNum=0&SearchTe rmsArray=null%7c26000%7cnull

[35] *About ISO.* (2011). ISO.org. Retrieved June 1, 2011 from: http://www.iso.org/iso/about.htm

[36] Fournet, E. (2011). *ISO Secretary-General's perspectives on ISO 26000.* Retrieved June 4, 2011 from: http:// www.iso.org/iso/sr_iso_26000-perspectives

[37] ISO 26000. *Guidance on social responsibility.* (2010) Nov. 1. ISO.org. Retrieved May 26, 2011 from: http:// webstore.ansi.org/FindStandards.aspx?SearchString=26000&SearchOption=0&PageNum=0&SearchTe rmsArray=null%7c26000%7cnull

[38] ISO 26000. *Guidance on social responsibility.* (2010). Nov. 1. ISO.org. Retrieved May 26, 2011 from: http:// webstore.ansi.org/FindStandards.aspx?SearchString=26000&SearchOption=0&PageNum=0&SearchTe rmsArray=null%7c26000%7cnull

[39] *Universal Declaration of Human Rights.* (1948). Dec 10. *General Assembly of the UN.* Retrieved June 6, 2011 from http://www.un.org/en/documents/udhr/index.shtml

Chapter 2

Systems Thinking Approaches and Environmental Metrics

2.1 Systems Thinking Approaches

Introduction

The first half of the chapter will focus on utilizing systems thinking as a management tool to map the current state to redesign how decisions are made. The second half of the chapter will focus on widely accepted tools to quantify only environmental metrics. (See Chapter 8 for Triple Bottom Line measurements.)

Systems thinking is a tool to quantify the input, throughput, and output of a product or process. Therefore, quantifying metrics gives the manager the data to evaluate and improve efficiencies using systems thinking. Systems thinking is an excellent management tool to manage environmental resource consumption and disposal in order to identify key areas for improvement.

Quantifying resource consumption into metrics, such as energy usage or water consumption, is the basis for understanding the organization's current state. Quantifying metrics is also a tool that managers can use to create future projections, performance indicators, and track progress on project management.

Depending on the size and complexity of your organization, use the metrics that are unique to the organization. This chapter is written for the span of small businesses to corporations, governmental agencies, as well as nongovernmental agencies (NGOs). Thus, sustainability management applies to any professional in any industry as the methodologies are the same, just the complexity will differ wildly.

Again, the second part of this chapter focuses only on environmental metrics to evaluate how to apply systems thinking. Chapter 8 will include intrinsic and extrinsic measurements of the TBL.

What gets measured gets managed. What gets measured can be reported, communicated, and celebrated. Effective change management will rely on quantifying positive and negative impacts.

Carrying Capacity of the Planet

Precious natural resources are being depleted faster than can be renewed. The carrying capacity of the planet is finite and not infinite. Carrying capacity is a limit, and pressure is put on any system when it overshoots beyond carrying capacity.[1] Overshoot is to go beyond the limits, whether accidentally or intentionally. Natural resource depletion occurs when a resource is consumed faster than it can be replenished. Daily demand for precious metals and gems, rock and stone, fossil fuels, natural gas, fresh water, and wood are stretching resource supply. Agricultural yields depend on healthy soil and topsoil management to maintain water retention. Fisheries rely on healthy fish stocks, oceanic temperatures, and healthy ecosystems. Cyclical weather patterns, oceanic temperatures, and climate change are all impacting ecosystems worldwide. The stretch on resources, plus human-made pollution of natural resources, is of major concern to sustainable development. Future generations will depend on how resources are used today.

Nonrenewable resources are limited, such as fossil fuels and coal that take millions of years to regenerate verses renewable resources, such as water and soil that are regenerative. Thereby, the planet's natural resources are limited and constrained to the output the earth can produce.

Prior to the 1970s, the United States used to be the largest oil producer in the world. Finite oil resources were drilled to depths that were easy to reach until it became too expensive or obsolete in regional areas. Since that time, America couples drilling for oil with domestic and offshore drilling, but relies on foreign suppliers as well. Imagine if Americans had recognized that the carrying capacity would soon be surpassed in the 1970s and had innovated technologies that did not rely on fossil fuels? How organizations and society use natural resources may be the biggest test to humankind in order to sustain a healthy natural environment for future generations. Are we up to the challenge? Absolutely. Innovation and technology will create the products of tomorrow to meet growing consumer demand to live a lifestyle that does not exceed the carrying capacity of the planet.

Exponential Population Growth

Can the planet sustain the current rate of consumption? The answer is no. The carrying capacity of the planet's nonrenewable resources is finite. Yet world population is growing at an exponential rate and population growth is accelerating material usage of natural resources. Exponential growth doubles over a given period of time, for example 2 then 4 then 8 then 16 and so on. Exponential decay is a negative growth rate.

The formula for exponential growth below is represented with x, r for the growth rate of a variable, and t representing time, such as 0, 2, 4, 6, 8.

$$x_t = x_0(1 + r)^t$$

Where x_0 is the value of x and time = 0.

For example, suppose a growth rate where r = 5% or 0.05, time is increased to the next increment, then x would be 1.05 or 5% larger the previous time integer.

Linear growth differs as growth occurs by the exact same amount during each consecutive time frame. Exponential growth can be further explained using the example of compound interest versus simple interest. A savings account or investment will exponentially grow over time due to compounded interest, whereas simple interest would not.

To compensate for population doubling every 35–50 years, there is an imperative to reimagine how natural resources are used to prevent overshoot without irreversible damage.

Can the planet withstand exponential growth of the human species? During October 2011, global population reached seven billion people. Roughly every 12 years, one billion more people are added to the planet. In 1974, there were four billion, in 1987—five billion, in

1999—six billion, and in 2011—seven billion. If this trend continues, there may be 10 billion people populating the planet before 2050.

Population growth is determined by the number of births minus number of deaths. Higher birth rates in Asia and Africa will continue growth. While in western nations, birth rates will hold steady and then begin to decline. The mortality rate in Western nations is declining because people are living longer due to advances in education, science, medication, and health care, etc. Population growth will continue to strain all natural resources on the planet. Strategic planning is an imperative to prepare for population growth. Growing enough food will rely on arable land and water to feed a growing global population. Smart planning will be a necessity and the entrepreneurial and political challenge of this generation.

Overshoot and Collapse

Humankind has already overshot the carrying capacity of the planet, according to *Limits to Growth—The 30-Year Update.*[2] Economic and political systems are slow to adjust to the limit as most people's behavior remains unchanged due to a lack of an emergency environmental crisis. Let's use oil as an example to demonstrate delay. Delay is caused due to either not recognizing the need or perceiving that there is not an emergency situation that requires immediate action. Since the 1970s, America has been in a state of delay to react to oil depletion because gasoline is prevalent in reserve stocks and from global suppliers. There is no sense of urgency, except for the uncertainty of fluctuating oil prices. Periods of delay will create even more extreme detriments and unforeseen constraints in the future. According to the authors of *Limits to Growth*, humankind will approach carrying capacity in four ways:

1. Grow without interruption as limits are far off in the future
2. Level off below the carrying capacity
3. Overshoot without doing permanent damage
4. Overshoot with severe and irreparable damage[3]

The authors define overshoot as to go too far accidentally. Overshoot is caused by a combination of 1) rapid change, 2) limits or barriers, and 3) errors or delays in perceiving or taking action.[4] Growing population and consumption of finite resources has already surpassed the carrying capacity of the planet, so numbers 1 and 2 are no longer possible. Humankind has a choice to overshoot without permanent damage or to suffer the long-term consequences of irreparable damage. The challenge to each person and every organization is to no longer delay and address overshoot so humankind does not cause irreparable damage and collapse.

Collapse occurs before natural resources are depleted. It can also occur due to prices being too expensive or energy intensive to sustain quantity and quality of materials.[5] There is a period of delay in time for the collapse to be recognizable. Growth must be sustainable in order to avoid collapse. Society has a responsibility to future generations. It is irresponsible to leave future generations burdened with environmental degradation, social discontent, and economic debt.

Sustainable growth is an oxymoron.[6] Growth is celebrated in Western economies as a measure of success, but growth requires the usage of materials and capital. Finite resources are being consumed faster than supply. Socially, success for many western cultures oftentimes comes down to high earnings or material possessions. At work, revenue generation and growth is a performance indicator tied to compensation and promotion. Western culture demands material output at a rate that overshoots the planets carrying capacity. Thereby, the earth cannot produce enough natural resources to support limitless material usage and economic growth. Can growth occur with materials consumption not exceeding replenished supply? Will Western culture ever accept that "sustainable growth" is an oxymoron?[7] Will there ever be a society that rewards stewardship more than profitability? If society continues to delay because growth is a measure of success, a collapse will sacrifice the quality of life of current and future generations.

The wealthier a society or person is, the larger the impact on the environment. The more a culture is technologically advanced, the higher the strain on natural resources increases. This is due to material goods being consumed at a higher rate by affluent consumers more so than those living in poverty. The equipment needed to produce goods to meet equipment demand also outpaces the carrying capacity of the planet. The more affluent a society is, the more people consume products and services. An important formula used to assess the impact on natural resource depletion is:

Impact = Populations × Affluence × Technology.[8]

1. Affluence offers the ability to consume more
2. The population size of a society impacts the rate of consumption
3. Affluent societies consume technology devices and equipment at a higher rate, thus making a larger impact than an impoverished country will
4. Emerging economies are experiencing population growth, consumption of technology, and greater wealth
5. Cumulatively the result will create a profound impact on materials and societal quality of life

Reimagining the System

The challenge of overshoot can be addressed by first reimagining everyday lifestyles and behavioral choices both at home and within the workplace. Material resource depletion is a global issue evidenced with regional consequences. *The goal is not to be less wasteful.* Instead, the goal is to reimagine lifestyle and work environments. Future challenges to all organizations will be higher costs for materials as they are more difficult to mine or costly to produce; or resources are located in hard to reach or hostile areas on the planet. Envisioning the risks and threats posed today is a necessity to reimagine and redesign the way work is conducted to include processes and flows. Positioning the organization for the future is the goal.

2.2 Systems Thinking and System Dynamics Approaches

Positioning the organization for the future requires a new way of thinking. Strategic thinking identifies areas of risk and opportunity. Society and the economy are dependent on a healthy natural environment. Without a healthy environment, the planet will not sustain a healthy society, nor will society be able to create a robust economy. Each realm of the TBL is interconnected dynamically in a complex system.

Systems thinking and system dynamics are helpful management tools. Systems thinking is a mapping tool to aid in decision making. System dynamics uses software to create the map and then conduct experiments, perhaps to simulate the outcome of a decision.[9] Systems thinking maps out inputs, throughput, and output to see the system as it exists today. Systems thinking enables us to identify complex causal loops within the system and find effective leverage points. By exploring inputs and outputs and how those interactions will change the outcome over time, it then enables behavioral changes.

Systems thinking reimagines how to utilize materials and resources by managing inputs and outputs and how those interactions will change an outcome over time. System dynamics takes this one step further and uses computer simulation models to experiment with potential solutions.

What Is a System?

A system is the interconnected elements that are organized to achieve a purpose.[10] A system is made up of three components:

1. A purpose or function
2. Elements or stocks
3. Interconnections: how all elements are interconnected around the purpose[11]

The purpose of a soccer team is to win games. The elements are the materials used: coaches, players, fans, stadium, and so forth. Each element also has a purpose. The coaching staff's purpose is to manage the team's strategy and improve the team's abilities. The stadium gives the players a place to play. The fans enjoy the players and create revenue for the stadium. The elements are all interconnected around the purpose of winning the game.

Every finished good has a source that comes from a natural resource. Understanding materials usage of sources is an important first step to understanding how each process or action impacts the economy, environment, or society. Next, those impacts are all interconnected to the elements that make up the system in order to achieve a finished good or other purpose.

Feedback Loops

Every action has a reaction. In system dynamics, the causal loop is referred to as a "feedback loop". There are two types of feedback loops:

1. Reinforcing (+); or
2. Balancing (-).

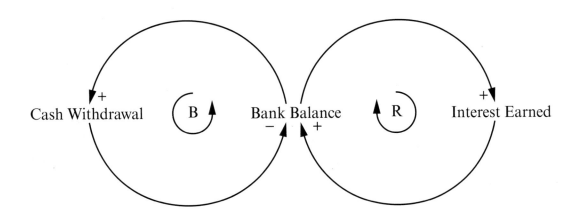

Feedback loops occur over time and the effects may be delayed. In the example above, interest earned is delayed over time from the net present value to future value. Reinforcing feedback loops generate either exponential growth or decline in the system. Balancing loops are stabilizing or goal seeking. Balancing feedback loops stop the reinforcing reaction. In the example above, the long-term goal is to invest cash into a bank account. Compound interest will exponentially grow over time in the account. If the customer withdraws from the account, the balancing feedback loop will diminish the returns of the interest and or the original investment.

Feedback loops are changes to stocks that affect the flows which change the interconnections of a system.[12] Feedback loops are either positive or negative, but the result is not a positive or negative result or outcome. The positive feedback loop represents self-reinforcing (R) to show exponential growth or decline. While negative feedback loops offset or reverse the direction of the change to strive to pull the system into equilibrium (B).[13] Jay Forrester, the founder of System Dynamics, ascertains that reinforcing loops that accelerate growth are unsustainable; while balancing feedback loops seek equilibrium.[14] Equilibrium is oftentimes not easy to achieve.

In a complex system, there are oftentimes solutions to resolve problems which generate short-term negative effects, which will deter people from implementing the solution. On the other hand, maximization of short-term profit can lead to the collapse of the whole system.

Tragedy of the Commons

Peter Senge's *Tragedy of the Commons* system dynamics model demonstrates how resources are used for individual gain or short-term profit. In the diagram below, the reinforcing feedback loops show how Individual A and B use material resources faster than they can be replenished and thus overshoot the carrying capacity of the resource's limit.

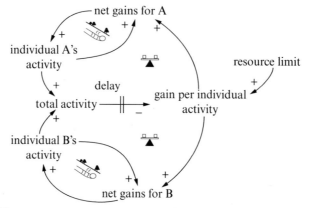

Tragedy of the Commons[15]

As a result of seeking short term gains, neither person A nor B recognizes the period of delay; then the resource depletes. Persons A and B experience diminishing returns, and end up depleting the resource even further to maximize profitability before obsolescence. "Nature does not foul her own nest," a famous saying, is a reminder to the human species that we are interconnected to the other elements in nature. Humankind foul's its own nest, such as litter, emissions, waste to landfill, sewage, etc.

In order to create long-term solutions to sustain a healthy environment, which every being relies upon, the first action an organization must take is to examine the root of the problem. The next step is to decide how to solve the problem. Deeply examining the interconnections of the problem will provide the details of why we need to solve the root problem. System dynamics is one tool to display all the puzzle pieces to see the big picture in order to find the root cause of the problem. The models also create a visual map to be able to make decisions for future plans.

Finding the Root Cause of the Problem with Systems Thinking

Evaluate the Sources and Sinks of the System

In order to create long-term solutions to sustain a healthy environment, which every species relies upon, the first action an organization should take is to examine the root problem of a system. In order to do that, each system must be identified. In order to visualize the systems thinking process, office copy paper will be used as an example.

Identify the separate systems first that make up the whole system. For instance, a tree is a system all in itself with elements, such as roots, branches, and leaves that interact with water (a separate system) and air (a separate system).

Next it is important to evaluate sources and sinks. Sources are raw materials, and also elements of the system; whereas sinks are the pollutants or waste products that are disposed of into the land, water, or air.

Office copy paper is used in so many work processes. The original source is a tree. The source is the raw material. The paper can then be disposed of or recycled. The disposal process leads to the "sink". Office paper sinks could include: disposed in landfill, littered into the natural environment, or recycled. Sources and sinks are the physical limits to growth. If trees were scarce, virgin paper would rise in cost due to scarcity or access.

The next step is to evaluate the interconnections of the elements. The elements in this case are the trees themselves plus the other separate systems that make up the processing of the paper. To evaluate one element at a time, the interconnections of the tree are the physical flows of water and chemical reactions that spur growth, protect from dehydration, or signal the shedding of leaves. The life cycle of a tree is a dynamic system to produce oxygen and sequester carbon dioxide. All of these systems are dynamic. The tree becomes the source for the paper product. The tree is the element—a tangible item as the source for the finished good: the paper.

The other elements in production are water, energy, labor, and machinery. These elements interact with other systems throughout the supply chain from raw material to retail; those systems include the elements needed for extraction, transportation, warehousing, and shelf space. All of these systems are separate yet interconnected with the purpose to extract a natural resource to sell a material good.

In system dynamics, the system in which office paper is manufactured into a finished good can be illustrated with the following stock and flow diagram:

© *Kendall Hunt Publishing Company*

- Stocks rise as inflows exceed outflow
- Stocks fall as outflows exceed inflow
- Dynamic equilibrium is achieved if inflow = outflow

Stocks are accumulations and are oftentimes used as the basis to make a decision.[16] For example, in the case of paper, the stock would be the number of trees used in production.

Controlling the flows, or volume of input and output, will change stock levels. Stocks change slowly as the flows are adjusted, which is another reason for delayed reaction as change takes time. Dynamic equilibrium of stocks can be achieved if inputs are optimized with output.

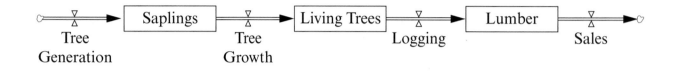

Extracting too many trees would create a surplus if demand were not as high. Therefore, inputs of sources need to be managed based on demand. The output of the transformation should be optimized to use inputs to the fullest capacity. Managing flows is essential to achieving throughput efficiencies of stocks. Maximizing profits can create short-term gains, but may also create long-term consequences to sources and sinks.

The next step is to determine the root cause of the problem by evaluating sources and sinks. Deeply examining the interconnections of the elements will provide the details of why the problem needs to be solved.[17] It is important to evaluate the following questions to get a clear picture of the current state:

- How could interconnections of flows be changed to create a better system?
- How could a system be designed to protect and rejuvenate raw material sources?
- How could a system be designed to reduce sinks? Sinks are the solid waste and byproducts of the flows and the location where it all ends up, such as in a river, the landfill, or emissions to air.

Sources would include any of the following choices for the paper manufacturer:

- **Forest:** is the tree from a sustainably farmed forest or what is the distance from source?
- **Tree farm specifically to grow trees for consumption:** is this a long-term reliable source?
- **Recycled paper:** is it affordable to purchase recycled content to remanufacture?

Sinks would include disposal and where pollutants end up:

- Processing chemicals–identify chemicals in processing and any harmful impacts to workers.
- Pulp byproduct–how is the byproduct disposed of or reused?
- Waste water treatment–is it cost effective to treat own waste stream?
- Paper is disposed by consumers into landfills.
- Paper is disposed by consumers by littering in natural ecosystems.
- Paper is recycled by the end user.

Deeply examining the interconnections of the elements will provide the details of why the problem needs to be solved.[18]

For each problem identified, draw causal loops to understand the current state. Next manipulate the feedback loops to experiment and map out the desired outcome by balancing reinforcing causal loops. Recall that a balancing feedback loop seeks equilibrium by stopping the reinforcing reaction that creates exponential growth or decline.

Let's say the office paper manufacturer compared the price of each source with the following outcomes:

- Forest is the cheapest option
- Tree farm is 500 miles further away than forest and more expensive for transportation
- Too expensive to purchase the equipment to remanufacture post-consumer recycled content paper

Feedback loops could be designed to balance the reaction into equilibrium. As an example, the manufacturer can purchase sustainably managed forest wood that is certified through either the Forest Stewardship Council or the Sustainable Forestry Initiative to mitigate the problem of clear cutting and deforestation. Certified forest managers do not clear cut, they usually extract 1 in every 5 trees, and plant saplings to rejuvenate growth. (See Chapter 7 for more on forestry certification.)

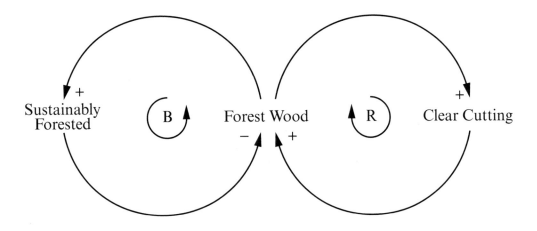

The paper and cardboard industries have been working on long-term solutions since the 1980s to create solutions to the problem of clear cutting hillsides or deforestation of rainforests. The system has been altered to achieve long-term solutions to clear cutting forests or rainforest destruction by changing the interconnections and feedback loops. Significant changes to stocks of the paper industry's problems were restorative, yet did create the decimation of the logging industry in the United States of America. It is important to understand that there will be consequences and constraints to short-term profit while creating long-term solutions. It is also important to understand while solving problems to the current system, unintended consequences will also occur. Looking at the entire system will help to ensure solutions not only solve the challenge at hand, but also do not create even worse problems.

By building a system dynamics computer simulation model, the model can further explore ways to intervene with the interconnections of elements and resolve the problems within a system. System dynamics is also a tool to visualize separate systems and how they are interconnected.

For example, we can experiment with simulation models to further understand how the system of office paper was reformed for long-term preservation of forestry and rainforests.

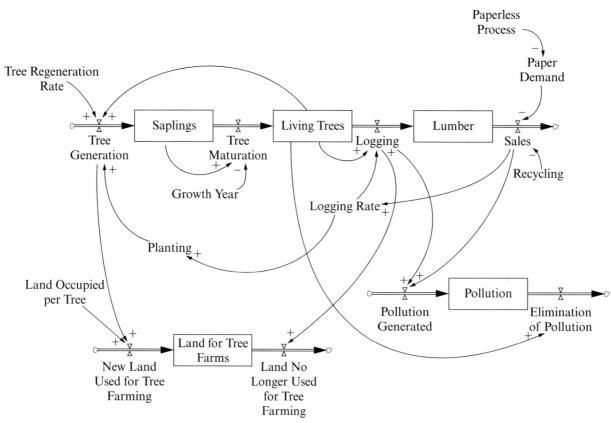

System Dynamics Model of Office Paper[19]

The solutions to deforestation are modeled in system dynamics to further explore how technology, recycling, tree farms, and certifications have mitigated pollution and reduced clear cutting and deforestation. Each solution has created a new system with elements that are interconnected. The interrelated systems are as follows:

1. The problem: clear cutting trees on hillsides and deforestation of rainforests. Deforestation and clear cutting release carbon into the atmosphere and reduce sequestration.
2. Certifications that have been established: Forest Stewardship Council and the Sustainable Forestry Initiative.
3. Tree farms became another way to produce trees specifically for paper that offsets clear cutting and provides use for land.
4. When consumers recycle paper, it can then be remanufactured. New jobs are created which offset jobs lost in forestry. Remanufacturing also reduces clear cutting as the need for virgin materials is reduced. It also reduces energy and water usage to create a product from recycled content rather than from virgin material.
5. Technology automation, archiving, and paperless work processes offset the entire system by reducing the need to use paper.
6. Email, smart phones, and social media offset the entire system as paperless communication systems.

System dynamics is one tool to display all the puzzle pieces in order to see the big picture in order to find the root cause of the problem. Mapping a dynamic complex system simplifies the purpose, elements, and interconnections.

What is your profession? Take a moment to think about the source or stock of the smallest items you use on a daily basis. What is the natural resource? Where does it come from? Does it create a sink, which is a byproduct or waste? Is there a solution to ensure there is an end-of-life solution to avoid waste to landfill or pollution? What are the problems associated with manufacturing a finished good? What risks will the industry encounter? Systems thinkers use a skillset to design feedback loops to reimagine self-reinforcing changes to positively impact the elements of the environment, economy, and social equity.

Understanding the dynamic systems of your industry, supply chain, and value chain will enable managers to plan, implement, evaluate, and control redesigning sources and sinks to seek long-term solutions. Sustainability management requires that professionals can identify the major risks and threats to the industry from raw materials to end-of-life management. Redesigning the organization will take time, collaboration across formal and informal networks, and working together as an industry to find long-term solutions. Redesigning the organization will require that risks become opportunities to transform systems.

Strategic thinkers can position organizations to maximize efficiencies. The case for sustainability management is that it will ensure longevity of the organization by reducing costs by maximizing efficiency, reducing risk for the organization and industry, increasing opportunities to open new markets, and protecting the organization's brand reputation. Internally, efficiencies of scale will be an imperative to achieve systemic change and create an organizational culture that understands how to make decisions by evaluating positive and negative impacts to the system of the economy, environment, and society. (See more on change management in Chapter 4.)

Systems thinking and system dynamics are tools to make strategic decisions and then experiment with future state outcomes. The same process can be used to drill down into the tactical and operational levels. Systems thinking is a tool that assists managers to quantify metrics along each process of work flow or during the product life cycle. Systems thinking can also be a tool to quantify metrics of sources through sinks and stocks and flows. The next section of this chapter will discuss general metrics to quantify an environmental resource's input, throughput, and output of a product or process. What gets measured gets managed.

2.3 Achieving and Measuring Efficiency

How do we not overshoot the carrying capacity of the planet? The answer is to no longer remain in a period of delay. Leaders in sustainability management have recognized the need to take action, improve the economy, restore the environment, and redesign their brands. The rest of this chapter will focus on suggestions that anyone can use to take action. The small impacts made by multitudes of people create enormous ripple effects.

The journey of sustainability management begins with understanding risks and opportunities, as well as the impacts made on the economy, society, and the environment. Organizational values and ethics are important to identify before the journey can begin. Other steps that should be taken before implementing cost reduction strategies are to:

1. Develop and communicate a clear strategic vision.
2. Evaluate life cycle analysis to identify the largest risks.

3. Evaluate the system dynamics of sources (materials) and sinks (waste and byproducts) of internal consumption of energy, water, waste, pollution, and solid waste.
4. Utilize systems thinking to identify the largest negative impacts to reimagine and redesign.
5. Identify partners to collaborate with to develop solutions, who may be competitors, experts, government entities, NGOs and business professionals, etc. Remember no one can solve these large issues alone.
6. Provide the organization with the case for engaging sustainability management—show the value of taking action on the bottom line of profitability or whatever matters most to the organization.
7. Obtain senior management level commitment to viable and feasible plans and proposals.
8. Form cross-functional teams to understand how resources are used today.
9. Cross-functional teams evaluate how to achieve internal efficiencies and develop tactical plans with clear targets of short-, medium-, and long-term goals.
10. Identify technology needs to manage the change.
11. Train frontline management and employees on how to implement, measure, track, and celebrate success. Train front-line staff on why it is important for each individual to manage for sustainability. Making the case for a personal vested interest inspires workforce motivation and dedication in which each employee is making a direct impact by making a difference. Knowledge will empower.
12. Motivate the workforce and have a plan to communicate and celebrate achievements.
13. Compile data and metrics for internal and external reporting to communicate efforts.
14. Prepare and deliver reports in a method that is effective.
15. Continue to move forward in reaching or exceeding target goals.

These 15 steps are important for change management to occur. Communicating the case for sustainability will be a key factor in engaging actions. Allowing bottom-up participation, empowerment, and collaboration will begin to spur new ideas and innovation to redesign the organization.

2.4 Environmental Management Metrics

The remainder of this chapter will focus on how to reduce internal operational resources and materials based on systems thinking. (External reporting is covered in Chapter 8.) Metrics are invaluable in evaluating sources and sinks. The quantified data can then be used to manage inputs and outputs to reduce strains on natural resources and reduce material and natural resources.

Each organizational setting is unique and will have varying degrees of what should be tracked and measured to gage performance. The tracking methods are not all-encompassing for every situation, but cover the basic metrics for any office environment.

The chapter will focus on tracking and measuring the following major categories for environmental metrics used for environmental accounting:

1. Solid waste management
2. Water management

3. Energy management
4. Pollution management

Most organizations track and evaluate all utility data to have a baseline measurement to benchmark future year outcomes. Any organization can reduce costs by managing material inputs. In some states, regulatory requirements will, or already do, require compliance with managing solid waste, water, energy, or pollution. Environmental regulations are already prevalent and will only become more stringent in the years to come. Sustainable organizations go beyond compliance to proactively manage materials inputs simply because it is the right thing to do and it is just smart business.

Organizations from business, government, and nonprofit utilize large amounts of materials on a daily basis. When you manage inputs, you will certainly reduce outputs. Striving for zero waste is a mantra that all employees can understand. Zero Waste can be defined as striving to eliminate inefficiencies. As an example, zero waste can be the action of turning off the lights when no one is in a room. Zero waste can also be fixing leaking water pipes. Zero waste can also be using natural fertilizers instead of chemical-based ones. Zero waste can also be the decision to buy foods that are not packaged. Zero waste is a mindset as well. When employees think Zero Waste with each process, they will automatically consciously make decisions to strive for positive impacts for people, planet, and profit. The framework Zero Waste mimics the Total Quality Management movement's Zero Defect. The evolution of management from the quality movement to the sustainability movement is well underway.

Tracking and Measuring Inputs and Outputs

What gets managed gets done. This popular statement is a key core competency in sustainability management. It is astounding to learn how much an organization can reduce inefficiencies just by tracking and measuring results of simple conservation methods.

Target goals are essential. In order to set target goals, the organization needs to know the current state. Goals should be formed after an assessment of how the organization currently processes a workflow. Complete projections of the outcome of the future state, then clearly state the goals and objectives to improve. Then the organization can move toward the desired future state. There are multiple software packages available to assist organizations in tracking, compiling, and evaluating progress. Technology will ensure that tracking even the smallest action can make a significant impact. Software to manage these small actions oftentimes makes the difference in ensuring that managing sustainability initiatives are not too daunting.

GreenTraks is an energy management software program that compiles all utilities, to include water, electricity, fuel, and carbon footprinting. Software enables managers to evaluate the current state and prepare reports and communication tools for employees and stakeholders. Comprehensive software programs make managing for sustainability more manageable as manually tracking and preparing projections is time consuming.

The following suggestions are broadly discussed and do not account for company-specific circumstances. Each organization is unique, yet the following environmental metrics and processes will apply to all organizations—large, medium, or small. For all accounting methodologies, environmental metrics should consider inefficiencies along the entire system that are controllable through operations. Assessing the current state of inputs, throughput, and outputs is the first place to begin. The next step is to determine the desired state and work toward achieving goals. Organizations that are collaborating throughout the value chain will also track and measure inefficiencies across the supply chain.

Environmental Energy Management tracks, measures, and evaluates material resource usage. Key performance indicators must be developed to ensure systemic change and to successfully build a mindset. Cost accounting can trace the social or environmental issues and then design projects and activities to reduce risk or improve positive impacts. Sustainability management has many tools for managers to evaluate and quantify risks and opportunities:

1. Activity Based Costing
2. Life Cycle Assessment—environmental impact of a product
3. Life Cycle Costing— a comparative analyses tool to benchmark environmental and social impacts of a product
4. Key financial ratios
5. Separate financial statements to track carbon emissions of greenhouse gases

Tracking and measuring environmental management is usually reported in operating or overhead expenses under Generally Accepted Accounting Principles (GAAP). GAAP currently does not allow for carbon accounting to be integrated into the balance sheet.

Solid Waste Management—Zero Waste to Landfill

Solid waste management is an excellent target goal to start with. Solid waste management is an immediate game-changer within an organization. Most importantly, solid waste is controllable; therefore easily manageable. Besides storing chemicals and hazardous materials to be in compliance, recycling systems can be set up. Recycling is low-hanging fruit and significantly diverts waste from the landfill. Employees feel good about their actions, and the organization can create a new revenue stream if enough materials can be sold to a recycling company, such as cardboard. In the early stages of sustainability management, recycling is a great place to start. After systemic change occurs, the organization will continuously reduce their recyclable material output due to procurement decisions that control sources coming into the organization. This change will take time to accomplish and it is recommended to phase in the goal with incremental target goals.

The process flow of implementing a systemic mindset for Zero Waste to Landfill can be broken down into low-hanging fruit to medium-range stages:

Low Hanging Fruit Stage
1. Conduct a waste assessment in order to determine the diversion rate.
   a. Weigh materials that are being thrown in the garbage.
   b. Assess what materials are in the garbage that can be recycled and diverted to compost, if applicable.
   c. Assess which materials in the garbage could be reduced or reused through procurement decisions. What materials do we pay to bring in that we also pay to throw out?
   d. Assess and weigh materials in the recycling that should be in the garbage to determine the recycling accuracy rate.
   e. Calculate the current diversion: **diversion rate = (total diverted / (waste + diverted))**.
   f. Calculate pounds per person of disposed waste.
   g. Calculate pounds disposed per unit manufactured.

    h. Weigh hazardous materials in the garbage and recycling.

    i. Evaluate the current disposal of hazardous materials from all business units.

2. Evaluate current reduction activities (paperless processes, shipping materials, office supplies, cleaning materials, etc.).

3. Evaluate if the company has a buy-back or reuse program so its customers can return materials that can be reused again or remanufactured.

4. Partner with the waste hauler to identify commodities they do not have buyers for and what materials are acceptable for recycling or composting. Waste haulers can oftentimes provide recycling posters, training for employees, and recommendations on long-term diversion plans.

5. Based on the current diversion rate, set incremental target goals so the organization has time to build awareness and learn how to divert materials and control inputs and outputs, such as 30% diverted within three-months; 50% by six-months.

6. Setup a tracking system to measure garbage and recycled materials to track diversion progress toward goals.

7. Train all staff and third-party suppliers, such as cleaning crews, on what to recycle and where to place the recycled materials.

8. Setup a two-way communication system for all departmental units to generate new ideas.

9. Setup recycling systems in all areas of operations:

    a. The key is convenience. Employees will recycle if it is easy.

    b. In workstations, offices, warehouses—place large co-mingle recycling containers, small garbage containers, and small shred boxes side by side.

    c. Designate areas for cardboard and large packaging materials and clearly label them.

    d. Lunchroom—place a large recycling station, compost station for organic waste, and small garbage container.

    e. Garbage cans can be small once recycling and composting are implemented.

10. Collaborate with your current waste hauler to discuss solutions and renegotiate contracts to add more recycling bins. Eventually reduce the number of waste hauls or the bin size. Reducing the frequency of pickup and bin size significantly reduces costs.

11. Enlist support from cross-functional teams to monitor, build awareness, and encourage.

12. Track and measure the financial savings.

13. Track and measure the garbage reduction by volume.

14. Track and measure the recycling success rate. What's in the recycling that should be?

15. Set up a composting system in break rooms and restaurants to divert organic materials, or partner with a composting company or waste hauler for removal.

16. Continuously communicate success to encourage, motivate, and inspire continued progress. Communicate specific results to employees, such as 400 pounds of organic material was composted this year.

17. Partner with local community non-profits and county services to divert materials that can either be reused or disposed of safely. Donating reusable items keeps materials out of the landfill and closes the loop to create end-of-life solutions. Items that can easily be donated are: furniture, appliances, e-waste (computers and cell phones), building materials and fixtures, scrap metal, scrap wood, cleaning materials, hygiene materials, finished goods that do not meet quality standards, etc.

18. Partner with suppliers to take back and properly dispose of materials, such as pallets, shrink wrap, pallet ties, packaging materials, and byproducts to be remanufactured.

Medium Range Stage

19. Increase the incremental target goal.
20. Train employees on new targets and how to partner with the community for success.
21. Partner with recycling companies to sell commodities to earn revenues instead of paying to haul away. Items such as cardboard, shrink-wrap, metals, and plastics can be baled and sold. It may be an organizational value to work with recycling companies that sell materials to the closest location to reduce transportation emissions and create and retain new jobs in the recycling industry.
22. Evaluate materials used within the facility. It is valuable to weigh and calculate diversion rates by department to track individual departmental target goals.
23. Evaluate how activities are planned and throw zero waste events to provide teaching moments. Contract caterers that offer zero waste solutions, such as reusable dinnerware and napkins.
24. Develop and implement an Environmental Preferable Purchasing policy and an Environmental Management System for specific resources that can be reimagined to achieve better efficiencies. (See the section in Chapter 3—Environmental Preferable Purchasing (EPP) Policy and Environmental Management System (EMS) Policy.)
25. Measure and track resources procured with pre- and post-consumer recycled content, as well as reusable items that replaced one-time use items.
26. Train employees on new policies.
27. Require ownership by placing responsibility in performance appraisals, job duties, etc.
28. Continue to track and measure.
29. Celebrate success and continue to strive for 99% waste diversion.

There are so many ways to achieve Zero Waste to Landfill. What can be recycled in most communities (if offered by the municipality or county)?

- All paper, newspaper, magazines, and cardboard
- All rinsed aluminum or tin cans
- Clean aluminum foil
- Glass
- Plastics 1,2,4,5.

Ask your waste hauler about plastics 3,6,7, and 8. Polylactic acid (PLA) is oftentimes labeled #8. PLA is biobased material manufactured with organic materials that contain high sugars and starches. They will break apart in the landfill eventually, but need a high heat of 140 degrees Fahrenheit to biodegrade. Table 1 is an overview of the types of polymers in each numbered plastic material.

Recycling is regionally based on the waste stream's available buyers of materials. Organizations that recycle just the basic materials listed above can divert 30–50% of waste from landfill. Properly disposing of organic waste, recycling, hazardous materials, metals, appliances, and electronic waste will divert another significant percentage. Many counties have a hazardous waste facility available for residential disposal. Commercial disposal is not prevalently available. Therefore, recycling centers can be excellent entrepreneurship opportunities if not already available within the county.

Some of the consequences of achieving Zero Waste are landfill tipping fees are reduced, thereby reducing county revenues. Loss of revenue will impact how the landfills are managed and staffed. Waste haulers will suffer revenue losses when organizations reduce frequency of pickup and increase recycling. The system needs to work together to ensure that the recycling industry becomes a vibrant industry to support jobs in a growing field that can offset jobs lost in waste haul and storage. Every action has a reaction. It is important that employees understand the scale and scope of their actions. Perhaps one day, garbage will be such a highly sought commodity that waste haulers will pay to take your garbage away. This is an early adoption of an existing business model. Companies such as Quest Recycling, LLC actually pay Walmart to haul away all of the organic waste materials. Quest Recycling then produces compost, animal feed, and recycles the vegetable oils into biofuels. Walmart has created a revenue stream, the recycling company wins, and the recycling industry wins.[20]

Table 1: Plastic Labels for Recycling

1 PETE	**Polyethylene Terephalate Ethylene** PETE goes into soft drink, juice, water, detergent, and cleaner bottles. Also used for cooking and peanut butter jars.
2 HDPE	**High Density Polyethylene** High Density Polyethylene HDPE goes into milk and water jugs, bleach bottles, detergent and shampoo.Also into plastic bags and grocery sacks, motor oil bottles, household cleaners, and butter tubs.
3 PVC	**Polyvinyl Chloride** PVC goes into window cleaner, cooking oils, and detergent bottles. Also used for peanut butter jars and water jugs.
4 LDPE	**Low Density Polyethylene** LDPE goes into plastic bags and grocery sacks, dry cleaning bags and flexible film packaging. Also some bottles.
5 PP	**Polypropylene** PP goes into caps, disks, syrup bottles, yogurt tubs, straws, and film packaging.
6 PS	**Polystyrene** PS goes into meat trays, egg cartons, plates, cutlery, carry-out containers, and clear trays.
7 OTHER	**Other** Includes resins not mentioned above or combinations of plastics.

Recycling images © patrimonio designs limited, 2012. Used under license from Shutterstock, Inc.

Zero Waste

Waste is defined as anything more than the very minimum needed to complete the job at hand. Waste would include parts, labor, electricity, gas, fuel, automation, injuries, inventory, or even physical space that does not add value to the outcome. Waste is broadly being used as a framework for inefficiencies. Managers at all levels are responsible for reducing redundancies, manual work processes, and processes that do not make common sense.

Creating a mantra of zero waste creates a culture within the workplace. The mantra is easy to remember, which helps each employee remember to find the efficiencies that create value and positively impact profitability, biodiversity, and social equity. The quality movement and lean manufacturing created similar terminology, such as Zero Defects. Zero Waste follows the same "Zero" to encompass equipment, health, and safety to human resource management, to facilities management, and so on.

When organizations implement practices to improve efficiencies, all of these actions can be quantified. Metrics give managers data to show how the organization is achieving efficiencies that are reducing expenses, driving brand value, increasing revenues, or even impacting stock prices. Metrics are key performance indicators that managers can now manage environment, social, and economic impacts. Metrics also allow organizations to compile information and benchmark results between business units, regions, multinationals, and even competitor to competitor. Results can further spur action to motivate the workforce to compete against one another in the spirit of pursuing zero waste with purpose.

Water Management and Metrics

Water is the most precious natural resource. It is a regional resource, but has global implications. All life depends on fresh clean water. How we consume it and manage water will be an imperative as future generations will depend on the decisions of past generations.

An effective water strategy will assess risks and opportunities of regional water supply or scarcity. Water is dependent on weather and therefore, risks are difficult to assess long-term. Sectors that are highly exposed to risk include food and beverage, manufacturing, energy generation, and mining. Yet all organizations use water, so water management is also an imperative for restaurants, stadiums, service organizations, property management, large office hubs, and schools.

What are some risks to consider? The Carbon Disclosure Project categorizes risk in six categories:

1. Physical
2. Regulatory
3. Litigation
4. Product standards
5. Brand damage
6. Insufficient infrastructure

Responding to risks and proactively seeking solutions will ensure value for the organization. The Carbon Disclosure Project not only provides tools to report greenhouse gas emissions but water footprinting as well. The Carbon Disclosure Project assesses these risks in water management:

1. Deteriorating water quality
2. Natural disasters, such as flooding, scarcity and drought, or water stress

3. Current and future regulatory requirements to standards of water consumption, land development, depletion, quality control testing, rising prices, permitting issues, etc.
4. Water limitations regulated by municipalities or regional governmental entities

Once risks are evaluated, the next step is to assess how much water is used and for what purpose. Basic evaluation criteria can be tracked and measured.

Assessing Controllable Water Usage

1. How much water do we use from sources in volatile regions? Areas of concern are regions with water scarcity or ones that negatively impact the ecosystem.
2. What are the future concerns of the natural ecosystem and supply?
3. Quantify by meter the total water consumption from year to year. Water is typically measured in the USA by the following:
   a. Liter: is .264 gallons—oftentimes used in consumer packaged goods (CPG)
   b. Gallons—sometimes used in residential billing as well as CPGs
   c. Cubic feet: 7.48 gallons in one cubic foot. 1 gallon = 748 CCF (hundred cubic feet)—oftentimes used in commercial billing
   d. Acre feet: 325,851.43 gallons—mostly used by water providers
4. Evaluate the utility bill. Separate meters and track water usage as an internal measurement for facilities, manufacturing, or consumption as well as external usage for irrigation. Subtract sewage costs from water usage to find the true usage cost.
5. Are there possibilities to reuse water in a closed loop system? If we already are, are we maximizing efficiencies as well as tracking and measuring volume?
6. How much water does the organization discharge? What are the risks of doing so and what is the cost to the ecosystem where water is discharged?
7. Is the city working toward sewage infrastructure improvements? How can the business and political communities work together to find viable solutions?

Next, evaluate the water usage throughout the supply chain to assess the entire life cycle. It is important to evaluate the risks and opportunities of the external environment. Evaluating the following questions will help to assess risk:

- What are the changes in availability and price volatility?
- Are high amounts of water used to produce goods?
- Is the supply chain using energy sources that require large amounts of water?
- What consumer trends and expectations could put us at risk?
- How can the supply chain be positioned to better meet the needs of the future?
- What partnerships exist to seek assistance in reimagining the supply chain?
- What are competitors doing to reduce risk?
- What government regulations exist or are upcoming?

Action Plan for Water Management Program
The next step is to determine a water strategy and develop a policy. The policy should focus on internal operations, as well as supply chain water management considerations.

Once the policy is established, the next step is to develop a plan. Target goals should be included for each of the following main water metrics:

1. Goals to reduce usage in operations and consumption by personnel, which is oftentimes called a "water footprint"
2. Goals to reuse water inside the facility and outdoor irrigation controls, such as: rain collection, swales, waste water treatment, and manufacturing closed loop systems
3. Goals to reduce discharge. Improve quality of water discharged as waste water through sewage and anaerobic and aerobic digestion treatment. Reducing toxins and chemicals and replacing with natural materials reduces waste water treatment

Incremental targets are oftentimes helpful to ensure employee motivation and the ability to achieve quick wins and long-term value. It is recommended to develop goals using volume or conservation, social impacts, and expense reduction. Rising costs oftentimes spur conservation or just simply doing the right thing motivates change.

Set Target Goals
There are so many easy ways to reduce water consumption inside a facility:

- Set a target goal to reduce water, such as 30% within the facility
  - Install low-flow fixtures such as sink aerators, shower heads, or toilets
    - Sink aerator—from 2.2 gallons per minute (gpm) to 1.6 or lower
    - Shower heads—from 3 gpm to 2 gpm or lower
    - Toilets—from 3 gallons per flush (gpf) to 1.6 gpf or lower
    - Commercial faucet hoses—from 2.2 gpm to 1 gpm or lower
  - Install water smart technologies, such as dishwashers and laundry machines
  - Recommend employees report leaks and have them repaired
- Set target goal to reduce outdoor water usage, such as 60% outdoor usage
  - Water efficient brooms are available instead of power washing sidewalks or pool sides
  - Install low-flow sprinkler heads for irrigation where water is sprayed directly on the ground to avoid evaporation
  - Calibrate sprinkler heads to only water what's intended and avoid hardscapes, such as sidewalks and parking lots
  - Install above or underground drip systems for bushes
  - Consult with a landscape architect or landscape maintenance company to recommend indigenous low-water tolerant plant species
  - Reduce turf areas, which will not only reduce water usage but also reduce costs on fertilizer and maintenance

Low-Flow Irrigation Solutions

Replacing conventional sprinkler heads with low-flow heads can save up to 60%. By meter, calculate the total water used, in this case one hundred cubic feet, and then calculate the projected cost reduction to ensure the project is feasible.

Irrigation Water Reduction		
	Meter #62053699	
Bill Date	CCF	Cost
6.25.10–7.27.10	352	$422.13
7.28.10–8.25.10	335	$410.83
8.26.10–9.27.10	344	$419.43
9.28.10–10.27.10	248	$327.71
10.28.10–11.29.10	107	$193.00
11.30.10–12.28.10	43	$132.04
12.29.10–1.27.11	57	$155.00
1.28.11–2.25.11	86	$185.74
2.26.11–3.25.11	95	$194.88
3.26.11–4.26.11	108	$210.98
4.27.11–5.25.11	172	$333.76
5.26.11–6.24.11	262	$384.41
Total	**2208.69**	**$3,369.91**
Gallons	**1,652,098**	
50% reduction	**826,049**	**$1,684.96**

- ° Install porous landscaping options, such as pervious granite instead of groundcover to reduce having to replace bark or rocks
- ° Reuse rain water for maintenance needs or watering potted plants
- ° Smart water meters use satellite technology to monitor the weather, test soil saturation levels, and interact with the sprinkler timer system to reduce watering times or shut off when it is raining or snowing

Taking actions such as these simple recommendations will reduce costs for water, maintenance, and supplies. It will positively impact the environment by conserving water. Finally, it will also impact quality of life as employees are asked to make very few changes and will be conserving without even thinking about it.

Calculate Projections

Using an example that every organization can relate to, water can easily be managed by changing behavior and taking simple easy-to-achieve steps. For example, an organization switches from providing bottled water for employees to a filtered tap system to reduce costs significantly. Calculating the project's viability would use the formula:

Price per unit of bottled water × Consumption = Total Employee Perk in $

$6 per Case × 30 cases per month = $180 a monthly or $2,160 annually

Reducing recycling of the bottles can also reduce the size of the outdoor bin. You can save even more money and shrink the recycling bin size:

Cost reduction = The difference between the garbage and/or recycling bin size and expense reduced

Environmental impact = # of bottles diverted from not being used

Many organizations reinvest the savings back into more sustainability practices to close the loop. The return on investment and payback period can then be calculated:

Return on Investment = ((Old amount − New Amount)) − Cost of Investment)/Cost of Investment

Payback Period = new price/old price

California Water Service Company provides water conservation kits to commercial and residential customers. Customers can order sink aerators, low-flow shower heads, leak detectors, and even water brooms. Pacific Living Properties, a property management company, partnered with California Water Service Company to reduce their water usage in their residential properties. In just one region alone, the cost benefit analysis of replacing toilets, sink aerators, and shower heads will make the following impact:

	# of Units	Old Gallons	New Gallons	Gallons Saved 3x per Day	Price per Gallon	Monthly Expense Reduced	Annual Reduction
Sink Aerators	606	2.2	1	65,448	$0.0017	$111.26	$1,335.14
Kitchen Sink	400	2.2	2	7,200	$0.0017	$12.24	$146.88
Shower Heads	520	3	2	46,800	$0.0017	$79.56	$954.72
Toilets	520	1.6	0.8	37,440	$0.0017	$63.65	$763.78
Total				**156,888**		**$266.71**	**$3,200.52**

Calculating Water Delivery or Discharge

According to WaterSense, the EPA's program to conserve water, the measurements used to deliver water is:

1.5 kilowatts to supply 1,000 gallons from the public supply.

This metric to deliver water includes pumping, filtration, treatment, and distribution to the public system.

The measurement to calculate waste water treatment is:

1.8 kilowatts per 1,000 gallons.[21]

Project metrics should then include all measurements for the following to account for the life cycle of the change:

- Water delivery volume and cost
- Water conservation per project for volume and cost
- Water discharge volume and cost
- Natural gas or electricity should be accounted for if the project includes water heating systems. (See metrics in next section.)

Financial Statement Impact: Reporting Metrics

Just as you would prepare monthly financial statements, internal environmental management reports should also explain the utility expense reduction in the Profit and Loss sheet. Each project outcome should be compiled by each business unit to report actions that impacted cost savings and usage overall.

Reporting actions will benefit the company in several ways:

- Track progress in meeting target goals
- Communicate success to employees
- Document performance in employee performance appraisals
- Provide lenders with documentation of managing costs and conservation methods
- Include intrinsic and extrinsic value in financial and sustainability reports

Water is the most precious resource and can easily be conserved by making small changes that add up quickly.

Water's Impact on Natural Gas or Electricity for Water Heating Appliances

Projects that replace hot water heating systems also impact reductions in cost for either natural gas or electricity. Appliances will use either natural gas or electricity to heat water, such as a water heater tank.

WaterSense uses the following assumptions to calculate the impact on gas or electricity:

- Electric water heaters are 90% more efficient (uses .18 KWh of electricity per gallon)
- Natural gas heaters are 60% more efficient (uses .9 cubic feet of gas per gallon)
- Water is heated from 55 degrees to 120 degrees Fahrenheit

Metrics can be calculated based on:

1 British Thermal Unit (BTU) per 1 pound of water raised 1 degree.

It is recommended to change therms to kWh for consistent reporting methodologies using this formula:

1 therm = 29.3 kWh where

1 Mcf of Natural Gas = 10.307 therms.[22]

Natural Gas Metrics

Cubic feet is the common measurement used when calculating natural gas. One cubic foot of gas is equal to the amount needed to fill a certain volume under temperature and pressure conditions.

1 therm = 100 cubic feet

Mcf = 1,000 cubic feet (Whereas M stands for the roman numeral 1,000 and cf is cubic feet)

When comparing fuels, the metrics are reported in British Thermal Units (BTUs). A BTU is approximately a pint, and is the heat required to heat one pound of water one degree Fahrenheit.

Table 2: Natural Gas Measurement

UNIT OF MEASURE	APPROX. HEAT ENERGY
1 cubic foot	1,000 BTU's
100 cubic feet (1 therm)	100,000 BTU's
1,000 cubic feet (1 mcf)	1,000,000 BTU's

Source: http://www.tulsagastech.com/measure.html[23]

WaterSense uses the following calculations to convert therms to kWh:

1 therm = 29.3 kWh

1 Mcf = 10.307 therms[24]

Be sure to include natural gas measurements for hot water heating projects or fuel usage in financial statements to show the full life cycle of the project.

Energy Management and Electricity Metrics

Energy metrics are quite easy to establish a snapshot view of the current situation and then develop programs for conservation and future state targets. All organizations can assess and measure the following common energy consumption within the facility:

- Building integrity—insulation, air leaks, awnings, shading, passive air
- Lighting
- Air conditioning and heating systems
- Appliances—plugload of refrigerators, dishwashers, ovens, microwaves, etc.
- Components or office equipment—computers, monitors, calculators, telephones, fax and copy machines, printers, etc.
- Phantom loads—identify components with a wattage reader that draw energy even when the device is turned off

Some organizations can further assess energy consumption of the following:

- Warehouse equipment powered by electricity
- Data centers
- Manufacturing machinery
- Power tools and equipment

Conservation Methods and Project Management

There are three types of energy usage:

1. Electricity,
2. Natural gas or alternative gases, and
3. Renewable energy on site.

Action Plan for Energy Program Management

Create an action plan for an energy management program with the following steps:

1. The first step is to assess how energy is being used on a 24-hour basis, and also seasonal anomalies both in the interior and exterior of the facility
2. The next step is to assess what inefficiencies exist by meter
3. Evaluate electricity bills to determine current costs and usage of electricity and gas. Identify peak periods and the largest sources of energy consumption
4. Develop a program that prioritizes inefficiencies
5. Develop short-, medium-, and long-term project management objectives
6. Commit to the Environmental Energy Management program
7. Perform life cycle costing to conduct a cost based analysis of potential alternatives that will reduce usage
8. Determine the cost of investing in alternatives and calculate the rate of return on investment and payback period of the project
9. Phase in project goals and communicate progress
10. Monitor, track, and measure performance
11. Communicate progress throughout the organization
12. Embed employee actions into formal accountability measures, such as incentives or performance appraisals
13. Maintain motivation to continuously improve

How to Measure Energy Usage of Devices
Energy Mix

The electricity bill will show total kilowatt hours used during a timeframe. The price of electricity is regional as it depends on how the electricity is created for the "grid" that is referred to as the "energy mix". Energy mix can be created by a percentage of electrical generation from hydro-electricity, coal, nuclear, gas, oil, renewable energy sources, etc.

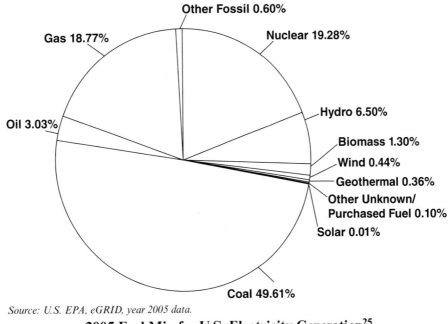

Source: U.S. EPA, eGRID, year 2005 data.
2005 Fuel Mix for U.S. Electricity Generation[25]

Electricity is also regionally priced by breaking the price into tiers based on a base load and then higher rates for higher usage or peak hour usage. Tiered rates are actually helpful to motivate conservation as companies can strive to reduce energy tiers or electricity usage during peak hours to reduce costs. Tiered rates incentivize conservation and charge higher prices for those that do not conserve.

Tools for Energy Management

Tools are available to measure the wattage of appliances or devices for a precise measurement to calculate the current state. It is recommended for an organization to know the electricity usage of major devices used on a daily basis, such as computers, monitors, printers, calculators, telephones, break room appliances, lighting in the interior and exterior, etc.

Companies such as GreenNet offer energy management dashboards that include the ability to measure the electricity being consumed by attaching a reading device to the circuit breaker, called submetering. The network is monitored and the company can have alerts sent via email or smart phone application to alert management of spikes or peak overloads. Being able to isolate power consumption by sub-metering enables project management to be more accurate and easier to manage. Monitoring electricity in real time is a smart way to manage energy.

Energy Metrics

Power is measured in watts or joules per second. Power is the rate of energy generated or consumed measured in watts. Power should not be confused with energy. One unit of energy is a kilowatt hour. Energy is calculated by watts multiplied by time. A 100 watt lightbulb is the power. If run for an hour, it consumes .1 kilowatt hour, usually calculated by the hour.

Energy is billed in the following increments:

watt	watt hour
kWh	kilowatt hour
MWh	megawatt hour
GWh	gigawatt hour
TWh	terawatt hour
PWh	petawatt hour

To measure kilowatt-hours or energy, use the wattage of the device, multiply by the number of hours used, and divide by 1,000 and then multiply by the price of electricity. (Dividing by 1,000 converts watt-hours to kilowatt-hours.)

cost of electricity = (wattage x hours used) ÷ 1000 × price per kWh

The electricity cost of each device should be measured and analyzed. Then conduct a cost benefit analyses to project annual savings with an alternative. For example, when considering upgrading lighting from 100-watt incandescent light bulbs to 25-watt compact fluorescent light bulbs a simple cost analyses would be:

- Cost of a 25 watt CFL light bulb = (25 × 10)/1000 × $.17 = $.04.
- Cost of a 100 watt incandescent light bulb = (100 × 10)/1000 × $.17 = $.17.
- Potential daily cost savings = $.13.
- Potential annual cost savings = $.13 × 260 days = $33.80.
- Retrofit of 150 light bulbs projected annual savings = $33.80 × 150 = $5,070.
- Total investment of 150 CFLs = $450.
- Total project savings = $5,070 − $450 = $4,620.

If an appliance does not list wattage, it may list amperages. You can calculate wattage by multiplying amperage times volts.

1.5 amps × 120 volts = 180 watts

Energy Reduction Suggestions

There are many easy and quick ways to reduce energy costs. Here are just a few suggestions to reduce costs immediately with little out of pocket expense:

- Open the shades during the day to maximize daylighting and reduce lighting usage.
- Close the blinds at night and during midafternoon hours in summertime to insulate.
- Install window tinting to reduce radiation and create an ultraviolet barrier.
- Assess if insulation is ideal thickness in the attic. Install temperature controlled attic fans to blow hot air out of the attic during summer months.
- Install weather stripping on all exterior doors or anywhere where an air leak exists.
- Regularly clean ducts, vents, and filters to ensure efficient air flow and quality.
- Test ducts for leaks.

- Insulate hot water pipes and duct system.
- Install motion lighting in infrequently used rooms.
- Summertime, open doors and windows in the morning and turn on ceiling fans.
- Set air conditioning temperature on the thermostat at 78 degrees during summertime.
- Use space heaters in winter and keep the thermostat temperature at 68 degrees.
- Use ceiling fans year round to control ambient air temperature.
- Install digital thermostats and set timers to control the temperature settings to reduce usage during non-working hours.
- Install surge protectors to protect computer equipment and turn them off to reduce phantom loads. Phantom loads are the energy draw electrical components can draw even when the device is turned off. A good indication of a phantom load is a light is on even in off mode. Service organizations and small businesses can save $350 on average annually just on phantom loads.
- Upgrade lighting to more efficient bulbs or tubes.
  ○ Tubing is based on diameter, the smaller the diameter the more energy efficient. For instance, upgrading tubing from a T12 to T5 fluorescent can significantly reduce energy costs, but T5 tubes are more than double the price to buy new. The investment cost to retrofit then becomes a barrier. Yet, as you can see in the next example, the T5 tube will double cost savings over a T8 tube

Table 3: Comparative Analysis of Tubing

Life Cycle Costing of Upgrading From T12 to T8				9 hours per day	
	Wattage	**Energy Cost**	**Units**	**Cost to Operate**	**Annual Savings**
Current T12	34	$0.0023	4	$0.31	
Current	0	$0.0023	0	$0.00	
Monthly				$84.46	
Yearly				$1,027.55	$0.00
New T8	25	$0.0023	4	$0.28	
Monthly				$62.10	
Yearly				$755.55	$272.00
New T5	15	$0.0023	4	$0.14	
Monthly				$37.26	
Yearly				$453.33	$574.22

a. Upgrading lightbulbs can significantly reduce energy costs
b. Light emitting diodes (LED) are the most efficient bulbs on the market today that also have a better life cycle impact than the compact fluorescent lightbulb due to mercury gas

Table 4: Lightbulb Comparative Analysis

Life Cycle Costing of Upgrading to CFL or LED Lighting					
	Wattage	**Energy Cost**	**Units**	**Cost to Operate**	**Annual Savings**
Current	60	$0.0023	18	$2.48	Total Units
Current	40	$0.0023	4	$0.37	
Monthly				$770.04	
Yearly				$9,368.82	$0.00
New CFL	25	$0.0023	22	$1.27	
Monthly				$341.55	
Yearly				$4,155.53	$5,213.30
New LED	15	$0.0023	22	$0.76	
Monthly				$204.93	
Yearly				$2,493.32	$6,875.51

Creating a Culture

The following ways can reduce energy pervasively throughout the organization:

- Train employees on how and why to conserve energy
- Behavioral changes of employees, such as turning off lights or installing motion detectors in infrequent usage areas
- Success will be dependent on making conservation easy for employees
- Communicate target goals and objectives and how each person makes an impact
- Track and measure progress
- Communicate progress
- Celebrate success of achieving milestones

The low-hanging fruit oftentimes can save the organization significant amounts of money that can be reinvested into more expensive capital investments in either environmental or social responsibility objectives. Environmental Energy Management makes a significant impact on the bottom line.

2.5 Emissions Management and Metrics—Carbon Footprint

The most widely accepted standards to account and report greenhouse gases were developed in 1998 by the World Resources Institute and World Business Council of Sustainable Development. To date, there is not a globally accepted accounting method for emissions though. Organizational measurements of greenhouse gases (GHG) account for manmade contributions based on secondary data to give industries a baseline metric to calculate carbon. On the other hand, in natural systems, greenhouse gases are produced in multiple ways such as through decomposition of plant life and wild fires. Yet nature devises ways to capture or sequester those gases, such as a tree absorbs carbon dioxide (CO_2) through photosynthesis and the sink is a biogas stored in trunks or branches. Nature already has a balancing mechanism. Yet, emissions created by mankind cannot be completely absorbed by the oceans, forests, or soil. Mankind does not have a balancing mechanism.

There are several methods to measure greenhouse gas emissions, such as Carbon Trust, Carbon Impact, ISO 14064, Open Eco, or the Environmental Protection Agency's eGRID, just to name a few. The Greenhouse Gas Protocol is a free online tool that is widely used.

The Greenhouse Gas Protocol issues many standards and calculation spreadsheet tools for the following:

1. GHG Protocol Corporate Accounting and Reporting Standard (Corporate Accounting Standard)
2. GHG Protocol for Project Accounting for Mitigation Projects

Greenhouse gases (GHG) are reported as an equivalent of carbon dioxide (CO_2e), based on the global warming potential (GWP) of each GHG:

- Carbon dioxide: CO_2 − GWP = 1
- Methane: CH4− GWP = 21
- Nitrous oxide: N_2O − GWP = 310
- Sulfur hexafluoride: SF6 − GWP = 23,900
- HFCs: hydroflourocarbons – GWP = 650 − 11,700
- PFCs: perflourocarbons

All greenhouse gases are reported in CO_2 equivalent.

$$CO_2E = GHG\ emitted \times GWP\ of\ emitted\ GHG$$

Industrial, transportation, residential, commercial, and agricultural are the primary activities that create manmade GHGs.[26] Burning fossil and biomass fuels are known to contribute to GHG emissions through activities such as:

- Gasoline or oil
- Coal
- Natural gas
- Cement production
- Flaring gas
- Open burning of agricultural and residential vegetative wastes
- Prescribed forest burning
- Wild fires (caused by mankind plus naturally ignited)

Major sources of an individual's GHG are: heating and cooling, electricity usage, and transportation. Oftentimes, the term "carbon footprint" is used as a framework to refer to GHG emissions. Calculating a GHG footprint can serve several different purposes:

- Required to report to comply with state environmental regulations such as California's AB 32
- Voluntarily report to non-profit organizations such as Carbon Disclosure Project or California Climate Action Registry
- Multinational firms that report in the voluntary and involuntary (Kyoto Protocol) carbon trading market
- Calculate projects that reduce GHG to meet strategic targets

- Offset GHG to collaborate as an industry or sector
- Compliance with the California Environmental Quality Act (CEQA)

Action Plan Greenhouse Gas Project Management

Tactical goals and targets will ensure project managers have clear directives. Recall systems thinking that sources are the release of GHG, while the sink is the removal or storage of emissions. Sources include activities such as combustion emissions from generating electricity, combustion emissions from generating energy or off-grid electricity, flaring, and emissions from pipelines and landfills. Projects will manage both sources and sinks. First, an organization will calculate a baseline measurement of GHG for direct emissions. Direct emissions are activities directly controlled by the organization. Whereas, indirect emissions are created while producing electricity.

Calculating Carbon Footprint

The Greenhouse Gas Protocol Project Accounting[27] is a free tool available to the public to calculate a baseline GHG measurement and to conduct activities within a project that will reduce emissions.

- **Project Activity Emissions$_y$** = (Production Level$_y$) $\times$ (Project Activity Emission Rate$_y$)
- **Baseline Emissions$_y$** = (Production Level$_y$) $\times$ (Baseline Emission Rate$_y$)

Explanations:

Project Activity Emission Rate$_y$ = tons of CO_2 equivalent per unit of production in a year "y"

Baseline Emission Rate$_y$ = tons of CO_2 equivalent per unit of production in year "y" for project's baseline

Production Level$_y$ = the amount produced in year "y"

Calculation tools are available that already integrate secondary data by sector on specific metrics and even include tools for service organizations to calculate employee travel.[28] For more detailed metrics, see the Greenhouse Gas Protocol website www.ghgprotocol.org.

Managing Sources and Sinks

The next step is to manage sources and sinks. Managing carbon will reduce negative environmental impacts, reduce expenses, and respond to stakeholder expectations.

Managing carbon is required in some states. Since January 2009, the California Air Resource Board, an arm of the California Environmental Protection Agency, requires the following sectors to report carbon emissions under the CA Assembly Bill 32 Global Warming Solutions Act:

- Stationary combustion
- Cement plants
- Electricity providers
- Electricity generators + cogeneration facilities
- Refineries: hydrogen, oil, and gas

In the state of California, mandatory reporting is required for facilities that use more than 471,520 MMBtu of natural gas or 12,000 short tons of coal. Reporting is also required if 1 MW of electricity can be produced or emits more than 2,500 metric tons of CO_2.[29]

Besides governance, organizations may choose to reduce their environmental impact, costs, and risks of brand damage by reducing emissions. According to the Greenhouse Gas Protocol Project Accounting, projects should be designed to set the organization up for success by following a logical process flow:

GHG Project	Activity	Primary Effect
Energy Efficiency Project	Lighting retrofit with energy efficient lighting	Reduce combustion from grid electricity generation

GHG Metrics

GHG are reported either by time or production.

For energy efficiency, energy generation, and industrial process project activities report as per unit of product or service expressed as:

GHG Emissions / Unit of Product or Service

For GHG emissions or sequestration:

GHG Emissions / (Unit of Time) × (Unit of Baseline Candidate Size or Capacity).

Primary and Secondary Effects

By reducing GHG emissions through activities there are two effects: primary and secondary. Primary effects are the removal or storage of GHG as either a source or sink. The secondary effect is the unintended consequence caused by the activity. Secondary effects can either be a one-time occurrence or occur throughout the value chain based on inputs up and downstream.

All complimentary Greenhouse Gas Protocol toolkits can be downloaded at: http://www.ghgprotocol.org/calculation-tools.

Air Pollution Abatement

Ozone

Fuels and burning materials also emit particulate matter and oxides of nitrogen (NOx). NOx can react with organic compounds in the atmosphere in the presence of sunlight to cause ozone, also referred to as smog. Smog should not be confused with GHG. High levels of particulate pollution, smog, in the atmosphere leads to unhealthy air for the public to breathe. Unhealthy air has negative implications to the human cardiovascular system and is known to also cause or exacerbate asthma and emphysema. Burning organic material not only releases particulate matter, it also releases greenhouse gases and other toxins, such as dioxin.

In the Sacramento Valley of California, ozone is a seasonal problem, typically occurring during the months of May through October. Sources for the pollutants which react to form ozone include motor vehicles, power plants, factories, chemical solvents, combustion products from various fuels, and consumer products.

Ozone acts as a strong irritant that attacks the body's respiratory system. Symptoms include shortness of breath, chest pain when inhaling deeply, wheezing and coughing. When ozone levels are high, people with lung disease (e.g., chronic bronchitis, emphysema, and asthma) are particularly susceptible to adverse health impacts.

Nitrogen Oxides

Nitrogen dioxide (NO_2), a toxic reddish-brown gas, and nitric oxide (NO), a colorless gas, comprise NOx (oxides of nitrogen). Because NOx is an ingredient in the formation of ozone, it is referred to as an ozone precursor. NO_2 is associated with adverse health effects and is formed in the atmosphere when NO is oxidized to NO_2. Both NO_2 and NO are produced as a result of fuel combustion.

Particulate Matter—PM10 and PM2.5

Particulate matter in the air is a complex mixture of tiny particles that consists of dry solid fragments, solid cores with liquid coatings, and small droplets of liquid. These particles vary greatly in shape, size, and chemical composition, and can be made up of many different materials such as metals, soot, soil, and dust. Particles that are 10 microns or less in diameter are defined as "respirable particulate matter" or PM10. These particles (PM10 and smaller) pose the greatest health concern because they can embed deep into the lungs. Particles that are 2.5 microns or less in diameter are defined as "fine" particulate matter or PM2.5. In addition to adverse health concerns, these fine particles can contribute significantly to regional haze and reduction of visibility.

Ambient PM can be classified into two groups; primary PM that is directly emitted from sources such as vehicle travel on paved and unpaved roads, forest management burning, agriculture burning, residential wood burning stoves/fireplaces, and combustion processes. The second classification of is secondary PM that is formed in the air from the reactions of precursor gases such as nitrogen oxides, volatile organic compounds, sulfur oxides, and ammonia. Therefore, to address the full scope of possible PM problems, measures to reduce both directly-emitted PM as well as precursor gases should be considered.

Particulate matter pollution tends to be worse in the Sacramento Valley during winter months on days when there is little or no air movement, cold temperatures and no precipitation. PM can build up locally until the weather pattern changes and the pollution dissipates. This can occur in a matter of hours or days, depending on weather conditions and pollution sources.

According to the Butte County Air Quality Management District, small particles that make up PM can easily penetrate deep into the lungs. Scientists have studied the effects of this type of pollution on human health. Both short- and long-term exposures to PM have been shown to lead to harmful health effects. People with heart or lung diseases, older adults, and children are more at risk to the adverse health effects from PM exposure. In addition, scientists have observed higher rates of hospitalizations, emergency room visits, and doctor's visits for respiratory illnesses or heart disease during times of high PM concentrations. Scientists have found a relationship between high PM levels and reductions in various aspects of the healthy functioning of people's lungs.[30]

2.6 Summary

Besides environmental metrics, metrics should also be accounted for TBL to account for performance beyond environmental impacts. Social, economic, and environmental metrics should be quantified. (See Chapter 8: Communication and Sustainability Reporting for more details on social, economic, and environmental metrics.) The quantifiable and tangible benefits of managing for sustainability will continue to motivate the workforce and spur action amongst employees. Quantifiable metrics will build a sense of pride within the workplace by clearly showing how much the organization invests in responsibility and how each employee makes a significant difference.

What gets measured can be managed. Quantifying reductions of inputs, throughputs, and outputs drives change. Quantifying metrics provides the data to make decisions, set clear target goals, implement program management, measure performance, communicate results, and then celebrate success.

2.7 Experiential Exercises

I. Stocks, Flows, and Sinks

Think about one process at work that you know creates waste to landfill. Draw the workflow process as it exists today and identify the raw materials (sources) and what happens to the byproducts, or waste, at end of life (sinks).

II. System Dynamics Flow Chart

Practice drawing a System Dynamics flow chart to change the system from the current state to a future desired state. Redesign the system to create a dynamic flow chart that changes the sources, stocks, flows, and sinks. How can inputs, throughput, and output be managed without negatively impacting TBL? Draw feedback loops to show how one action can be balanced by a reaction—a positive or negative feedback loop.

III. Fabricating Target Goals and Project Management Timelines

A. Identify Environmental Impacts

What are most serious environmental impacts within your organization or throughout the supply chain? List some operational functions or processes that both positively and negatively impact the environment.

Solid Waste	Water Consumption	Energy Consumption	Air Pollution	Land or Water Pollution

B. Identify Economic Impacts

What are most serious economic impacts within your organization or throughout the supply chain? List some operational functions or processes that both positively and negatively impact profitability or the local economy.

Internal Inefficiency	Sunk Costs	Local Commerce vs. Global Supply Chain	Financial Statements

C. Identify Social Impacts

What are the most serious social impacts within your organization or throughout the supply chain? List some operational functions or processes that both positively and negatively impact your employees or society.

Benefits	Performance Based Incentives	Employee Retention or Turnover	Philanthropy and Volunteer Programs

IV. Developing Target Goals and Project Management Timelines

A. Brainstorming Continuous Improvements
Identify some ways your organization can improve negative impacts.

Economic Impact	Environmental Impact	Societal Impact

B. Setting Target Goals and a Project Management Schedule

Now organize your ideas into goals that can be implemented within your organization and set clear targets to achieve in a given timeframe.

Short-Term TBL Goals	0–6 Month Timeframe and Project Manager
Medium-Term TBL Goals	**6–12 Month Timeframe**
Long-Term TBL Goals	**2nd Year and Onward**

V. Metrics

For each goal, determine the target goal and how often it will be evaluated to measure progress.

Practice calculating environmental management metrics to determine if a new project will be financially viable and feasible in the timeline you imagined.

- Solid Waste: Goal is to recycle 30% of materials within three months. You currently have a 3-yard trash bin that costs $150 every week to pick up. You have now ordered a 2-yard trash bin for $110 and a recycling bin for $10.
  ○ What is the cost benefit?
  ○ What are the TBL benefits?

- Water: Goal is to reduce water usage within the facility by 10% by installing more efficient sink aerators.
  ○ You have four bathroom sinks with 2.2 gpm aerators that can be replaced with a .5 gpm aerator that costs $.50 for each aerator.
  ○ Your breakroom sink has a 2.2 gpm aerator that can be replaced with a 1 gpm aerator that costs $2.00. Create your own assumptions based on the number of employees and frequency of breakroom and restroom usage.
  ○ What is the total projected water reduction in gallons? What is the cost savings to the company?
  ○ What is the ROI and payback? Is this a feasible and viable goal?
  ○ What are the TBL benefits?

- Energy: Goal is to reduce energy by using natural daylighting for three hours in the morning. Your workplace has 24, 25-watt compact fluorescent lights and all of them will remain turned off during this timeframe. The price of energy for your electric company is $.17 per KWh.
  - What is the cost reduction to the company?
  - What are the total KWh reduced per day, month, and year?
  - Is this a feasible and viable goal?
  - What are the environmental and social impacts?

- Air Pollution: Goal is to reduce the carbon footprint of employee travel by 20%.
  - You have 10 employees that drive to work each day. You will need to find out their total round-trip mileage.
  - Access www.ghgprotocol.org and calculate employee carbon footprint using the Service Sector toolkit
  - Devise 4 ways you can reduce employee travel to reach your goal
  - Will your organization invest in transportation incentives or employee recognition programs? If so what will it cost the company to implement these goals? Calculate ROI, payback, and a cost benefit analysis for a feasibility study
  - What are the environmental, social, and economic impacts?

SAMPLE QUESTIONS

Systems Thinking

1. A system is made up of three components. Which of the following is not a component of a system?

   A. Purpose or function
   B. Interconnections
   C. Elements
   D. Overshoot

2. What does "overshoot" mean?

   A. Missing your target
   B. Being late
   C. Go beyond limits
   D. Growth at any cost

3. Sources and sinks are the physical limit to growth. Is this true or false?

   A. True
   B. False

4. Sources are necessary to sustain life. Which one of the following is an example of a source?

   A. Raw materials
   B. Landfills
   C. Waste water treatment
   D. People

5. Which of the following does not explain the acronym or formula IPAT?

   A. Impact
   B. Population
   C. Authority
   D. Technology

6. Positive feedback loops reflect a positive outcome. Is this true or false?

   A. True
   B. False

7. CCF is a measurement of?

   A. Energy
   B. Natural Gas
   C. Water
   D. Pollution

8. Energy is measured in what metric?

   A. Therms
   B. BTUs
   C. CCF
   D. kWh

9. Natural gas is measured in what metric?

   A. Therms
   B. BTUs
   C. CCF
   D. kWh

10. Greenhouse gases are reported by converting to what equivalent?

    A. Methane
    B. Carbon dioxide
    C. Nitrogen oxide
    D. Sulfur dioxide

Answers:1D, 2C, 3A, 4A, 5C, 6B, 7C, 8D, 9A, 10B

ENDNOTES

[1] Meadows, D., Randers, J. & Meadows, D. (2004). *Limits to growth: The 30-year update.* White River Junction, VT: Chelsea Green Publishing Co. (p. 5).

[2] Meadows, D., Randers, J. & Meadows, D. (2004). *Limits to growth: The 30-year update.* White River Junction, VT: Chelsea Green Publishing Co. (p. 137).

[3] Meadows, D., Randers, J. & Meadows, D. (2004). *Limits to growth: The 30-year update.* White River Junction, VT: Chelsea Green Publishing Co. (p. 137).

[4] Meadows, D., Randers, J. & Meadows, D. (2004). *Limits to growth: The 30-year update.* White River Junction, VT: Chelsea Green Publishing Co. (p. 5).

[5] An Interview with John Sterman. (January 2009). A sober optimist's guide to sustainability. *MIT Sloan Management Review, reprint 50320.* (pp. 1–5).

[6] An Interview with John Sterman. (January 2009). A sober optimist's guide to sustainability *MIT Sloan Management Review, reprint 50320.* (pp. 1–5).

[7] An Interview with John Sterman. (January 2009). A sober optimist's guide to sustainability. *MIT Sloan Management Review, reprint 50320.* (pp. 1–5).

[8] Meadows, D., Randers, J. & Meadows, D. (2004). *Limits to growth: The 30-year update.* White River Junction, VT: Chelsea Green Publishing Co. (p. 126).

[9] Sterman, J. (2001). Systems dynamics modeling: Tools for learning in a complex world. *California Management Review.* 43(4). (p. 21).

[10] Meadows, D., Randers, J. & Meadows, D. (2004). *Limits to growth: The 30-year update.* White River Junction, VT: Chelsea Green Publishing Co. (p. 11).

[11] Meadows, D., Randers, J. & Meadows, D. (2004). *Limits to growth: The 30-year update.* White River Junction, VT: Chelsea Green Publishing Co. (p. 11).

[12] Meadows, D. edited by Wright, D. (2008). *Thinking in systems.* White River Junction, VT: Chelsea Green Publishing Co. (p. 25).

[13] Meadows, D., Randers, J. and Meadows, D. (2004). *Limits to growth: The 30-year update.* White River Junction, VT: Chelsea Green Publishing Co. (p. 147).

[14] Forrester, Jay. (1969). *Urban dynamics.* Cambridge, MA: MIT Press.

[15] Senge, Peter. (1990). *The fifth discipline: The art and practice of the learning organization.* New York, NY: Doubleday, (p. 387).

[16] Sterman, J. (2000). *Business dynamics–Systems thinking and modeling for a complex world.* Boston, MA: McGraw Hill Companies. (p. 192).

[17] Hopkins, Michael, S. (2009). An interview with Jay Forrester: The loop you can't get out of. *MIT Sloan Management Review, reprint 50201.* (pp. 9–12).

[18] Hopkins, Michael, S. (2009). An interview with Jay Forrester: The loop you can't get out of. *MIT Sloan Management Review, reprint 50201.* (pp. 9–12).

[19] Kim, Hyunjung. (2011, personal creation). Vensim Model–Ventana Systems, Inc.

[20] *Quest Recycling.* Retrieved October 17, 2011 from: http://www.questrecycling.com/pdf/Quest_and_walmart _global_sustainability_milestone_meeting-PR-3-21-11.pdf

[21] *Methodology and Assumptions for Estimating WaterSense Annual Accomplishments.* (n.d.) Retrieved on April 19, 2012 from: http://www.responsiblepurchasing.org/watersense_methodology.pdf

[22] *Methodology and Assumptions for Estimating WaterSense Annual Accomplishments.* (n.d.) Retrieved on April 19, 2012 from: http://www.responsiblepurchasing.org/watersense_methodology.pdf

[23] *How Natural Gas is Measured.* Retrieved on April 17, 2012 from: http://www.tulsagastech.com/measure.html

[24] *Methodology and Assumptions for Estimating WaterSense Annual Accomplishments.* (n.d.) Retrieved on April 19, 2012 from: http://www.responsiblepurchasing.org/watersense_methodology.pdf

[25] *Energy and You.* (November 14, 2008). Retrieved on April 19, 2012 from: http://www.epa.gov/cleanenergy /energy-and-you/index.html

[26] *2011 U.S. Greenhouse Gas Inventory Report.* (April 2011). *Inventory of U.S. Greenhouse Gas Emissions and Sinks: 1990-2009.* USEPA #430-R-11-005. Retrieved on 10-23-11 from: http://epa.gov/climatechange /emissions/usinventoryreport.html

[27] *The GHG Protocol for Project Accounting.* (Dec. 2005). Retrieved on 10-20-2011 from: http://www.ghgprotocol .org/files/ghgp/ghg_project_protocol.pdf

[28] *Calculations Tools.* Retrieved on October 19, 2011 from: http://www.ghgprotocol.org/calculation-tools

[29] *FAQs - ARB GHG Reporting and Verification.* (May 2011). Retrieved on 10-23-11 from: http://www.arb .ca.gov/cc/reporting/ghg-rep/updated_faq.pdf

[30] Wagoner, J. Butte County Air Quality Management District's Air Pollution Control Officer. (March 6, 2012). Personal interview.

Chapter 3

Policies for Decision Making and Change Management

3.1 Introduction

Embedding sustainability management into strategy is just the first step. Creating policies that clearly outline the values of the organization and a clear roadmap will ensure employees adopt new work processes to make informed decisions. Decision making can only be improved through developing clear policies and then training employees on the why, what, how, how much, and how often details, etc. Achieving better efficiencies and brand value through responsibility is clearly a benefit to any organization. Creating tools for employees, which guide behavior, will create lasting benefits.

Recall from Chapter 1, that a Sustainability Management System (SMS) is a planning document that establishes an organization's policies based on values and integrity. Tailor the SMS to fit the culture of your workforce. For example, Pacific Living Properties, Inc.'s SMS clearly outlines the vision and mission of the organization:

> *Pacific Living Properties, Inc. positively contributes to the health and well-being of many communities throughout the west coast. Our vision is to provide sustainable living environments and our strategy is "Be Green because We Care." Our mission is to help our residents learn to live healthier lifestyles and to learn about the environmental impacts that each person makes. For our employees, our mission is to strive for zero waste and reimagine how we process our daily responsibilities.*
>
> *Managing for sustainability is simply strategically positioning the organization's employees to be excellent stewards of society, the natural environment, and improve economic conditions for our residents. Our employees are an essential game changer within the local community. We serve a purpose that is so meaningful in that we change people's lives for the better. We make a difference.[1]*

Pacific Living Properties, Inc. also outlines the values of the organization by TBL:

> *The SMS policy is to always strategically manage our properties as stewards of society, the environment, and the economy. Our goal is to make choices that positively impact people, planet, and profit to the best of our ability.*

- *Social Equity Values*

  Our efforts to transform communities positively impact many people every day. Our work ensures that people have the support and services they need to live a high quality lifestyle. The company is only successful because of your kindness and generosity. We believe in fostering a healthy lifestyle to improve quality of life. We believe in leading by example and helping others learn about sustainability.

- *Environmental Stewardship*

  Pacific Living Properties, Inc. strives to learn about the environmental impacts of each action or operational practice. We encourage employees to recommend savings that will reduce energy usage, water usage, solid waste, and pollution to the waste water system and soil. We uphold a policy of environmental stewardship to help make decisions in our daily routines that could reduce material consumption and to reduce any wasted resources.

- *Economic Stewardship*

  Every resource we have should be used to end-of-life so we can reuse it over and over again to save money and divert waste from landfills. If an item is to be thrown away, perhaps another organization could use it. Other ways you can help be economic stewards is to think about your daily routine. In what ways could you conserve energy, water, waste, or reduce pollution?[2]

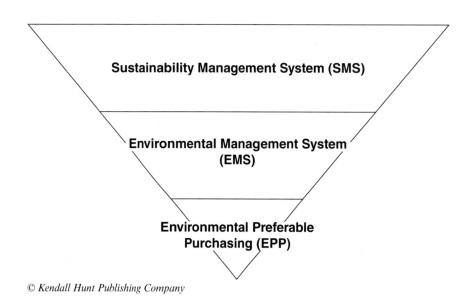

© Kendall Hunt Publishing Company

3.2 Chapter Overview

The chapter will focus on describing the key components of policies that will build awareness and create guidelines and standards:

1. Sustainability Management System (SMS) explains the strategic priorities of the organization. An SMS focuses on the big picture and the values of the organization.

2. Environmental Management System (EMS) focuses on addressing and improving specific work processes or activities that specifically impact the natural environment internally and throughout the value chain. An EMS is a subset of an SMS.
3. Environmental Preferable Purchasing (EPP) focuses on guiding decision-making on inputs—specifically conducting life cycle costing to evaluate procurement decisions.

3.3 Sustainability Management System (SMS) Policy

Recall from Chapter 1, a Sustainable Management Systems (SMS) policy establishes the following:

Planning

- Vision statement that clearly communicates values and ethics to stakeholders
- Mission statement to establish organizational mindset of long term value through Triple Bottom Line

Organizing

- Understand external environment opportunities and threats and develop strategies to gain competitive advantage through long-term planning
- Evaluate constraints on natural resources or raw materials facing obsolescence or future unaffordable costs
- Evaluate social responsibility impacts of all stakeholders throughout the value chain
- Evaluate industry's impact on economic responsibility
- Develop short-, medium-, and long-term goals for internal strengths and weaknesses
- Establish internal decision-making processes that focus on moving toward the triple bottom line values articulated in the mission statement
- Establish partnerships within the value chain, to include suppliers, government entities, and nongovernmental agencies
- Create an Environmental Management System policy specifically for directions on how to handle environmental aspects, such as hazardous materials and chemicals at the frontline or operational level
- Create an Environmental Preferable Purchasing policy to communicate organizational values to guide employee purchasing decisions

Leading

- Create frameworks/terminology to talk about sustainability
- Implement operational goals
- Training and development of talented employees
- Change management techniques to benchmark progress and continuous improvement
- Create monitoring systems that measure desired environmental, economic, and social outcomes and critical indicators for undesired or unintended outcomes

Controlling

- Capital budget consideration for quick wins and long-term resource efficiency
- Financial expectations for long-term project management for return on investment, payback periods, and profit margins

- Define key metrics to benchmark and measure organizational TBL progress and outcomes
- Define how and when to report metrics across systems
- Establish how the organization will communicate achievements and challenges to stakeholders

Evaluating

- Clear key performance indicators to benchmark when the organization achieves a mindset of sustainability, as in evaluating when employees consider TBL as a job function while making decisions at all levels within the organizational structure
- Establish incentive and reward programs to celebrate success
- Empower employees to take action so change is driven top down and bottom up
- Revise policy as needed and seek continuous improvement
- Effectively communicate success and challenges to internal and external stakeholders, with a high priority focused on reporting the facts and metrics to show progress

Established Codes of Conduct

There are established codes of conduct that prevalently exist worldwide. Referencing or adopting existing codes is another way to establish and communicate values. Existing codes of conduct address responsibility in social equity, economics, and environmental arenas:

- The United Nations Global Compact:
  www.unglobalcompact.org
  Ten principles for business regarding human and labor rights, environmental responsibility, and anti-corruption.

- The Caux Round Table's Principles for Business:
  www.cauxroundtable.org/principles.html
  Business leaders established globally responsible business practices, such as human rights, education, and the welfare of contributing positively to local communities.

- Coalition for Environmentally Responsible Economies (CERES) Principles:
  www.ceres.org
  A nonprofit organization that developed principles for biodiversity, environmental responsibility, natural resource usage, energy conservation, and reducing risk.

- International Chamber of Commerce:
  www.iccwbo.org
  Promotes international trade, open markets, and investment favoring responsibility over regulation.

- United Nations Universal Declaration of Human Rights:
  www.unhchr.ch/documents/udhr/
  Declares universal freedoms from discrimination, slavery, abuse, and inhumane treatment.

3.4 Environmental Management System (EMS) Policy

Creating a policy that gives guidance for employees will increase the likelihood of successful changes in management and pervasive alignment toward meeting strategic goals. Every organization has pollutants and toxins within the facility, such as paints, cleaning materials, and air fresheners. Building awareness takes time to successfully grow an organization's culture.

An EMS focuses on the decision making process to improve efficiencies and impacts of workflows, purchasing decisions, and end-of-life management. Based on the strategic goals of the organization, the EMS should outline operational goals at the frontline level. Target goals for environmental management should focus on five key activities:

1. Solid waste prevention
2. Energy conservation
3. Water conservation
4. Pollution prevention of water, land, and air
5. Specifically address procedures for known chemicals or hazardous materials on site

ISO Certifications

ISO 14001 is a certification an organization can obtain by establishing an EMS and having it audited and verified. The International Organization of Standardization will certify an organization's process and has thorough guidelines for how to set up an EMS. ISO 14001 is the guideline to set up an EMS, while ISO 14004 are the requirements for the EMS.[3] Most manufacturing and governmental agencies prevalently certify their EMS. Certification is also a competitive advantage that can differentiate your organization against competing suppliers and/or to attract new business by showing a commitment to establishing workplace policies focused on responsibility to the environment.

Creating Realistic Goals and Key Performance Indicators

Programs can be devised to achieve goals and objectives for energy, water, waste, and pollution.

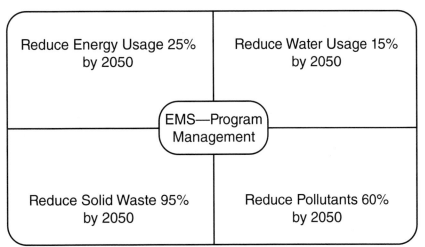

© Kendall Hunt Publishing Company

Projects should then be planned to achieve stated program goals. Key performance indicators should be established for all projects to know when milestones are achieved and should be communicated.

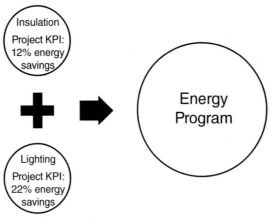

© Kendall Hunt Publishing Company

Tracking and measuring progress is critical to successful project management. Life cycle costing should be calculated for each project to determine the feasibility and viability of alternatives to the current state in order to reach the desired future state. It is an excellent tool to make decisions by comparing the benefits and drawbacks of different alternative choices. Then tracking tools can be designed for the evaluation stage to report progression.

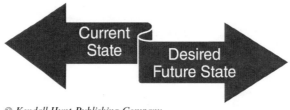

© Kendall Hunt Publishing Company

Life Cycle Costing Example

To achieve the energy program target of 25%, an organization should assess the current state. In the following example, Zebra, Inc. evaluates a lighting strategy project. The company currently uses 9,876,753 kilowatts per hour and pays an annual expense of $1,382,745 in energy costs just for lighting.

Lighting Project Management—Target Goal 22% Reduction

	KwH per meter	**Current Cost**
Current Interior	1,273,558	$178,298.12
Current Exterior	8,603,195	$1,204,447.30
Annual Total	**9,876,753**	**$1,382,745.42**

The next step would be to evaluate available alternatives to reach the future state of 25% reduction. Zebra, Inc. assesses different lighting options to replace bulbs and fluorescent tubing for the interior and exterior lighting.

Life Cycle Costing—Projected State

Interior		Kw per bulb	# Units	Daily Hours	Daily Total kWh	Annual Total kWh	Total Daily Cost	Total Annual Cost	Per unit Investment	Projected Investment
	LED bulbs	6	10	10	600	219,000	$84	$30,660	$15	$150
	CFL bulbs	25	10	10	2,500	912,500	$350	$127,750	$3	$30
	Fluorescent T5 Tubing	14	20	10	2,800	1,022,000	$392	$143,080	$8	$160
Exterior										
	LED fixtures	23	60	14	19,320	7,051,800	$2,705	$987,252	$200	$12,000
Best Choice in Bold					22,720	8,292,800	$3,181	$1,160,992	$223	$12,310

The final step is to evaluate if the alternative choices would meet the target goal.

Cost Benefit Analyses

	Current kWh per meter	Current Cost	Future kWh per meter	Future Cost	% Reduction	Cost Reduction	Minus Investment	1st Year Savings
Current Interior	1,273,558	$178,298.12	1,241,000.00	$173,740	0.30	$4,558.12	$310	$4,248.12
Current Exterior	8,603,195	$1,204,447.30	7,051,800.00	$987,252	0.18	$217,195.30	$12,000	$205,195.30
Annual Total	9,876,753	$1,382,745.42	8,292,800.00	$1,160,992	0.24	$221,753.42	$12,310	$209,443.42

Zebra, Inc. would invest $12,310 to purchase new lighting before applicable rebates. The total projected lighting reduction of 24% would nearly meet the 25% target. If the organization is able to invest in new lighting, the savings within the first year would be $209,443. If the investment would need to be phased in due to affordability, Zebra could implement the interior lighting and phase in exterior lighting over time.

Another consideration would be to evaluate product features to continue a broad evaluation of life cycle costing options between lighting options.

Life Cycle Costing	Raw Material Toxins	End of Life Toxins	Life Span	Benefits
LED	yes	no mercury	30,000	low heat radiance
CFL	mercury gas	mercury gas	8,000	many low cost styles

Zebra, Inc. has determined that the best option is to replace incandescent bulbs with LED bulbs due to low toxicity, better end-of-life disposal options, low heat radiance, and higher savings on energy costs. Although the initial investment is higher for LED over CFL, the product life cycle is longer for LEDs. The payback period will be faster and the rebates are also higher. By taking into account all of these considerations, the LED light was chosen as the best option.

Business Process Management

Once the EMS programs are defined and written into guidelines, the implementation, evaluation, and reporting processes are the next steps.

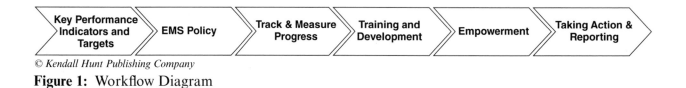

© *Kendall Hunt Publishing Company*

Figure 1: Workflow Diagram

Training and Development

Training and development is critical. Employees cannot perform life cycle costing without knowing the positive and negative impacts a product or process incurs. They cannot make better choices without knowing why and how they are making improvements. For instance, most people don't really think about what happens to the garbage after it's hauled away. Most know that it goes to a landfill, but some people are not aware that the landfill emits dangerous methane gas due to the decomposition of organic materials, and that the county has to manage those landfills with taxpayer dollars. Most people do not know that the landfills are filling up fast and that counties have to purchase new locations or transport the garbage to another county or state. When employees are shown how they fit into the system of an entire process, they are more apt to participate in improving the system. Equipped with information, employees are more apt to question their everyday work processes and find new ways to reimagine, redesign, reduce, reuse, repair, recycle, and even practice rot (composting).

Empowerment

Empowerment is the next step. Give employees and departments target goals that stretch their capabilities. First employees need to know what to accomplish, then they need to know why, next is how, then how to track progress, and finally how and when to communicate progress. Employees should also be aware of authority parameters and budgetary allocations in order to be able to make decisions and then implement them.

Let's say the project is to reduce office paper usage by 50%. Training would include: just not printing unnecessary documents, filing documents electronically by archiving, printing a document on both sides of the paper by using the duplex printer setting, or purchasing new paper that contains recycled content. Training on why should include the difference between raw materials, such as using virgin and recycled paper content and the manufacturing process of each. Employees should evaluate the following when tracking and measuring progress:

- Office paper units purchased by volume in current state and the annual cost to procure
- Office paper purchased during the implementation stage
  - Virgin material volume
  - Recycled content volume
- Peak periods of office paper usage
- Reporting progress at the end of the year will compare year-on-year results Reporting should include volume reduction plus cost reduction and what actions were taken to achieve the goal
- Efforts should be documented for accountability, such as commendations in performance appraisals
- Communicate specific results to employees and within sustainability reports

Empowerment should be closely linked to celebrating success. When employees suggest new ideas, it is beneficial to give them authority to implement those ideas and report on the progress. Empowerment leads to cultural change and building excitement. When employees report progress, it is very important to celebrate successes of the small actions. This is because the small actions really add up and make huge positive impacts. As an example, recycling systems may reduce garbage expense by $1,000 a year for a small business. Procurement choices can oftentimes save another $1,000 just from buying in bulk. Energy conservation can oftentimes reduce expenses at a minimum of $2,000 for a small office. See how it all adds up quickly to $4,000? The company can then reinvest these savings into more expensive sustainability projects that require capital investment funding and approval.

© *Kendall Hunt Publishing Company*

Figure 2: Empowerment Workflow Diagram

Taking Action

Taking action should also be documented and lauded in performance appraisals, incentive reward programs, or public praise. Lack of activity can also be documented in performance appraisals so all employees know the organization takes sustainability management seriously. Embedding responsibility into formal and informal systems of human resource management will also continue to reward employees for great new ideas. Motivating the workforce long term can be very challenging to keep the momentum flowing; consistently recognizing employees is well worth the effort and will build excitement and motivation throughout the workplace.

An EMS will provide procedures and establish major programs to conserve or mitigate within an organization's span of control. An EMS is a tool employees can use to make everyday decisions that make a significant impact on reducing expenses, material usage, and pollution.

3.5 Environment Preferable Purchasing (EPP) Policy

Another widely used tool is to establish a policy specifically for purchasing decisions—Environmental Preferable Purchasing (EPP) policy. Procurement policies should align with strategic goals and reflect the values of the organization. An EPP policy will guide purchasing decisions to consider many factors prior to purchasing inputs.

Procurement decisions should be based on evaluating the source—raw materials of the product. Throughput should be evaluated for how it's made and the consequences or impacts to the environment and social issues, such as working conditions. Procurement decisions should evaluate sinks—where waste products end up as pollutants and wastes, whether finished goods or byproducts. Evaluating sinks questions end-of-life management.

© *Kendall Hunt Publishing Company*

When organizations spend money on products twice, they are paying once as an input and paying again as a waste product. There are even further costs, such as fees and fines for improper disposal. End-of-life considerations are just as important as considering how raw materials are obtained and transported. Life cycle costing is an excellent framework to teach employees to evaluate the pros and cons of a product, service, or vendor to choose the better option.

Environmental Preferable Purchasing Outcomes

The outcome of an EPP policy should be to ensure that products and services contracted or purchased would meet the needs of the organization's strategic imperatives, values, and goals. Some "green" products have a price premium, such as organic vegetables; while others are well established and market demand has created competitive pricing, such as recycled content copy paper. It may be valuable to set a price ceiling of 10–15% to purchase products or services that are new to the market or continue to sell at a premium price.

Another outcome should be to continue to evaluate products and services on the quality, price, functionality, and feasibility. Yet policies assist employees in researching existing environmentally preferable products on the market. The outcome transitions to supporting sustainable and social entrepreneurial companies and growing the economy by investing in innovation and design.

Life Cycle Costing of Alternatives

Prevalent examples of EPPs exist on the Internet. The Natural Resource Defense Council has multiple case studies available to the general public free of charge.[4] The following purchasing criteria should be tailored to the needs and unique environment of the organization:

- The entire value chain should be considered to identify where raw materials were sourced.
- How are raw materials assembled and manufactured?
- How far did the product travel to reach the retail store?
- If a product is purchased online from a local source, will it come from a local distribution channel?
- What are the labor conditions of the manufacture and has the company been inspected for social responsibility by a third party auditor?
- Is there an end-of-life solution or will these products have to be disposed of in the landfill, or even worse, in a hazardous materials facility?

Some purchasing considerations to include in an EPP will help to determine which product or service is a better choice:

- Products made with significant content of pre- or post-consumer recycled content
- Products that reduce the use of chemicals to protect human and environmental health
- Products manufactured by renewable energy sources
- Products that reduce particulate matter or greenhouse gases to reduce air pollution
- Products that reduce water pollution
- Products that reduce waste
- Products with packaging materials that are truly compostable or biodegradable such as paper or wax paper
- Products with minimal packaging materials
- Reusable products or refillable office supplies
- Products that are durable and dependable
- Products that have multiple functions
- Products that have buy-back options from manufacturers
- Repairable or remanufactured parts or products
- Products that are recyclable
- Products manufactured with high labor standards
- Products from local merchants to spur economic growth
- Products that can be obtained locally to reduce transportation emissions
- Products that are designed for the environment or have closed loop manufacturing processes
- Products sold in bulk or concentrated materials
- Product is low maintenance during usage stage

Employees will require information to make decisions. Training is an essential action to implement an EPP. Evaluating criteria will become easier through time as awareness builds and everyone is more comfortable evaluating the products' life cycle benefits and features. Universities, nongovernmental entities (NGO), and manufacturers oftentimes are great resources for assistance in learning more about environmental impacts.

Product Labeling

Some product labeling and marketing can be confusing. Employees think they are making the right choices, but need to know the entire picture. The next section will address a few commonly confused terms in product labeling.

Biodegradable:
Organic materials can decompose back into natural elements through aerobic (air and oxygen) or anaerobic (bacteria) digestion. Bio-degradable materials are plants, or products that are made from plants, such as paper or cotton shirts. What chemicals were added during the manufacturing stage may allow the material to still biodegrade, but will not be a healthy additive for soil enhancement or compost. For instance, a paper plate with a plastic lining will biodegrade but will not be a soil enhancement due to the plastic only "breaks apart".

Compostable:
Organic materials that when degraded can be used again as fertilizer. Composting requires a ratio of carbon to nitrogen ratio at 30 to 1 or less. Greens and browns are easy ways to ensure the pH level or acidity will be an excellent soil enhancement. Anaerobic digestion by micro-organisms breaks down organic material. The hotter the compost, the faster it breaks down. In-vessel compost machines reach high temperatures of 140–180 degrees. These in-vessel composters can break down the new bio-based plastics and packaging materials.

Natural:
A product that is produced by nature and not by mankind. The Food and Drug Administration does not have a definition, but refers to natural as plant or animal products that are not produced synthetically.[5] The United States Department of Agriculture specifies for meat and poultry that it must not contain artificial ingredients, preservatives, and does not fundamentally alter the raw material.[6]

Organic:
Organic farming maintains and replenishes soil fertility. Organic foods must not contain toxic and persistent pesticides and fertilizers, antibiotics, synthetic hormones, or genetic engineering. Even more so, organic production does not include sewage sludge, or contamination. Organic foods are minimally processed and do not contain artificial ingredients or preservatives.

Biodegradable Plastics:
Plastic alternatives are prevalent on the market today and often marketed as biodegradable. They are biodegradable in an in-vessel composter machine or large wind rows that reach high temperatures of 140 degrees Fahrenheit.

Some of the new polymer innovations on the market today are:

- PHA (polyhydroxyalkanoates)
- PHBV (polyhydroxybutyrate-valerate)
- PLA (polylactic acid)
- PCL (polycaprolactone)
- PVA (polyvinyl alcohol)
- PET (polyethylene terephthalate)

These polymers are made from byproducts that have enough sugar and starch such as, corn, wheat, or sugar cane. These plastics are referred to as hydro-biodegradable plastics (HBP) and oxo-biodegradable plastics (OBP). While breaking down, both will degrade by hydrolysis and oxidation. HBPs degrade faster than OBPs. At decomposition, the result is carbon dioxide (CO_2), water (H_2O) and biomass.

Finding Suppliers and Products

The U.S. Environmental Protection Agency also has some invaluable resources for the general public on their website: http://www.epa.gov/epawaste/conserve/tools/cpg/index.htm. The EPA publishes a Comprehensive Procurement Guideline (CPG) program in support of reusing materials remanufactured from solid waste. The CPG includes eight product categories:

- Construction products
- Landscaping products
- Non-paper office products
- Paper and paper products
- Park and recreation products
- Transportation products
- Vehicular products
- Miscellaneous products

The CPG also provides a supplier directory to locate available suppliers of these products.

Supplier Relations

Every decision has an impact on the environment, society, and economy. With each dollar we spend, we show our support. Consumers increasingly hold the entire value chain responsible for all the actions and activities throughout the whole process. Damaging your brand based on supplier relations is an increasing risk. Aligning your organization with other entities that share the same respect for people, planet, and profit is another way to support sustainability management and protect your image. Some choices to consider are:

- Support local communities by buying local
- Purchase from manufacturers that do not pollute or destroy the environment
- Support suppliers with verified fair labor conditions
- Purchase products that are third party certified, such as Green Seal for cleaning products
- Work with suppliers that have a sustainable mindset that aligns with yours
- Support innovation of entrepreneurship to create the products of the future

The Green Hotel Association is a nonprofit organization headquartered in Houston, TX. The goal of the organization is to provide hotel managers, engineers, and employees with guidelines on how to reduce negative environmental impacts without sacrificing quality or hospitality. Green Hotel Association's first major public campaign was the signage found in hotel rooms to "hang up your towel" or "we change sheets every other day" in order to reuse hotel materials to reduce water, energy, and labor costs. Today, the association is a central communicator and collaborator to offer hotels resources and information. The pace of innovation and new ideas can be overwhelming. The association takes on that task and provides members with a bi-weekly newsletter to keep members up to date. Membership is very affordable, and the members range from small business bed and breakfasts, military bases to major chains. The trend today of the association is to help new startup entrepreneurs inform the membership of new product innovation and development available on the market. The services provided by the Green Hotel Association are excellent examples of how to help buyers find suppliers, and how an industry can work together.

Besides supplier relations, EPP policies can open new markets due to government regulations. Many state and federal government agencies have well-established EPPs in order to support entrepreneurs whose values align with stewardship and responsibility. In the state of California, the CA Public Contract Code's Environmentally Preferable Purchasing, sections 12400–12404) and the State Agency Buy Recycled Campaign, section 12153, require state agencies to make better purchasing decisions that protect human health and the environment.[7] The government is a dependable buyer of goods and services. Establishing and implementing an EPP can be a competitive advantage to secure new government contracts or open new markets to beat the competition in the RFP process.

3.6 Summary

The SMS, EMS, and EPP may certainly be created as one policy to reduce redundancy, especially for small- to medium-sized businesses. An organization does not have to complete any of these policies; they are just excellent tools for change management, employee training, vetting suppliers, or contracting new products or services.

3.7 Experiential Exercises

Chapter 1 focused on organizational values and the terminology used in sustainability management. In Chapter 2, you have already begun thinking about goals and objectives you can achieve. Writing a policy for the employees of the company is great practice. The policy is an excellent training tool, and a clear road map for employees to understand their roles in the organization and how they each make an impact—both positive and negative.

I.   Write a Sustainability Management Policy that clearly states your values and expectations of each employee.

II. Write an Environmental Management System Policy that clearly identifies the major priorities of the organization. This document should be a training tool to build awareness of chemicals or hazardous materials onsite, waste to landfill and properly disposing of items, waste water treatment impacts, air pollutants used on premise, energy and water conservation, and why conservation is important.

III. Write an Environmentally Preferable Purchasing Policy that clearly outlines procurement decisions employees should make regarding achieving a Zero Waste culture. Some organizations specify that all office supplies must be reusable and made of recycled content.

SAMPLE QUESTIONS

1. Decision making of frontline staff can be improved by creating _____.

    A. policies and training materials
    B. social equity statements
    C. evaluation tools
    D. scorecards

2. Which policy includes the strategic vision statement of an organization?

    A. Environmental Purchasing Policy
    B. Environmental Preferable Purchasing Policy
    C. Environmental Management System
    D. Sustainability Management System

3. Which policy focuses on addressing and improving specific environmental work processes?

    A. Environmental Purchasing Policy
    B. Environmental Preferable Purchasing Policy
    C. Environmental Management System
    D. Sustainability Management System

4. An Environmental Management System focuses on the strategic priorities of the organization.

    A. True
    B. False

5. _____ is defined as giving employees the authority to implement action plans.

    A. Empowerment
    B. Training
    C. Austerity
    D. Synergy

6. What is the acronym for the policy that specifically focuses on purchasing?

    A. SMS
    B. EPP
    C. EMS
    D. AMS

7. What does the acronym EPP stand for?

    A. Environmental Purchasing Policy
    B. Economic Procurement Procedure
    C. Environmental Preferable Purchasing
    D. Environmental Purchasing Preference

8. Procurement decisions should focus on inputs and outputs, but further evaluates _____ and _____.

    A. gasoline or diesel fuel
    B. electric and water usage
    C. sun and wind
    D. sources and sinks

9. There are many regulations on product labels, such as "biodegradable" or "natural".

    A. True
    B. False

10. Which product is the best choice based on life cycle assessment?

    A. Natural apple juice
    B. Organic apple juice
    C. No sugar added apple juice
    D. Light Apple Juice

Answers: 1A, 2D, 3C, 4B, 5A, 6B, 7C, 8D, 9B, 10B

ENDNOTES

[1] Miller, J. (2011). Personal interview. Pacific Living Properties, Inc.

[2] Miller, J. (2011). Personal interview. Pacific Living Properties, Inc.

[3] *ISO 14000 essentials.* Retrieved on October 28, 2011 from: http://www.iso.org/iso/iso_14000_essentials

[4] *An Environmental Preferable Purchasing Policy.* (n.d.) Retrieved on October 29, 2011 from: http://www.nrdc
.org/enterprise/greeningadvisor/gpp-purch_policy.asp

[5] *What are Natural Ingredients?* The Natural Ingredient Resource Center. Retrieved on October 28, 2011 from:
http://www.naturalingredient.org/naturalingredients.htm

[6] *What are Natural Ingredients?* The Natural Ingredient Resource Center. Retrieved on October 28, 2011 from:
http://www.naturalingredient.org/naturalingredients.htm

[7] *Laws and Regulations.* CA Department of General Services. Retrieved on October 29, 2011 from: http://www
.dgs.ca.gov/buyinggreen/Home/BuyersMain.aspx

Chapter 4

Aligning Business Systems to Achieve Systemic Change

4.1 Introduction

Chapter 1 introduces major frameworks and positioning the company for long-term sustainable growth that meet the needs of future opportunities and risks. Chapter 2 focuses on identifying sources and sinks and evaluating the current situation. Systems thinking will identify the environmental impacts an organization makes. Chapter 2 also includes how to measure environmental impacts. Chapter 3 outlines the policies organizations create to meet strategic imperatives. In this chapter, the procedures that can be deployed within departments are discussed as well as the roles of management and departmental functions. This chapter is a guide that discusses the many ways sustainability management is implemented through change management. Each organization is unique, but aligning business systems can be achieved by any entity in business, government, or nonprofits. It is recommended to use this chapter to assign responsibility and job duties for the function where it is most applicable within your own organization. As a reminder, this study guide is written for professionals at all levels of management in cross-industry, public, and non-profit entities that are each in different stages of embedding sustainability management across the organization's culture.

4.2 Aligning Business Systems

What does aligning business systems mean? To align business systems is to give clear directives to leaders and employees to meet the strategic goals of the organization by each person aligning process, action, and behavior to successfully meet strategic goals. In sustainability management, the values of the organization play a major role. Aligning business systems around the organization's values will create a culture or mindset of ethical decision making. If employees do not know or understand the organization's values, they cannot align their actions and processes to meet organizational expectations. Therefore, continuous communication of the organization's values and codes of conduct is necessary.

The stakeholders of an organization make up the elements of a system, such as owners, investors, management, employees, customers, and competitors. The processes and procedures of that system determine how the organization communicates, interacts, and functions. With a clearly defined system, employees understand how to interact, bring value, and great new ideas to meet the needs of stakeholders.

The success of managing for sustainability relies on creating a culture within the organization. The culture then drives systemic change to achieve the vision and mission, where all units and departments are committed to participating, taking action, driving new ideas, and continuously improving. Cultural transition must be driven from the senior management as top down, but embraced and accepted by employees.

4.3 Change Management

In order to align business systems to meet strategic future plans, change management is the most important aspect to manage for sustainability. Change management is the transition from a current state to a desired future state. Employees at all levels of the organization should clearly understand defined values, attitudes, norms, and beliefs within an organization that support how work is processed. Resistance to change will need to be managed with tools to help employees understand and embody new values or norms. Change management is a journey that will take time, but with the proper management to reduce barriers and build awareness, change management can oftentimes be invigorating and meet the personal values of employees. Therefore, change management creates value because it instills employee loyalty to the company through a proud sense of accomplishment and achievement.

Change management can be accomplished by establishing a clear strategic vision, then developing tactical and operational goals.

© Kendall Hunt Publishing Company

In sustainability management, each employee at all levels of the organization plays an integral role in developing a culture of responsibility. When employees understand that values transform to value, the culture can rally around attitudes and beliefs that exceed the expectations of stakeholders. Clear expectations and target goals that achieve the long-term needs of the organization must be clearly defined and communicated.

This chapter will focus on the future desired state on the journey of sustainability management.

The Journey of Sustainability Management

The journey of sustainability management begins internally with senior management support, a clear vision, values, and direction so change management will not be met with too much resistance.

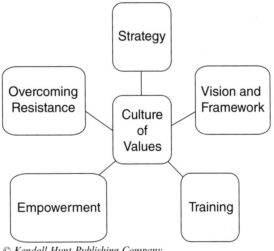

Creating a culture centered on values requires time to build awareness through communicating frequently to all employees. Communicating with a framework will give employees an easy mantra to follow. For instance, Pacific Living Properties' vision is simply "Be Green". Then it is necessary to create an implementation plan, align business systems around the strategy, and ensure all processes and reporting are transparent.

To achieve the desired state, the organization should focus on five key steps:

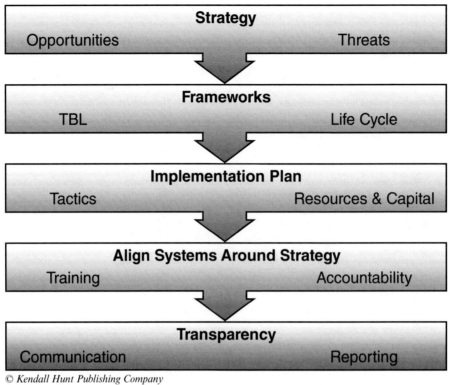

© *Kendall Hunt Publishing Company*

Figure 1: Process Map

Empower and Train

Regardless of the size of your organization, sustainability must be supported by senior management. Senior managers empower employees to seek better ways to create value. Each employee plays an integral role in building the culture from the bottom up to meet senior management and stakeholder expectations.

A culture, or mindset, of sustainability cannot be achieved if sustainability is a centralized function and employees in other business units or departments are not expected to participate. Therefore, aligning business systems starts with building awareness, training and development, and empowering employees with clear job responsibilities and expectations.

The rest of the chapter will focus on the role that managers play and the departmental processes that are important to achieving a culture that creates value through values.

4.4 The Role of Senior Management

The process of integrating a sustainable mindset within an organization can be achieved by recognizing that the environment, economy, and society are intimately dependent on a healthy natural ecosystem. Oftentimes, organizations practice backcasting to create strategic goals. Backcasting is the process of imagining the industry position 25 to 50 years into the future and positioning the organization for sustainable growth. Backcasting assists the organization to recognize future opportunities and risks in the external environment that will impact the industry. Management can then design tactics to achieve goals that start from the futuristic standpoint and drill backward to reach long-term goals.

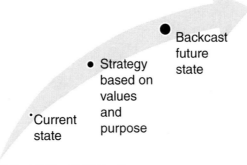

© *Kendall Hunt Publishing Company*

To recall, Phase I of a sustainable strategy focuses on internal redesign based on the impacts the organization makes on the environment, society, and economy. Phase II focuses on collaborating throughout the supply chain to achieve common supply chain strategies. Phase III focuses on partnerships with external stakeholders to achieve broad positive impacts to the environment, society, and economy.

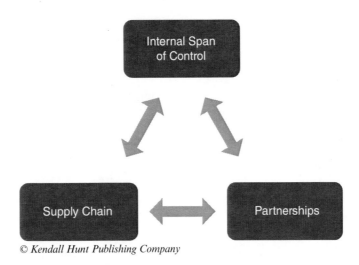

© *Kendall Hunt Publishing Company*

Role of Senior Managers in Phase I: Internal Control

Long before sustainability management became a popular management practice, the company Smucker's Quality Beverages was practicing sustainability as a core business approach. Acquiring brands such as K. W. Knudsen and Santa Cruz opened up new markets in the natural and organic beverage consumer market. Senior managers crafted the "Smucker's Experience" as a vision statement and added the "sustainability pillar" in all 14 plants. Senior managers delegate tactical goals in pillars, such as quality, sustainability, safety, etc. The parent company, J. M. Smucker, crafts strategy on "Basic Beliefs." Since 1897, the "Basic Beliefs" of quality, people, ethics, growth, and independence drive strategy and achievements.[1] These basic beliefs are embodied by all senior managers to protect the brand. They are driven from the top down, yet embedded into the culture to achieve a mindset of values and integrity. Creating a culture based on ethics and sustainability drives performance as the core business at J. M. Smucker.

The role of senior management is to position the company to meet the future needs of stakeholders and the environment while maintaining a profitable business. Senior managers play an integral role by granting authority and funding to lower-level managers to achieve organizational goals.

The first step is to understand how the organization impacts the natural environment and people throughout the value chain. It is essential to view the positive ways the company impacts the community and local economy in which the business operates. It is important to understand that the environmental and societal issues throughout the supply chain are outside the span of control of management, but stakeholders are demanding that organizations take responsibility for all impacts that occur throughout the value chain.

Environmental Scanning

The next step is to project natural resource price and availability over the next few decades, and then understand how those risk factors could become opportunities to diversify, open new markets, or maintain a competitive advantage, etc. Conduct environmental scanning to identify the risks and opportunities. Based on scanning, backcast and determine a strategy to create the future desired state.

Vision

Senior managers should craft a vision statement that reflects the values of the organization and its purpose. PepsiCo's "Performance with Purpose" means delivering sustainable growth by investing in a healthier future for people and our planet. PepsiCo. focuses on human, environment, talent, and responsible sourcing sustainability.[2] With a strong purpose statement or framework, employees can clearly understand how to achieve performance and can easily remember their purpose with an easy mantra "Performance with Purpose".

Leadership

The role of senior managers is also to lead by example or "walk the talk." Employees expect leadership and want to know that the company is committed to values. Employees will be more inclined to emulate senior management's behavior, attitudes, and beliefs if sincere and genuine. Senior managers should be committed to sustainability if they expect to create a culture based on values. If not, internal and external stakeholders will view strategic statements as a public relations or marketing tool instead of a commitment to managing for future generations. In the same respect, even if senior management is highly committed to a sustainable future, if the employees are not, then stakeholders will definitely view sustainability statements as a public relations tactic. Therefore, it is so important to align departmental functions and responsibilities to achieve strategic goals.

Forming the Strategy

Next, strategic priorities are created to chart the path to sustainable growth and development of the company. It will also be important for senior managers to provide capital budget funding and delegate necessary authority to middle-level and operational managers to achieve sustainable goals. Senior managers play an integral role by granting authority and funding to lower-level managers to achieve organizational goals. Training and education of all managers will be essential before tactics can be created to ensure the needs of the organization meet stakeholder expectations on societal, environmental, and economic performance indicators.

It is important that senior management empower middle-level management to accept ownership to achieve the sustainable vision. Feasible and viable tactical plans will need to be crafted that include the best ways to communicate, educate, collaborate, track, measure, and report on performance. Ownership and empowerment will ensure proper authority and decision-making roles will be clearly defined.

Role of Senior Managers in Phase II: Supplier Engagement

Senior management plays a pivotal role in aligning business systems, but will also need to concentrate time and effort in achieving sustainable goals through external collaboration. Phase II requires working upstream and downstream throughout the supply chain from C-suite to C-suite or CEO to CEO. Remember, sustainability cannot be achieved alone, working together will achieve far greater results. Collaboration with external partners from raw material extraction to the product's end of life will better align the organization to meet stakeholder expectations and be able to respond to very high demands for responsibility. Quick wins and multiple benefits will arise when the entire supply chain works together.

No matter the size and scope of operations, all organizations impact TBL in positive and negative ways. Even in a service business, non-profit, or governmental office, the major environmental impacts are energy usage, equipment, employee travel, and office supplies. Thereby, supplier relations are imperative to procuring new innovative materials or products that will enable the office to support using technology and office supplies that reduce materials usage. Teachable moments held in the office foster building awareness, such as throwing "zero waste and local food" events with local vendors, or even partnering with utility companies to reduce energy, water, and solid waste management solutions. These teachable events also engage and support suppliers to participate and learn together.

An organization's greatest impacts are made by working through the supply chain because of management and procurement decisions that manage inputs, throughput, and outputs of goods, people, and services. Collaborating externally creates internal solutions that could not be met without forming long-term external relationships.

As an example, California Water Service Company procures office supplies that are made from post-consumer waste materials, such as pens, paper, staples, etc. These products are readily available from office supply retailers that offer sustainable products. The company makes upstream impacts by making decisions to support companies that are in the recycling waste stream industry and manufacturers that make products from the waste stream. The company finally closes the loop when employees recycle materials again. As a buyer, these decisions support economic growth and longevity for companies that are innovating new products through the waste stream. They are also supporting retailers willing to create shelf space for new product innovations. The whole supply chain wins.

Supplier Scorecards

For companies that manufacture products, collaborating through the supply chain is also an integral aspect to gain access to materials that meet customer expectations and the values of the organization. Procter and Gamble (P&G) has collaborated with the Supplier Sustainability Board to create a supplier scorecard for all suppliers based on their values, purpose, and principles. Supplier scorecards help organizations benchmark the sustainable practices of suppliers and clearly communicate P&G's expectations to their suppliers. Suppliers report to P&G in order to demonstrate progress year over year on their handling of materials resource usage: water, solid waste, energy, and carbon metrics. P&G has also publicly

Table 1: P & G Supplier Scorecard

Supplier Environmental Sustainability Scorecard	(FILL IN ALL APPLICABLE SHADED CELLS; OTHERS ARE OPTIONAL)							

Submit Date (M/D/Y):

Company Name (below):

Scope Code & Annual Data:
Enter Scope Code (based on your capability to measure):
P = P&G-specific materials and services (DESIRED)
S = Site(s) (combined total) that create for P&G
C = Corporate level
NA = Measure does not apply to my industry/service (explain)

INTERIM RATING: 0 (Auto-calculated)

Overall comments/exclusions regarding data scope:

Core Measure	I Status	Unit (from dropdown menu)	2010 (Current Year) Jan - Dec Scope	2010 Data	2009 (Past Year) Jan - Dec Scope	2009 Data	yyyy Jan - Dec Scope	yyyy Data	Comments (Use additional pages/attachments as needed to explain)
(Electric) Energy Usage									
(Fuel) Energy Usage									
(Input / Withdrawal) Water Usage									
(Output / Discharge) Water Usage									
Hazardous Waste Disposal									
Non-Hazardous Waste Disposal									
Kyoto Greenhouse Gas Emissions Direct (Scope 1)									
Kyoto Greenhouse Gas Emissions Indirect (Scope 2)									
Annual Output	N A		C / P / S		C / P / S		C / P / S		
P&G Sustainability Ideas & Initiatives Supported	N A	Description (Attach detail as needed)							
Fines & Sanctions	N A	USD and # (absolute)	C		C				
Environmental Mgt. System	N A	Yes, Partial or No	C		C				
Data Protocol	N A	Description							
Optional Measure									
Renewable Energy	N A								
Kyoto Greenhouse Gas Emissions Indirect (Scope 3)	N A								
Potential Waste Material Recycled, Reused, Recovered	N A								
Transportation Fuel Efficiency (Transportation Suppliers Only)	N A	Grams of CO_2 / ton-km							(Specify mode of transport used)
Industry Certification		TBD							
Other		TBD							

shared the scorecard and it is available to be used by others. The following is an excerpt of the scorecard, and the accompanying instructions can be found on the Supplier Environmental Sustainability Scorecard: http://www.pgsupplier.com/pg-launches-enhanced-supplier-environmental-sustainability-scorecard-and-training-materials.[3]

Another example of collaboration is the Electronics Industry Citizenship Coalition's Code of Conduct. The electronics industry is collaborating on requiring the same code of conduct from all global suppliers to improve working and environmental conditions, such as labor conditions, equipment, health and safety, management efficiencies, ethics, and environmental management. They require all vendors go beyond legal requirements and meet the minimum standards of materials usage, components, labor conditions and wages, and health and safety standards. The EICC has five key areas:

1. Section A Labor
2. Section B Health and Safety
3. Section C Environment
4. Section D Applying Standards
5. Section E Ethics[4]

A scorecard can help a company choose suppliers that are meeting standards of the industry to award contracts. Scorecards achieve several benefits:

- Enables suppliers to meet one standard for all members of the coalition
- Opens new markets to do business with the entire coalition
- Creates clear common standards and expectations
- Creates strong relationships through collaboration
- Creates expectations that are standard across industries
- Creates a process for selecting suppliers
- Creates a process for procurement
- Meets or exceeds customer expectations
- Reduces risks
- Opens new markets
- Ensures business is meeting all government regulations

Closed Loop Management
Senior managers engage in supply chain collaboration to create closed loop systems by managing inputs and outputs. To recap, closed loop systems utilize all material resources throughout the supply chain to reduce inputs to achieve efficiencies, reuse byproducts, and recycle to reduce waste output. Closed loop systems reduce costs and oftentimes create new revenue streams.

Smucker's Natural Foods juice plants are able to work with local farmers within a 50-mile radius to pick up fruit byproducts for cattle feed, which reduces waste hauling and landfill tipping fees. Farmers fund the cost of hauling in exchange for cattle feed. The smash provides an excellent source of nutrients for herds in the local area. They also work with packaging designers to reduce the amount of cardboard and shrink wrap used in packaging materials. All products are sold in recyclable glass or aluminum containers, which offers the end customer recyclable packaging. The plant bales all recyclable materials and sells them to Smurfit Stone Recycling, which creates a new revenue stream. The revenue generated from recycling was used to hire a recycling coordinator position to align business systems. In addition, the company reinvested revenues generated from sustainability practices into funding new sustainability research and development, job creation, renewable energy investment, and funded new capital projects. Closing the loop is a strategic priority to reduce costs, provide new revenue streams, all while meeting customer expectations.

Creating Partnerships

Senior managers play a pivotal role in collaborating with external partners on research and development. When a sustainable alternative does not exist, senior managers can work through the supply chain to develop solutions. Lundberg Family Farms, the largest organic rice farmer in the United States, works with many organizations to create sustainable innovation and design. They conducted a life cycle assessment impact study with SAP, AG, and California State University, Chico, and found their largest waste material was packaging. Since then, they have pioneered a sustainable packaging research program. One of the programs they are experimenting with involves collaboration with local universities to create polylactic acid packaging made from their own waste product of rice bran. Polylactic acid (PLA) will biodegrade in an in-vessel compost machine and looks very similar to plastic packaging. Lundberg Family Farms strives to close the loop by creating packaging materials from their own byproducts. In addition, they have been experimenting with packaging size for their finished goods. By shrinking the size of the box and the shape, they can increase efficiencies in transportation volume and maximize shelf space too.

Another area that senior managers are extremely effective is collaborating C-suite to C-suite. For many years, sustainable companies have been collaborating directly with competitors to find solutions for the industry. In addition, many Boards of Directors are forming cross-functional BoDs to explore new relationships to resolve global issues, and partnerships are being formed in local communities in which the organization works and plays. Collaboration is a key success driver in sustainability management to create regional, national, and global solutions through working together. As you know, this is not business as usual. This is the opposite of being first to market or possessing a competitive advantage with a trade secret. This is creating trade secrets and then sharing them with your competition. As odd as it may seem to share trade secrets, smart companies understand they cannot solve global issues alone.

The Ripple Effect

The supply chain's impact on society, the environment, and the economy is enormous. If senior managers can collaborate and find solutions across industries and global borders, they can achieve sustainable wins both internally and externally.

Role of Senior Managers in Phase III: External Collaboration

Collaboration in Phase IIIs role is to establish relationships with local, state, and federal government entities plus external stakeholders such as customers, investors, nonprofits, and local residents. The role of collaboration in the external environment can have implications that can benefit the greater needs of society, the environment, and the economy. As society grasps that there are strains on natural resources due to increasing global population and affluence, society will expect government to enact more regulations that may be mutually exclusive to either society or business.

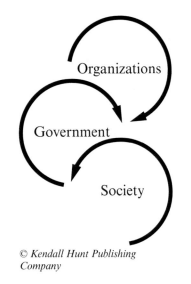

© Kendall Hunt Publishing Company

Evolution of the Field of Management

Business plays an important role in society by meeting stakeholder needs with products or services. Thus, it is important that business engage in sustainable development. For decades, as the field of business management progressed, organizations have proved that you can run a profitable company based on governance, ethics, social responsibility, and environmental stewardship. Environmental stewardship is the latest arena for business to engage in and learn about the impacts on the ecosystem. Many businesses have been proactively managing inputs and outputs of energy, waste, water, and pollution. Many have conducted life cycle assessments to identify the major impacts and learn how to improve them. More importantly, business makes a difference in local communities through philanthropy and actively encouraging their employees to volunteer in the local community.

© Kendall Hunt Publishing Company

Collaboration: Business and NGO

In many cases, these businesses are collaborating with NGOs to understand impacts on people and planet. Managers are not expected to be experts in biology, chemistry, or geology. Therefore, working with nonprofit organizations can be mutually beneficial. Waste

Management, Inc. collaborates with Habitat for Humanity to preserve the ecosystems around landfills. Landfills are large bodies of land that are covered up in many states. The ecosystem can thrive if protected from leaching and off-gases. Together the two organizations ensure a healthy natural system is preserved for plant and animal life.

Another example is Mars Chocolate. Mars works diligently with cocoa farmers upstream in the supply chain and collaborates with third-party auditors from Fair Trade and the Rainforest Alliance nongovernmental agencies. Not only does this support a collaborative effort to protect soil longevity, improve working conditions, access to education, and fair wages to farmers, the NGO assists Mars in finding innovative ways to ensure plentiful yields even with multiple risks. Mars also assists the NGOs in publicizing their important work with labels on their brands. In turn, consumers become more aware of the actions that Mars Chocolate takes to ensure the quality of the chocolate, which also entails quality of life for all of those throughout the supply chain. Mar's CEO strongly believes he has a tremendous responsibility to do the right thing. Collaborative efforts such as these create value throughout the entire value chain.

Collaboration: Business and Government

Another example of building relationships is Sierra Nevada Brewing Company. Sierra Nevada Brewing Company collaborates within the external environment in a myriad of ways to find solutions. The internal trucks and outsourced fleets participate in the Environmental Protection Agency's Smart Way program to increase aerodynamics, reduce emissions, and reduce transportation miles. They also work with the City of Chico, CA to reduce waste water output to the city with an onsite waste water treatment plant that also acts as a closed loop system. Managing water input reduction is a key imperative at the company. On the manufacturing line, engineers switched to a dry lube eliminating water altogether, and also re-circulate water from the brew process to clean the new bottles being filled on the bottling line. In addition, California Water Service Company also assists the organization in reducing water inputs through employee education programs, water brooms for cleaning, and the use of highly efficient appliances and aerators. Senior management participates in many research and development programs, but their latest effort is working with organic farmers to grow organic hops and barley. The company subsidizes farmers to grow organic crops for the loss of yield, or to compensate for periods in which a field must rest to restore soil fertility and top soil, for organic certification. This agreement has created a collaborative of farmers, suppliers, and manufacturers to ensure a sustainable future due to soil management and further secures stable suppliers of organic raw materials.

Xerox has been managing for sustainability for decades with repairable and replaceable parts as their core business model. Collaborating with the Department of Energy and the Environmental Protection Agency, Xerox helped to create the Energy Star certification. Microsoft Corporation has been working with local police to design systems to locate child pornographers and human traffickers. As society learns about the detriments or benefits an entity has on the environment and society, collaborating with government officials becomes a smart strategic priority for senior managers.

Many businesses are also collaborating with local, state, and federal government entities to enact policies based on long-term solutions. For instance, the Department of Energy is working with utility companies and entrepreneurs to find solutions to upgrade an antiquated electrical grid system. The U.S. Department of Agriculture is working with rural communities by fostering economic growth and offering solutions to America's farming industry. The Environmental Protection Plan is working to ensure clean water and air for future generations. All of these governmental bodies are interrelated to business needs as well as societal needs. Yet government oftentimes does not understand business and vice versa, so working together to form policies or regulations is an imperative to ensure solutions are mutually beneficial to business, government, society, and the environment.

Sustainable Communities

Working together to find solutions to regional issues is called "building a sustainable community." Sustainable communities rely on local leaders to work together to find solutions to local issues or risks. If your organization can navigate the external environment, you have a strong chance of building relationships in the community that will benefit its citizens.

IBM has repositioned the Global Business Services unit by using systems thinking to create efficiencies to flows—energy grids, water delivery and discharge, traffic congestion, bioengineering seedlings, and clothing. By looking at the interrelated elements of systems, IBM is able to create smarter software solutions to manage the interconnections of elements, reduce impacts throughout the supply chain, increase throughput efficiencies and reduce sinks—pollutants and waste streams. IBMs "Smarter Planet"[5] is designing smarter systems worldwide and helping communities to work together to find solutions to regional problems.

All-Points Petroleum's president serves on multiple Boards of Directors within Solano County, CA. All-Points Petroleum is a fuel tanker business that drives within a 100-mile radius to make deliveries. The company is highly engaged in volunteering in the community, contributing to society by creating jobs, sponsoring events and race teams, holding employees accountable to a code of conduct, and participating in building sustainable communities. The president serves as the Vice Chair for the City of Benicia and serves on the Planning Commission for the City of Fairfield in California. He is also a trustee of the Benicia Industrial Park, and serves as the Chief Financial Officer for Living Grace Fellowship. His philosophy is that stewardship can be embedded into any organization's strategy and works tirelessly to improve the quality of life within the community. He is a mentor to children, advocates on the behalf of a prosperous industrial business park, and collaborates to ensure a robust community that cherishes a high standard for quality of life.

Communication with Customers

Social media is now playing an interesting role in two-way communication. Companies are exploring how to receive feedback from stakeholders. For years, McDonald's sustainability director has held two-way blog conversations with customers regarding issues from packaging, sourcing ingredients, energy and solid waste management, global supply chain issues, to the caloric content of the meals served in the restaurant. These dialogues are intelligently discussed between multiple stakeholder groups and are transparent approaches by McDonalds to share details with the public on their research and development.

Another example, Timberland tried a new game on their Facebook page. When a customer purchases a new pair of "Earthkeeper" shoes, he or she could plant a tree on their Facebook page and then invite five friends to water it. Once the tree reached maturity, Timberland would then plant a real tree to offset their carbon footprint. Emotional appeals and positive approaches seem to work best to engage external stakeholders.

Investors

Another important stakeholder to engage is investors. Investors react to financial wellness, but are increasingly asking questions about social responsibility and environmental management. Since 1999, the Dow Jones Sustainability Index (DJSI) in cooperation with Sustainability

Asset Management (SAM) rates companies on how they are responding to risks and opportunities in their sustainability strategy. Key performance indicators are corporate governance, risk management, branding, climate change mitigation, supply chain standards and labor practices, environmental performance, social responsibility, and economic performance. Since then, Standard & Poor's Rating Service, Moody's, and the NASDAQ are all following suit. Not only do companies receive value from being listed on the DJSI, but investors use it as a tool to invest in responsible companies that are best in class. The DJSI provides an essential tool for benchmarking performance of the world's largest businesses.

Bank of America plays an important role in financing the "low carbon economy" by increasing accessibility to financing for innovative products and driving sustainability development. Access to financing improves community economic development worldwide. Bank of America even fosters programs to offer low interest rates and longer repayment terms to intermediaries in low-income communities to improve energy efficiency.

Formal Communication
One of the best ways organizations communicate with stakeholders is to issue either a sustainability report or an integrated financial statement for all stakeholders to view. The issue is transparency. Transparency is heavily regarded in reporting. Organizations should report both challenges and achievements to social, environmental, and economic improvements to be transparent. Sustainability reports are one-way communication tools to report metrics and actions that the organization has achieved. (See more on sustainability reporting in Chapter 8—Communications and Sustainability Reporting.)

Senior managers play a crucial role in developing strategies that will enhance internal processes and external collaboration with stakeholders. Sustainability management takes bold moves in a risky and uncertain future. The next step is to develop tactics to accomplish a successful implementation of the plan.

4.5 The Role of Middle-Level Management—Tactics

Sustainable strategic management can be achieved through tactics that align business units to achieve sustainable goals and objectives. The role that middle level managers play is to create feasible and viable plans to translate and communicate the strategic goals of the organization. They are also responsible for assigning talented people to implement the plan by engaging the frontline with inspiration, motivation, and tools to succeed.

Middle-level managers accomplish the planning stage by devising long-term, medium-range, and short-term goals. Tactics should be designed to be manageable, feasible, viable, and achievable. The functions of management are to plan, organize, lead, control, and evaluate strategic goals. Middle-level managers play an important role in achieving success by anticipating and eliminating barriers to success and reducing resistance to change.

Senior managers should ensure middle-level managers have the tools to succeed by empowering them and ensure capital is available to invest in sustainability management. Thereby, managers can create plans that are viable based on budgetary constraints or requirements.

Managers should create long-, medium-, and short-term goals. The next step is to organize the talent needed for each of the goals, identify the departments needed for implementation, and the external stakeholders that should be involved.

Policies and procedures should be created based on the Sustainability Management System (see Chapter 3—Policies for Decision Making and Change Management). The organization should clearly communicate the sustainability policies, the values and purpose of the organization, and the key performance indicators expected from employees. The policies should also explain the impacts the organization makes on the environment, society, and economy so all employees clearly understand what the organization already does well and what should be improved. The policies should clearly state the objectives and goals the organization will pursue to address future opportunities and risks. The policies should be a tool so that employees understand expectations for behavior, attitude, and actions needed to participate in the strategy. In addition, an SMS should also include the ways the employer will share information and communicate success and pitfalls of organizational goals.

Tactical goals should then be devised for internal control and external collaboration of key leaders in the organization that include the following:

- What programs should be planned?
- What partnerships need to be formed?
- What are key areas in which more expertise is needed?
- Who should we collaborate with externally?
- What key performance indicators would be meaningful?
- How much funding will be allocated?
- What timelines are expected for short-, medium-, and long-range goals?
- What is needed from employees?
- What are the responsibilities of employees?
- Who should participate and in what capacity?
- Who will lead the effort?
- How and when will the organization implement goals?
- How will the frontline communicate metrics and progress?
- When should progress reports be communicated and to whom?
- How will employees receive feedback on how the organization is progressing?
- How will employees be recognized formally and informally?

The planning stage should also consider unintended consequences. Changes to the system will inevitably create unintended results. Contingency planning will ensure solutions are created that don't make problems worse, or create new problems internally and externally.

Change Management

Change management will be a key tactic to engage internal and external stakeholders to achieve the organization's strategy. Resistance to change can occur due to multiple reasons: barriers, unintended consequences, and lack of participation may all be management challenges. Anticipating and eliminating barriers should be accomplished by developing solid plans to reduce resistance and overcome hurdles. Organizations must identify the barriers managers and employees will face when tackling sustainability management plans. Procedures should set employees up for success.

Making sustainability management personal is an excellent motivator. For instance, choose issues that are important to employees. As an example, Lundberg Family Farms is in a remote rural area and they incentivize their employees to carpool to reduce gas expense and increase workplace relationships. High employee participation increased during periods of higher gas prices, and then became systemic as employees liked spending informal time together while carpooling to and from work. In other words, employees should be responsible for their actions and how they impact the organization individually. When employees take ownership of the change, they will expand planned goals and objectives and continuously improve far more than expected. Most companies find that employees care a great deal about environmental, economic, and social issues. Employees will strive to continuously make positive impacts when the change directly impacts them personally.

Sustainability Management Consulting, a strategic management consulting company, believes that sustainability practices work hand-in-hand between the home and workplace. Practicing resource management at home creates actions that can be mimicked at work. SMC conducts training seminars for management teams to have employees practice the six R's at home and within the workplace:

1. Reimagine
2. Redesign
3. Reduce
4. Reuse
5. Rot
6. Recycle

Managing change is time consuming and a long-term commitment, but worthwhile. If time is not invested to developing clearly communicated policies, goals, and objectives, strategic goals will never be achieved. Lack of commitment from senior- and middle-level managers will place the organization at risk of being perceived as greenwashers—or all strategy and no action.

Change management is crucial to help employees understand the organization's impacts on people, planet, and profit. Tactics will appoint talented people within the organization who will be agents of change. These change agents will help educate, inspire, and motivate others so that change can be simultaneously driven bottom up and top down. Tactics driven by talented human resources will drive change and position the organization to achieve a mindset of sustainability.

A good place to begin is to develop training and education materials for employees to fully understand how to achieve the sustainable vision and how each employee has a vested interest in the success of the long-term goals of the company.[6] Information will be the driver to understanding positive and negative impacts the organization poses on society, the broader economy, and the natural environment. Training tactics can be approached with several methods:

- Formal training
- New employee orientation
- Cross-training
- Cross-functional training
- Shadowing a competitor to share tactics
- Attend conferences, seminars, and workshops

Many organizations set up formal taskforces and allow employees to form voluntary green teams to continue developing ideas in order to keep people motivated and focused. Middle-level managers devote time and funding toward employee education to give everyone the opportunity to learn about sustainability and how to recognize positive and negative impacts. This will benefit the organization by empowering employees to recognize more ways they can achieve efficiencies through environmental and social impacts to benefit the bottom line.

Key tactics such as process maps will help to steer employees toward the strategic vision with a visual reference. Process maps create a clear roadmap to follow and demonstrate how each department function is a key player. The process map will help employees visualize how each job function and departmental function plays an integral role in achieving strategic priorities to align business systems. The process map should include ways employees can engage right away and also show how they can offer solutions in the future. Training should allocate time to showing employees how to track and measure progress and how to complete the metrics needed by departmental function. Process maps will allow employees to identify inputs and outputs that are inefficient or could be improved through sustainable practices.

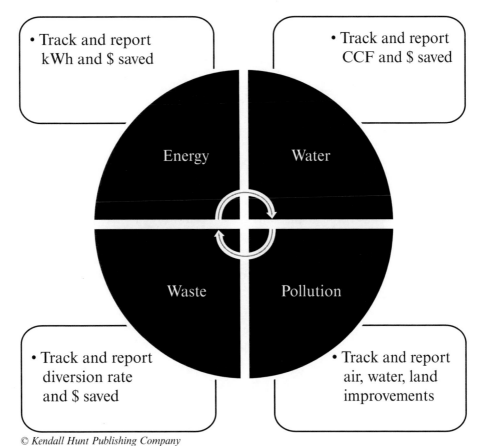

Figure 2: Human Resource Department's Reduce Process Map

A process map is a tool to manage performance, progress, communication, and achievements of all departments. A process map will also provide key performance indicators for reporting. As an example, SAP Enterprise Resource Planning assists their customers to manage for sustainability with technology solutions to create systems that help manage metrics, performance, and achievements.

Table 2: SAP Solutions for Sustainability[7]

Executive Management	Strategy Management	Engagement & Corp. Citizenship	Benchmarking & Analytics	Materiality & Assured Reporting	Financial Risk & Performance
Environment, Health & Safety	Environmental Compliance	Industrial Health & Safety	Process Safety	Risk Assessment & Reduction	Emergency Management
Operations	Facility Energy Management	Production Energy Management	Carbon Management	Natural Resource Management	Smart Grid Participation
Supply Chain	Sourcing & Procurement	Traceability & Recall	Green Logistics		Supply Chain Design & Planning
Product	Product Compliance	Material & Product Safety	Recycling & Reuse	Sustainable Design	Product Footprint
Consumers	Personal Footprint	Mobility		Residential Energy	
Human Resources	Diversity	Strategic Workforce Management	Labor Compliance & Human Rights	Travel Management	
IT	Availability, Security, Accessibility & Privacy		Green IT		

Reprinted with permission by Scott Feldman, Senior Director, SAP, AG

The SAP sustainability map is a roadmap that ensures business units are systemically aligning business systems. A roadmap also depicts clear business process direction and establishes a culture of responsibility.

There are so many ways to encourage change quickly. But the most important factor is to choose short-term goals that have immediate results that employees and management can see and clearly discern the benefits. Quick wins, or low-hanging fruit, are great ways to motivate and inspire people as they will save money. In addition, low hanging fruit projects will reduce materials, energy, water, waste, and even create a healthier workplace atmosphere. Recycling is an excellent example of low-hanging fruit. Teaching employees what can be recycled should be the first step, and then implementing target goals to achieve zero waste to landfill will help ensure systemic change. Another benefit is that selling recyclable materials creates a new revenue stream. Employers can then reinvest the funds into new sustainability programs. Keep publicly touting these wins, and don't let the momentum die.

Building a culture of sustainability will ensure the SMS is integrated and will become systemic. How is this achieved? Multiple tactics that build excitement, reward achievement, and get employees involved immediately will bring desired outcomes. There are several ways to motivate employees:

- Quick wins celebrated and lauded immediately
- Encourage suggestions from employees
- Employee suggestions are implemented quickly if feasible
- Inspire employees through walking the talk
- Consistently encourage and talk about sustainability wins often
- Manage by walking around to encourage employees to remember small actions
- Involve employees in decision making by creating formal and informal teams
- Encourage social media to talk about wins at work with friends and family
- Encourage sharing ideas on internal portals or instant messaging
- Publicly celebrate success in consistent intervals
- Add responsibility and accountability in performance appraisals
- Tie goal achievement to bonuses or incentives

- Use public events as opportunities to learn about zero waste
- Encourage healthy lifestyles or wellness programs in the workplace
- Allow time to research alternative solutions, life cycle costing takes time to find the best solution
- Have fun with sustainability management, allow people to play and be competitive
- Use a framework that is memorable and perhaps create a jingle or mantra that will resonate to brand the culture change
- Hang up posters and signage to remind people to take certain actions
- Post results in the break room or other high traffic areas
- Setup visible reminders, such as recycling centers or composting bins

Many organizations integrate sustainable management as a mindset into every person's job function to decentralize the function in order to create a mindset of sustainability. For instance, PepsiCo and California Water Service Company both rely on individual responsibility to achieve goals. Meanwhile, other organizations appoint sustainability coordinators or directors to formally centralize the function to easily gather data and record organizational improvement. Still some employers hire public relations sustainability managers to speak at conferences about the organization's achievements. It is important to understand centralization and decentralization tactics will depend on organizational structure and the complexity that is unique to each entity.

The role that middle-level managers play is to engage both senior- and front-line managers to support long-term, medium-range, and short-term goals. Tactics should be designed to be manageable, and oftentimes sustainability begins with low-hanging fruit, which are sustainable practices that can be achieved quickly and at low cost. Inspiring a culture of sustainability will take time, but it will become pervasive as long as the organization and its management are committed to continuous improvement and celebrating success. After tactics have been planned and organized, the implementation of those plans should take place at the operational management level.

4.6 The Role of Operations Management

The role of operations managers in sustainability management is to execute, evaluate, and report on the progress of tactics toward achieving strategic goals. Frontline managers will determine the success or failure of the strategy. The operations manager role is integral to systemic change and continuous improvement.

The key function of operations management in sustainability is to 1) clearly understand how each department affects the whole system, and 2) be able to successfully execute key performance indicators. Managers will still maintain their normal duties and responsibilities, but new job duties and responsibilities will rely on making decisions based on benefitting TBL.

Managers will need to build awareness through training and education on the following:

- Why the organization manages for sustainability
- How each employee makes an individual and collective impact
- How each employee will play a major role in participating in the strategic goals of the organization

Everyone within the organization should be working together to achieve organizational goals. Therefore, interdepartmental communication will be a key driver in success. If each employee understands the following reasons behind the strategic imperative, the higher probability a culture of sustainability will be established:

- Understand that economic and social responsibility is dependent on environmental responsibility
- Understand the strain on natural resources or transportation modes used within the industry and supply chain
- The opportunities for new business and future risks
- Be trained on what the organization already accomplishes in sustainability management
- Understand how to make decisions that improve efficiency to input, throughput, and output regarding process flows
- Understand how each employee makes an impact
- Establish and meet KPIs
- Understand how to track and measure KPIs
- How to continuously communicate new ideas and share accomplishments

Aligning business systems means that all departments are working toward achieving the strategic goals of the organization. This concerted effort will ensure that a culture built around values will be pervasive and systemic. To align business systems, managers should communicate the following on a regular basis:

- Sustainable strategy and values of the organization with a clear Sustainability Management System Policy
- Short-, medium-, and long-term goals and objectives
- How the department is impacting people, plant, and profit in both positive and negative ways
- How the employee is making direct and indirect impacts
- How employees will learn about societal and environmental goals
- How employees benefit from sustainability
- How customers benefit from sustainability
- How the industry benefits from sustainability
- How other external stakeholders benefit from sustainable practices, such as suppliers, investors, etc.
- How the industry and organization make societal and economic impacts based on achievements
- How employees should make suggestions
- How to request proposals to make changes on inputs and outputs
- What employees can do both at home and at work to make a positive impact
- How employees can engage with community partners to make a difference
- How employees should communicate progress internally and externally

When employees understand why the organization is managing for sustainability the organization is well-positioned to align business systems with bottom up support. Operations managers execute tactical plans and set employees up for success with the following key tactics:

- Formal employee training to identify process improvements
- Frameworks that clearly communicate the values of the organization
- Policies and procedures to guide actions and decisions
- Feasible and viable goals and objectives
- Clear expectations for behavior and actions

- Recognition systems for achievements formally and informally
- Formal structures to drive suggestions and continuous improvement

Operations managers are critical players in implementing new policies by using change management skills and techniques. The following section discusses methodologies operations managers can use to manage the change.

Change Management

Change management is not an easy or quick process. Sustainability is a long-term strategic repositioning of the organization and it will take time. Excellent communication will increase the chances of systemic change and create a mindset that pervades the organization's culture. If managers treat sustainability as a fad, systemic change will never occur. Sustainability management changes the way employees will process how work is performed. Employees will be better able to recognize negative and positive impacts and learn how to develop processes to improve.

Methodologies, such as the Natural Step, help organizations align business systems to achieve sustainable strategies. How do organizations clearly identify impacts both upstream and downstream? The Natural Step framework uses four key indicators for operations to evaluate and make decisions for continuous improvement:

1. Amount of substances extracted from the planet,
2. Substances produced by humankind,
3. Environmental degradation, and
4. Human rights are met and respected.[8]

Find the Appeal—Choose a Framework

Choosing a methodology, as well as choosing a framework, that is complimentary to the organization's values is an important step to engage in sustainability. Frameworks will help employees talk about sustainability in an engaging manner. Every employee cares deeply about some aspect of the TBL: family, money, enjoying the environment. Find the appeal to give employees a reason to care.

Examples of Frameworks

The triple bottom line is a framework that helps employees remember to make decisions not just based on profitability, but to consider people and planet. Green to Gold is another framework to help employees remember that sustainable strategies will derive long-term value for the organization.[9] Zero Waste mimics the quality movement of Zero Defects, IBM uses Smarter Planet, Pepsi uses Performance with Purpose, HP uses Design for X to show the complex variables to consider in designing for the environment with consideration of product materials, design, packaging, transportation, etc. Choose a framework that engages employees and encourages them to explore sustainability. The framework should be easy to remember and become a mantra repeated often throughout the organization.

Change management is achievable if managed well. Every single employee cares deeply about something. When employees know their organization cares just as passionately about making a difference, they will align actions to help the organization do just that. Change management relies on finding the appeal that employees care about, communicating stakeholder expectations, and meeting the needs of both.

4.7 Aligning Business Systems—How Each Department Plays a Role

The next sections of the chapter will focus on departmental roles and functions that are key drivers of success to manage for sustainability.

4.8 The Role of Human Resource Management

Human resource managers have several roles in sustainability management, but it is oftentimes not clearly evident to them. Foremost, human resource management (HRM) is the social realm of TBL—people. Department functions focus on the process of attracting, training, and retaining talent through:

- Recruiting
- Retention and succession
- Training and development
- Employee benefits program
- Employee incentives program
- Performance appraisal
- Coaching and counseling
- Workplace satisfaction

Another integral role is that human resource managers are catalysts of change. They are an impartial and unbiased department within the organization. Managers are key players in reducing resistance to change and are excellent leaders in change management.[10]

Human resource managers are catalysts of change. They are excellent communicators, possess interpersonal skills, highly regard confidentiality, handle conflict resolution well, and are able to diffuse volatile situations. They are highly effective change agents to achieve systemic change.

The next sections will focus on how HRM can play an integral role in systemic change, plus a section on how to control intern processes within the HRM department itself.

Change Management and HRM Strategy

Aligning business systems cannot be accomplished without strong change management tactics to achieve the organizational strategy. Change management in the human resource department will rely heavily on employee education, development, communication, accountability, motivation, and metrics to communicate progress.

Key performance indicators can be developed by asking key questions, such as:

- What opportunities does the industry face in the future?
- What risks does the industry face in the future?
- What information do our employees need to know to position the organization to meet industry needs in the future?
- What are our internal impacts on the environment, society, and economy?
- What are our external impacts on the environment, society, and economy?
- What departmental functions can be measured to track change management and progress?

- Do we already include sustainability management responsibility into performance appraisals, job descriptions, and expectations?
- What do we already reward employees for and what can be improved?
- How can we communicate employee benefit and wellness programs to all stakeholders?
- What are the human resource practices expected by our external stakeholders and are we meeting those expectations?
- Are we recruiting new hires with values that align with the organizations?
- What training programs should be developed and continuous educational programs implemented?

Change Agents

Another effective tactic is for the HRM department to become change agents. Change agents motivate the workforce to focus on building a culture and mindset of sustainability. Change agents build excitement and drive motivation through building awareness. The process is a journey and will only be successful with commitment to the organization's strategy alongside senior management support. If HRM can drive change from the bottom up with top-down support, the organization can achieve systemic change. The success of the strategy will rely on the talented people within the organization.

HRM—Recruiting

Recruiting talented people will ensure the success of sustainable strategies as this is a journey not a short-term goal. Organizations can try various approaches to ensure they find talented people that fit well within the organizational culture:

Entry level
Recruiting an individual with a sustainability mindset does not have to be a hiring criterion, but organizations may want to focus on attracting applicants that prioritize integrity and values. New hires that respect safety and operational soundness, governance, ethics, and social responsibility can all be trained on specific organizational processes, but already possess a high sense of integrity. New hires with integrity will easily integrate into sustainable organizations. Second, selecting applicants with formal education in environmental issues, social responsibility, sustainability management, and environmental economics will also bring value to the organization. Third, recruiting individuals that are personable and adaptable will also be a successful recruitment strategy. Many organizations assess fit by having the applicants meet with different departmental managers and staff. Assessment of ethics and values will also be key indicators for recruiting and can evaluate applicants based on morality. Recruiting change agents and educated employees will swiftly move the organization toward successful implementation of strategic goals.

Managerial
Hiring criteria should be based on the needs and requirements of the position. Whether an organization is promoting internally or recruiting externally, the hiring criteria should focus on experience in lieu of education. This will ensure the applicant will provide long-term value and quickly adapt to the position and function. Other attributes to seek in evaluating excellent candidates will be a commitment to managing for the TBL and the ability to engage and motivate employees to do the same.

HRM—Training, Development, and Retention

1. Training

Training new hires and the development of existing staff is a key function of HRM. The department can assist the organizational goals in identifying, purchasing, or creating training materials to learn about TBL approaches. They can offer other managers tools to conduct training at the departmental level. They can also foster a spirit of lifestyle management during training sessions. If employees practice sustainability at home and at work, one reinforces the other. Plus employees will be better prepared to identify workplace systems that can be improved.

2. New Employee Orientation

New hire orientation (NEO) is a key area to embed sustainability training. The most effective training on sustainability begins in new hire orientation and then continues. As the employee's experience expands, they can then easily identify sustainable opportunities and make TBL decisions. New employee orientation should clearly help the employee understand the organization's culture and also how to interact effectively within it.

Recology informs new hires of sustainable initiatives in NEO. Formal training in NEO helps new hires immediately understand the company's values, what the expectations are, and how to make decisions that positively impact. Recology firmly believes that formal training programs bring long-term value. In addition, the organization outlines expectations that employees practice, such as reducing inputs and outputs both at home and work in order to help them build a mindset that meets the values of the organization.

Bi-annual (or even more frequently) training materials should be supplied to departmental managers. Annual or periodic training updates will be an effective way to help employees retain information. Training that is highly automated, such as webinar tutorials, provide workplace flexibility and convenience to complete organization-wide training. Webinars also offer a paperless process and reduce waste.

The training sessions should be tracked and measured and documented in several ways. First, it should be recognized on the employee performance appraisal as recognition for completing training. Second, operations managers can then receive reports as to the percentage of staff trained. Human resources should take this one step further and request feedback from operations as to the effectiveness of training in productivity, generating new ideas, instilling intrapreneurship, employee motivation, and inspiration. Third, the HR department can assess how well the culture is formalizing with surveys, observation, and scanning. Finally, HR managers should spot check retention of information of employees at all levels of the organization. All of this information should be included in the organization's sustainability report, if applicable, to show the concerted effort in providing employee tools to learn and engage in sustainability.

3. Reinforcing Training

Human resource management can ensure that training is reinforced in several ways:

- Work with operations, middle-, and senior-level managers to address sustainability progress in all meetings and interaction with employees as often as possible
- Management meetings can allocate time to sustainability reporting by all departments
- Assign task forces or steering committees to create a culture of sustainability
- Support voluntary "green teams" formed by motivated employees

- Assist departments in providing updates on sustainability progress
- Create signage to help employees remember to practice sustainability
- Set the example for employees and walk the talk

Human Resources—Benefit Programs

Quality of life is a key deliverable in sustainability management. How can organizations improve the quality of life of human talent? Benefit programs are a key investment in human capital. Health care, vacation and sick pay, disability, workman's compensation insurance, investment opportunities, tuition assistance, professional development, and coaching and counseling are just a few benefits that foster employee satisfaction. The investment in people should be a high priority when a company can afford to offer benefits. This will result in higher employee retention rates.

Sustainability is complex, but should also be fun! Having fun and being creative at work can recharge employee motivation and increase productivity. Sustainability oftentimes does just that! When employees win, the organization wins. Celebrate success with fun activities that are low cost. The following suggestions can be fun ways to celebrate success:

- Host success parties and recognize employees who have made contributions. Oftentimes, employees begin expecting monetary rewards, but pizza and BBQs served at a no-waste event can also be highly motivating
- Design peer awards for those employees who do not tout achievements to build a competitive peer system
- Reward employees with "lunch with the boss" or "lunch with the sustainability taskforce"
- Encourage peer pressure to get all employees moving toward sustainability
- Focus on workplace safety—be careful that monetary rewards do not incentivize employees hiding accidents or not reporting them. No employee wants to be the person that made the department miss out on the pizza party
- Encourage and recognize volunteer programs. Some organizations successfully have employee-led committees to nominate and review candidates for peer awards
- Green teams consist of volunteers who participate in sitting on a committee to share ideas. Devise ways for this team to be effective and accountable for action
- Cross-functional sustainability teams can be excellent cross training and expand employee scope as to organizational impacts
- Offer carpooling or mass transit incentives
- Give away a free bicycle to those employees that ride or walk to work
- Offer a secure place to store and lock bicycles or install a covered outdoor rack for inclement weather
- Offer customers carpool priority parking
- Allocate a "sustainable winner" parking spot each month
- Onsite doctors and wellness programs motivate and reduce absenteeism
- Hold contests periodically for extended lunch breaks
- Have managers of all departments hand out "caught you caring" awards for on-the-spot recognition and praise

Any of these low-cost rewards can motivate and foster a culture of sustainability.

Finally, HRM should track and quantify all of the ways the organization is motivating employees and include the metrics in sustainability reports. (See Chapter 8—Communications and Sustainability Reporting, for details on social metrics.)

Human Resources Department—Internal Span of Control

Internally within the department resources can be continuously improved for greater efficiencies. The human resource department is responsible for maintaining highly confidential information. Some of the key drivers to sustainable practices internally can focus on simple functions, such as motivation, training and development, technology, and safety. Here are a few examples.

Motivation
- Employees may be more apt to make suggestions directly to HRM as they may feel safe in reporting issues. The department can be a centralized source for employees to communicate suggestions in many types of modes: online intranet access, biannual training to refresh on sustainability training, face-to-face meetings, or monthly meetings requesting employee feedback
- Access to information for telecommuting or shift-work employees
- Email newsletters that drive motivation and report workplace success stories
- Instant messaging or using social media to request employee feedback
- Online surveys to assess workplace satisfaction for quantitative and qualitative results

Technology
- Use automation and technology to reduce paper and increase productivity in employment applications, hiring packets, benefit packages, performance appraisals, training and development records, payroll processing, retirement programs, succession planning, and risk management
- Reduce travel expenses by using online recruiting methods
- Create training materials accessible online or via tele/videoconference
- Automate assessment materials online
- Automate volunteer hour tracking system
- Automate philanthropy tracking system
- Scan and electronically store data archives
- Automate professional succession plans

Health and Safety
- Physical and mental health programs
- Wellness programs
- Safety programs
- Training on workforce development skills

Training and Development
- Encourage sustainable lifestyles in the workplace and strive for zero waste in all areas of the workplace
- Hold zero waste events to have fun with sustainable practices
- Hire caterers that offer zero waste events and locally sourced materials
- Personal Sustainability Practice—personal pledges employees can do to reduce TBL impacts at home or at work
  - Recycling
  - Taking mass transit, carpooling, or biking and walking

- ◦ Closed loop systems at home
- ◦ Take stairs instead of elevator programs
- ◦ Encourage smoking cessation programs
- ◦ Buy local to support local economy
- ◦ Reduce air pollutants. Support natural food products, such as grass-fed beef, cage-free chicken, organically grown vegetables and fruits, and snacks with natural ingredients

Simple steps such as these foster behaviors and processes that can be easily integrated into process and workplace practices. All of the above practices can also be tracked and measured to communicate progress to employees and report to external stakeholders. The metrics that should be reported to internal and external stakeholders should focus on the all three realms of the TBL. It is challenging to measure qualitative value, such as quality of life through wellness programs. Yet, the HR department can track retention rates and periodically survey the workforce to ascertain if wellness programs are meaningful to employees and at what rate does that improve their loyalty or quality of life.

Summary

Human resource management's main role focuses on social equity, yet the department itself can also contribute to major impacts to improve TBL performance. First, the department is the catalyst for change management and sets the organization up for success by developing and providing training materials to foster action and retention. Second, the department can automate many of the daily departmental functions to reduce material usage with technology and automation. Third, health and wellness programs internally can focus on improving social equity and increase retention and employee happiness. Finally, the department's performance metrics on philanthropy and social equity contribute to the value of the company's communication and reporting of sustainability management.

4.9 The Role of Equipment, Health, and Safety (EHS)

The role of Equipment, Health and Safety (EHS) managers in sustainability management is to be experts in the regulatory environment. EHS managers are already managing for the TBL, oftentimes going beyond compliance with OSHA, FDA, Public Safety, Public Health, etc. First, workplace health and safety are a key focus of the TBL for both internal and external stakeholders. Second, maintenance and procurement of equipment are important aspects in sustainability management. Third, EHS professionals are experts in compliance with regulatory requirements and work with many government agencies to reduce risks for the organization. Therefore, EHS managers play a key role as experts.

Asset Management

Many organizations have changed the EHS acronym from Equipment, Health, and Safety to Environmental, Health, and Safety; thus, appointing the EHS department with sustainability management control. From an organizational standpoint, EHS managers are experts in environmental, health, and safety compliance issues that mitigate risk. The expertise of EHS managers is a vital organizational role, as EHS managers already manage for the triple bottom line. Yet, sustainability management should not be controlled from this department alone, as the strategic imperatives of the organization will never be achieved.[11] This is due to other departments believing sustainability is the job function of the EHS department and not committing to executing the strategy. It is important to align all departments to meet the strategic goals of the organization and not centralize the responsibility. Aligning business systems cannot be achieved when sustainability is controlled in just one department. The internal practices that EHS Departments practice are broken down into six major categories:

1. Safety and training
2. Maintenance
3. Fleet management
4. Hazardous materials
5. Pollution
6. Technology and automation

1. Safety

Safety is an organizational imperative to prevent workplace accidents, litigation, public safety, and risk management in general. There are numerous governmental, federal and state, organizations that regulate safety. EHS managers are experts in compliance and work closely with multiple inspectors. Going beyond compliance will reduce risks, workman's compensation insurance premiums, disability benefits, fines, and negative perceptions by internal and external stakeholders. Not only does compliance positively impact the bottom line, it shows the workforce that the organization cares about employee safety. Another effort is to create a culture of safety that ensures employees look out for the well-being of one another to prevent accidents and injuries.

Reducing accidents due to establishing a culture of safety is a cost reduction technique. Workman's compensation insurance is expensive. The more claims, the more expensive it becomes, and the more difficult it can be to retain a policy. Safety meetings, voluntary safety and fire monitors, contingency training, and emergency response play a key role in educating employees on how to reduce risks. Compliance with OSHA or Public Safety regulations can be daunting, yet is an organizational imperative. EHS managers reduce expenses, accidents, and keep employees safe because it is the right thing to do.

Safety Training

EHS managers provide safety training materials for frontline managers to ensure organizations reduce risks and the costs associated with them. Monthly training materials should be provided via online tools to reduce mailing documents and printing materials. This method will reduce transportation cost, greenhouse gases associated with transportation, printer ink and paper, and time and effort organizing materials.

2. Maintenance

Maintenance of equipment is a long-term investment that reduces costs and protects assets. Capital investments on equipment are large expenditures for organizations. Maintaining expensive assets is a key role of the EHS manager. From a closed loop perspective, procuring assets that will bring value and meet the organization's goals are key decisions. Procuring equipment, machinery, or supplies that will be durable, provide long-term value, and can be repaired or upgraded are all procurement decisions that prolong valuable assets. It is important to take the time to understand new products to market in order to differentiate attributes and determine if claims are valid or just marketing ploys. Research the product for validity.

New products to market may also demand a premium price. The higher expense should then be considered in the life cycle costing in order to justify higher capital budget items.

Another way to increase the value of capital assets is routine maintenance and end-of-life disposal. Routine maintenance prolongs the equipment life of any asset. In addition, end-of-life management is a key role of the EHS as well. Disposing of old equipment can be challenging. Most counties have disposal locations for all electronics, appliances, toxins, hazardous materials, wires, metals, and recyclable materials. Counties post commercial information for disposal locations, fees, and limits to how many pounds of material that can be transferred without a permit.

The goal of disposal is zero waste. Be sure to ask yourself, can someone else use this? Can I sell this to another business? Can this part be broken down, refurbished, and used again? Can I find a buyer for materials that are normally thrown away, such as scrap metal? Creating new revenue streams from waste is a motivator and reduces landfill tipping fees. A win-win!

3. Fleet Management

Fleet management is as key area to reduce expensive maintenance. The most important risk objective is to protect employee and public safety by reducing hazards with well-maintained equipment and safety policies. Tire rotation, tire pressure, and tire tread all increase fuel efficiency. Routine engine oil changes and routine inspections also reduce expensive repairs. Driver training to consistently inspect the vehicle is an imperative to pre-empting expensive repairs. In addition, even clutch management—acceleration and deceleration techniques will reduce fuel expense and pollution.

Fleet managers are held to tight budgetary controls. Maintenance expenses run high, but in the long run prolong the useful life of equipment. Be prepared for budgetary needs increasing as sustainable alternatives are explored that may have a longer return on investment. Again, senior managers need to support sustainability management efforts by approving capital budget priorities that do not fit the status quo 1- to 3-year ROI, but allow longer-term investments for long-term value.

4. Hazardous Materials

In many workplace settings, EHS managers will be heavily engaged in monitoring Material Safety Data Sheets to assess what comes in and goes out of the organization. EHS managers can be catalysts of change to seek alternate products or choose suppliers to procure fewer volatile organic compounds. They can also ensure that materials sold to customers are not toxic or blacklisted. (Blacklisted materials are banned and greylisted chemicals are being phased out.) The everyday items used in an organization can be very unhealthy to workers, such as cleaning materials, air freshener, paints, flooring, adhesives, equipment, ink toner, colored paper, and textiles.

5. Pollution

Pollution and air quality are other areas where EHS managers play a pivotal role in sustainability. Going beyond compliance or preempting environmental regulations are excellent strategies for EHS managers. For diesel fleets, pollution concerns from exhaust of particulate matter (PM), and greenhouse gases of nitrous oxide are of concern. PM creates smog and GHG are trapped in the stratosphere. The more a fleet can reduce both NOx and PM the more compliant the organization will be.

Air quality within the facility is also a major function. EHS managers understand that clean air quality and circulation improve employee health and productivity. Working with the department managers to add more living plants that create fresh air, replacing dust collecting on flooring or wall covers, and cleaning ventilation screens and ducts are all ways EHS can improve worker health.

6. Technology and Automation

Using technology and automation will help EHS managers manage, track, and control data and increase efficiency in reporting metrics on progress. Transitioning to a paperless office environment, network management, and archiving data systems will enable managers to manage internal and external inputs, audits, inspections, and increase efficiency. Employee logs for vehicle inspections, driver logs, safety inspections, and fire inspections can all be automated or archived with technology in order to reduce paper, filing, and tracking operational readiness.

For organizations with fleets, there are many software options to manage the fleet costs, repairs, inspections, compliance with regulatory bodies, and other data. GPS technology improves efficiency and communication with on-road employees, reduces costs of fuel to select most efficient routing, accelerates logistics planning, and also improves inventory management due to loading and unloading times and waits. GPS also reduces driver stress as it can divert drivers away from highway congestion or accidents, notifies dispatch if a driver is out of operation, and the driver doesn't get lost as often.

Other technologies that reduce driver stress are PrePass and electronic highway toll devices. PrePass is a technology that is available to heavy highway diesel tractors once the company has passed a Department of Transportation inspection. Scales are placed on the highway prior to a weigh station. The scale weighs the full vehicle weight and then a device communicates with Highway Patrol at the weigh station. The driver receives a green signal to bypass the weigh station or a red signal to pull in. Each time a driver is pulled into a weigh station it is normal for blood pressure to raise due to anxiety. PrePass and electronic toll devices reduce traffic congestion and also emission from deceleration and acceleration. PrePass also saves the company money on savings from fuel to decelerate and accelerate plus the five-minutes lost to pull into each weigh station. Time is money!

Incremental Goals

Because the scope of work can be vast in this department, incremental goals are essential in planning priorities and reducing impacts.

Summary

When you keep equipment updated and people safe, you are managing for the triple bottom line. EHS managers already manage for sustainability. For systemic change to occur, all employees should work toward implementing sustainability management. The responsibility should not lie solely on the shoulders of the EHS manager. Just remember, the strategic vision will never be accomplished if only one department is charged with managing sustainability.

4.10 The Role of Facilities Management

The key role of Facilities Management (FM) is to manage resources, both people and materials, at low-cost efficiency and effectiveness. Facility managers are key players in sustainability that already drive change and seek continuous improvement. The next step is to understand the impacts on how the facility and the people within it impact the environment by managing sources and sinks. The final step is to work toward reducing and eliminating negative impacts by reimagining how the facility can operate optimum TBL levels, not just be less unsustainable.

The following section on facilities management will focus on how managers can maximize the building's assets and the valuable workforce and customers within it. The rest of this chapter will not focus on building planning, design, structure, etc. Leadership in Energy and Environmental Design certification created by the U.S. Green Building Council section will focus on new construction, expansion, remodeling, and deconstruction in Chapter 6.

Building Integrity
The building is a long-term investment for the organization. Maintaining the building's integrity refers to structural soundness of the building. Managing asset longevity is a key role of the facility manager. Building integrity is the first place to assess impacts on sunk costs. Proper insulation, dual- or triple-paned windows, air leaks between doorways and window sills, shading with awnings, energy management practiced by employees, and even how the natural sunlight impacts the building are all major areas that can be improved to reduce energy usage and costs. Whether you lease or own the building, building integrity should be the very first assessment to identify how to improve the energy efficiency of the building.

As renovations, expansion, or repairs are needed, there are many factors facilities managers should consider. New building, expansion, renovating, and deconstructing are all straining the carrying capacity of the planet due to the need for new products and precious materials used in manufacturing. On the flip side, deconstruction or byproducts of materials become a burden to society and the environment as materials quickly fill up landfills. Facilities managers play an integral role in how an organization responsibly procures and throws away building materials by carefully considering inputs and outputs and closed loop management.

Assess the Current State to Reimagine the Future State
Facilities management needs to also understand the positive and negative impacts made on employees, customers, and the natural environment. Understanding the organization's impacts begins with an assessment of the current operations of the facility. Managers should begin to understand life cycle assessment and how reducing, reusing, and recycling can improve societal, economic, and environmental impacts.

Facilities managers can create an Environmental Management System to focus on these four key areas of environmental and social impacts:

1. Energy
2. Water
3. Waste
4. Pollution

Refer to Chapter 2s Metrics section to review how to quantify the metrics.

All of these key areas will become the programs to implement. Program management is the large picture in which sub-goals are then created for project management. For instance, a company may set a KPI for 20% energy reduction in an Energy Program. Then individual projects will be planned to meet the KPI, such as creating projects to improve building integrity, lighting retrofits, fleet fuel usage, or natural gas reductions.

Energy Program Management

The most important area to assess first is the building's integrity. Does the building lose heating or air conditioning through the windows, ceilings, door jams, or flooring? Where does heat come in or go out of the building? Improving insulation in the building is the most important investment an organization can make. You can spend your entire budget on energy efficient lighting, but still not achieve conservation goals as the integrity of the building is not sound. Next, shading or awnings can reduce heat from direct sunlight, which then reduces air conditioning expense. Window integrity is also another insulating barrier against weather conditions. Dual- or triple-pane windows are an expensive initial investment, but a long-term energy saving tactic. Single pane windows let heat and cool air escape unabated and is just like throwing money out of the window. Window tinting can be an affordable solution. Tints on the market block 99% of ultraviolet rays and 79% of heat radiation.

Facilities managers can assess the following energy projects to reduce costs and make short- to long-term goals:

Lighting
- Daylighting is the practice of utilizing natural sunlight to light the building. Maximizing daylighting will immediately reduce electricity expense by keeping lighting off on sunny days.
- Energy efficient lighting, such as the light emitting diode (LED), compact fluorescent lights (CFL), should be assessed to understand how much energy is used to light the building. Fluorescent tubing should also be evaluated. The smaller the diameter, the more energy efficient (T12 more, T8, T5, T3 less energy).
- Delamping, the process of removing lightbulbs and ballasts, can reduce energy costs and remove unnecessary light in many areas where it is not required. Many lighting fixtures will have multiple tubes. Removing one or two can be easy low-hanging fruit. Be sure it is safe to delamp before doing so and be careful to consider eye strain of employees in highly trafficked areas or workstations where lighting may be too dim. The goal is to have enough lumens, not too much or too little light.
- Are motion detectors utilized in areas of the building that are not frequented often, such as breakrooms and bathrooms? The easier you make lighting strategies the less you rely on employees to turn off the lights.
- Ambient lighting technology uses skylights, daylighting, and motion to sense the lighting levels throughout the day. These systems will turn off and on lighting automatically.
- Timers and motion sensors can be excellent ways to reduce indoor and outdoor lighting.

Insulation
- Invest in a digital thermostat and create energy settings and timers to control the temperature in the building. Make it easy so employees do not have to remember to turn off the air conditioning when closing at night.
- Leave windows and doors open in the early morning hours can reduce the need for air conditioning during summer months.
- Thick shades or curtains will reduce heat or cold entering the building.
- Reflective window tinting can retract UVB rays and heat during summer months.
- Dual pane windows can keep the air conditioning and heat inside the building.
- Tight window seals and door plates can reduce heating and cooling from escaping.
- Weather stripping door seals and caulking windows reduce heating and air conditioning loss.

- Ceiling tiles can allow a tremendous amount of air conditioning and heating to escape.
- Insulate water heaters or boilers.

Energy Efficiency
- Assess appliances for energy efficiency labels such as Energy Star. Look for wattage usage on the manufacturer label or measure it with a watt reader.
- Invest in highly energy-efficient appliances, televisions, game stations, or equipment.
- Phantom loads—use a wattage reader to identify what appliances or equipment draw power even when they are turned off. If a device draws power, plug it into a surge protector that has a sensor or timer so it will automatically turn off to reduce plugload.
- Many energy companies will perform energy audits and consult on efficient lighting strategies at low or no cost.
- Renewable energy sources such as wind, solar, and thermal can be a large initial investment, especially if the building is leased. Long-term investments may be worthwhile budget proposals, but must be viable.

Energy reduction strategies are more successful when they are easy for employees. Energy programs should focus on the integrity of the facility to reduce energy costs. Externally, energy to the grid is reduced and communities benefit from conservation methods by being able to grow and develop using the same power to the grid. Reducing energy costs and usage reduces indirect carbon emissions.

Water Program Management

Water management is another environmental impact to assess. Water is inexpensive in the United States and does not create the incentive to conserve as the cost savings can be minimal. Yet, the environmental impact of conservation is tremendous. Water is a precious resource and should be managed as one. Water scarcity or abundance is regionally dependent on weather, so an organization's impact on the local community can be significant. Collaborating with local water resource departments and water companies can be beneficial to organizations. California Water Service Company offers customers assessments, free water saving tools, and educational materials. They go above and beyond to promote water conservation and work with local government, business, and citizens to achieve conservation methods.

To understand your water footprint, it is important to assess three water aspects within the facility.

1. Consumption or inflow
2. Reuse
3. Discharge or outflow

Assessing the water footprint should focus on the facility itself as well as any outdoor irrigation systems. The purpose of the assessment is to determine how water is used. How could it be used more efficiently? What processes could be reengineered to closed loop management systems for discharge reductions to be reused? The following are important assessment steps to take:

1. Assess ways in which the organization already conserves water and ways to improve.
2. Assess if all water appliances are equipped with aerators, which push air and reduce water flow, but maintain excellent pressure.
3. Do industrial sinks have low-flow fixtures and high-efficiency aerators?

4. Are low-flow toilets installed?
5. Can water displacement in the toilet tank be used for models older than 1996?
6. Does landscaping require constant water, or could water-tolerant landscaping be redesigned? Are sprinkler heads highly efficient and only watering the area required?
7. For manufacturers, can waste water be treated on site?
8. Can cleaning solvents be used that are oil based vs. water based or low voc or even better natural?
9. Reuse grey water, such as rainfall in landscaping or bathrooms
10. What closed loop systems exist and what possibilities could be implemented in the future?

Water program management makes a tremendous impact on the local community and conservation will reduce expenses. Conservation methods will ensure that the organization is not using water faster than it can be replenished.

Waste Program Management

Another important impact to assess is waste management. To begin the assessment, conduct a waste audit. Find out exactly what materials are put into the garbage and what materials are put into the recycling bins. Just like energy and water, waste haulers offer many solutions for the communities in which they serve. Companies, such as Waste Management and Recology, will conduct waste audits, offer recycling education, and offer solutions for waste control.

The waste audit should include physically inspecting the trash bins in all areas of the facility both indoors and outdoors. Assess the following steps to understand sources and sinks:

1. What types of materials are in the garbage?
2. What are employees bringing to work that is thrown away? Fast food, household appliances, household waste, yard waste, etc.
3. What materials in the garbage could be reduced, reused, or recycled?
4. Weigh the materials in the garbage per material source to audit how much could be diverted by reducing, reusing, or recycling.
5. Assess the materials in the recycling containers for accuracy.
6. Assess if recycling receptacles are in convenient locations to make it easy for employees to recycle.
7. Are the employees using the recycling containers?
8. Does the volume of recycled material warrant baling and selling to a recycling company? Most recycling companies prefer to pick up a minimum of one ton of cardboard at a time.
9. Materials such as cardboard, shrink wrap, plastics, metals, and glass can all be sold to recycling companies and creates a new revenue stream.
10. What do employees need to learn about recycling?
11. What procurement strategies will help reduce waste?
12. What material inputs are being wasted and not utilized to maximum capacity?
13. Are all byproducts being reused or sold to other companies to be reused?
14. Are smaller garbage receptacles available from the waste hauler to reduce expense?
15. Should the frequency of garbage pickup be increased, decreased, or remain the same?
16. Is there a location for an onsite composter? Is it legal to compost in the municipality?
17. What end-of-life strategies would reduce waste?

Zero Waste to Landfill in the Sustainability Movement mimics the Total Quality Management Movement's Zero Defect. The Zero Waste mantra, or framework, helps employees remember to reduce in the first place, reuse what they can, and if all else fails can the waste at least be recycled? Sending valuable commodities to the landfill is waste in several ways. First, the materials require complex transportation and logistics by waste haulers, the materials going to the landfill can be remanufactured in many cases, the materials going to the landfill may never decompose or breakdown, the organic decay process releases methane gas, and the land is wasted on burying material goods.

Participating in waste management has several positive impacts to the Triple Bottom Line. Recycling and remanufacturing goods creates new job growth and fosters industrial growth in the country. Food grade plastics mostly are remanufactured in the United States, but most other plastics are sent to landfill or transported overseas. When America establishes a strong closed loop system to recycle locally, economic development will be enhanced. Environmentally, the benefit of only procuring what is needed reduces the strain on raw materials. Socially and economically, purchasing remanufactured or post-consumer recycled material supports a growing industry. Raw material extraction for simple everyday items should never exceed the carrying capacity of the planet.

They key to reducing costs in waste management is to reduce the frequency of pickup or reduce the size of the outdoor bin. Pacific Living Properties had a waste audit conducted by Sustainability Management Consulting. PLP worked with Waste Management to implement recycling for residents. They held a training seminar for residents to learn what can be recycled and encouraged them to reach for 30% accuracy the first year and then 75% the following year. The outcome of reducing outdoor garbage bins and replacing with recycling receptacles saved the company more than $14,000 in the first year.

Pollution Program Management

Pollution control is another environmental impact to assess. To understand the organization's impact on pollution, the following steps can be assessed:

1. What risks are posed by the pollutants from the organization? Use the formula:

   Risk = Hazard × Exposure.

2. What pollutants are released to land, air, and water by the organization?
3. What alternatives exist?
4. Can the pollutant be sequestered and engineered to be a reused?
5. What are the volatile organic compounds (VOC) in the cleaning materials used onsite?
6. What VOCs are in the interior design of the building, textiles, paints, and fixtures?
7. How do employees travel to work?
8. How do customers travel to the location?
9. How are employees traveling for business purposes?
10. How do suppliers transport goods and people?
11. How does the community support mass transit to offer solutions for employees?
12. Can the pollutant be filtered and removed from the air?
13. What pollutants are put into the municipalities waste water treatment?
14. Do our products have pollutants or dangerous chemicals that pose risks to consumers? Do products have chemicals that are greylisted?

Pollution control oftentimes requires an expert, or a significant allocation of time to research and find out what the problem is. A tremendous amount of time will be invested in researching feasible and viable alternatives existing on the market. Collaborating with government, nongovernmental agencies, suppliers, and customers will oftentimes lead to greater resources and information for pollution management.

Create Project Management and KPIs
After the assessment is completed, the facility manager should strive to develop short-, medium-, and long-range program and project management goals and timelines. Quick wins, or low-hanging fruit, will help the organization understand that sustainability management is not always expensive. In fact, sustainable programs generate new revenue streams, which can be reinvested into more expensive capital budget items.

The Facilities Management department is not in charge of implementing all of the goals. In order to build a culture and ensure systemic change, each department will play a role in implementing the programs.

Summary

To recap, managing environmental and social impacts will absolutely save money. The most significant cost savings will be realized by energy reduction, and the most expensive investments will be for pollution abatement or mitigation.

The challenges facing facilities managers can be overwhelming. They face many barriers, such as requesting budget allocations for upgrades, maintenance, or replacement are oftentimes long-term capital budget item requests. Resistance to change by lower-level and senior-level employees can also impede progress and damper motivation. The key to success is to foster employee suggestions and then empower them to make the changes. It will be important to have the support of senior managers to fund improvements or projects will fail and sustainability management will become just a fad.

4.11 The Role of Information Technology

The information age automated processes and transformed the way work is performed. The sustainable movement in the technology industry is spurring innovation and entrepreneurial opportunities. Information Technology (IT) will continue to adapt with intelligent software, reduction in raw materials for hardware equipment, and cloud computing. The IT sector creates enormous waste streams throughout the entire value chain, such as pollution to land, water, and air during manufacturing, as well as assembly to e-waste at end of life.

Another issue is designing for obsolescence. Consumers have choices to either buy new or repair. Oftentimes for consumers, it is just more cost effective to buy new—rather than repair electronic equipment. Innovation in technology is quickly evolving, which makes many computers, laptops, and cell phones obsolete every few years. It is a cycle of waste.

Role of IT Industry
Fortunately, leaders in the IT sector have recognized this and have made drastic designing for the environment engineering breakthroughs. Brands such as HP, Intel, Apple, IBM, SAP, NetApp, Cisco, Samsung, SONY, Panasonic, etc. have all been leading the sustainability movement. The following are just a few examples of innovative supply chain sustainability strategies.

HP resolved the end-of-life problem of Styrofoam packaging by replacing it with made-to-fit corrugated cardboard or paperboard. End-of-life management has become a priority for manufacturers.

In addition to packaging, end-of-life programs have been more successful with buyback programs. Buyback programs are slowly being encouraged by working with retailers to accept electronics and appliances back from suppliers and consumers by diverting them from landfill. Buyback programs are supply chain partnerships to return materials to the originator to be reused again. Packaging, parts, shipping containers, electronics, etc. are returned by suppliers and end consumers that are sent to partners who refurbish, repair, or remanufacture them. Staples incentivizes customers to return ink cartridges that are sent back to the manufacturer. Best Buy is known to give away gift cards for e-waste returns from customers. Monetary incentives are not required, but oftentimes make the customer feel really good about doing a good deed. Incentives bring attention to the buyback program and are a great way to advertise for a great cause.

Product designs have been pioneered to reduce materials usage by manufacturing items to be smaller, lighter, and more energy efficient during usage. Ridding manufacturing of black-listed chemicals and treating waste water onsite are huge milestones of companies from Intel, HP, and Apple. Cell phones were quite small in 2010, until widespread adoption of smartphones dominated the cell phone market. The same technology then diversified into the tablet. Yet, the tablet is smaller and more resource efficient than a laptop computer.

Dematerialization is another added value. Companies have removed the installation CDs, owner's manual, warranty leaflets, and connection chords that are infrequently used by the customer. Consumers rarely receive owner's manuals or CDs to download software. Every aspect is now completed online between the consumer and company. Instead of buying a CD, many companies offer the option to download software directly from their webpage. The resources reduced because of dematerialization are making huge ripple effects throughout the supply chain.

The technology sector is making strides in managing the life cycle costs throughout the value chain and redesigning how the information technology industry will position itself for the future.

The Role of the IT Manager
The role of IT managers is to improve efficiency in the process of the business through equipment and hardware, software, data management, data storage, risk and security protection, and innovative critical thinking. Procurement and work processes are major functions in sustainability that will enhance IT objectives. The role of IT managers in all organizations, besides manufacturing, will be discussed in the following section.

Strategies
IT management strategies for long-term sustainability can be broken down into seven major functions:

1. Data center management for internal facility efficiency
2. Data center management for customers
3. Client and employee desktop and mobile solutions
4. Electronic archiving
5. Virtual technology tools

6. Energy management software
7. Environmental procurement practices and policies both internally and externally focused

1. Internal Data Center Management

Data center management is the physical or virtual storage of digital data. A company's data center will have equipment, such as servers, routers, computers, etc. The data center within a company hosts the Internet and Intranet connectivity, telecommunications, and web hosting.

Efficiencies can be achieved by focusing on the following:

- Networking capability
- Efficient server equipment
- Server virtualization to run multiple operating systems on a single physical host to offer flexibility
- Thin clients instead of personal computers
- Data center management. Server rooms oftentimes require just as much electricity to cool the equipment as it does to operate it. Most large datacenters are using outside air to cool data centers to reduce energy. NetApp servers' cool sides face one another, while the rear faces outflow vents so cool air is drawn in and hot air is blown out. NetApp was able to achieve a 1:2 ratio of Total Facility Power:Facility Equipment Load Costs. Normally, a ratio of 2 is considered energy efficient
- Energy efficiency of the server room can be a tremendous cost reduction. Ventilation systems, fans with HEPA filters, and clean air ducts increase energy efficiency. Automated temperature controlled dampers reduce energy usage more than perforated flooring
- Data storage and archiving on high-capacity drivers and storage efficiency technology, such as deduplication to store more data on less physical storage space on a disk
- Cloud computing data storage
- Automate all processes to improve efficiency and reduce materials usage, such as printing needs of the workforce. Securely archiving information is faster and more efficient

2. Data Center Management for Customers

The business purpose of some companies is to host data for clients, such as NetApp. Small businesses oftentimes hire a data center company for web hosting and archiving services. Some ways to achieve efficiencies:

- Thin clients instead of personal computers,
- Materials reduction in packaging,
- Lease contracts with buy back options, and
- Lease contracts with upgrade options.

3. Client and Employee Desktop and Mobile Solutions

IT managers make many decisions on integrating new technology to improve organizational efficiencies. The following are just a few ways efficiencies can be achieved:

- Thin clients instead of personal computers
- Lease contracts with buy back options
- Lease contracts with upgrade options
- Reduce energy consumption on PCs and laptops by setting defaults to sleep mode
- Have employees turn off equipment when not in use or default to hibernate settings

- Unplug equipment when not in use to eliminate phantom loads or plug them into timer surge protectors to automatically shut down when a device is no longer drawing power
- Donate old equipment, participate in a buyback program, or dispose of it safely
- Training of workforce to identify IT solutions
- Supporting telecommuters as it reduces energy usage, pollution from commuting, valuable workstations, and oftentimes increases productivity

4. Electronic Archiving

Archiving and securing sensitive confidential data is a well-established activity that reduces costs. Documents no longer need to be physically stored, saving costs on storage space. Production increases due to reduced filing. Information is readily available, which also maximizes efficiency.

Another cost saver is sending and receiving electronic documents. Accounts receivable, payables, online banking bill payments, credit card processing, automatic clearing house and electronic funds transfer are all great electronic efficiencies. Electronic documents arrive faster, and improve productivity and communication. Electronic methods also reduce paper, envelopes, stamps, postal service transportation, and fuel costs.

5. Virtual Technology Tools

Employee travel is one of the largest transportation service that nonprofit organizations and government agencies incur. Meetings also cost travel time plus employee payroll expense. Conferences are great networking opportunities, but create large carbon footprints for transportation. To reduce time and costs, many organizations hold videoconference meetings, webinars are common for training, and free voice over internet protocol (VOIP) allows small to large organizations to communicate for free, as well as very quickly and effectively.

6. Energy Management Software

Software to manage sustainability metrics is very valuable to organizations. Collecting and compiling data is time consuming and cumbersome. Software enables an organization to process information efficiently and evaluates results in an effective manner. Dashboards can be accessed to assess performance and progress. New technologies are emerging where alerts can be set up when energy spikes or overloads are detected. Water leaks can be detected due to changes in pressure. Emissions can be monitored based on GPS tracking of fleets. Employee travel emissions can also be tracked and monitored. Making sustainability management easy will substantially increase the likelihood that employees and managers will track, monitor, and evaluate data.

GreenTraks offers an energy management software solution that is more comprehensive in that it compiles data on electricity, fuel, water, and calculates carbon emissions from these activities. GreenTraks works with the utility and card lock fuel vendors to sign agreements to allow GreenTraks to upload client data into a portfolio, which reduces manual accounting entries. Managers can use multiple reports to manage resources, identify problems, identify performance enhancement, and report progress. The dashboard captures robust data to compare year-on-year results.

7. Environmental Preferable Purchasing Policy

Environmentally preferable purchasing practices and policies are extremely important in the IT department. Procurement decisions need to be made with a focus on both internal operational needs and externally focused on the supply chain. The goal is to manage for the entire product life cycle to reimage how impacts can be mitigated throughout the entire value chain:

- High-efficiency cables and wiring to reduce heavy metals
- Procuring reduced material electronic equipment
- Toxicity reduction in components and equipment procured
- Procure equipment designed for reuse or repair instead of obsolescence
- Collaborate with the supply chain to create solutions that don't exist on the market
- Materials reduction in packaging
- Materials reduction by posting user manuals, user registrations online
- Packaging material should be reusable and 100% recyclable
- Lease contracts with buy back options
- Lease contracts with upgrade options
- Procure equipment with end-of-life solutions
- Procure equipment that is energy efficient
- Procure Energy Star rated appliances and equipment
- Procure equipment that has been third-party certified or meets international standards, such as Restrictions of Hazardous Substances (RoHS), the European standard for low toxicity, REACH, and WEEE (See Chapter 5 for details on these standards.)

For more details on setting up a policy, refer to Chapter 3—EPP.

Organizations are increasingly being called to accept responsibility for the activities and practices throughout the entire supply chain. IT managers can also collaborate throughout the supply chain by participating in the Electronics Industry Citizen's Coalition (EICC) that establishes strict criteria for suppliers to be able to obtain contracts with sustainable manufacturers. Criteria are evaluated using a single scorecard methodology that is accepted by all members. The members use the scorecards to select responsible suppliers in order to ensure the organization exceeds the expectations of stakeholders.

The EICC also works with third party inspectors to conduct onsite audits. The EICC developed a code of conduct and an external audit process to make it easier and convenient for vendors to follow a consistent standard.

The EICC sets the bar high to work together to achieve sustainable policies and practices together as an industry. Imagine the widespread impacts an industry can create by working together and encouraging suppliers to participate.

Summary

IT managers play an important role in achieving organizational TBL efficiencies and effectiveness. Technology innovation can completely change workflow processing, materials usage and discard, and environmental management of natural resources.

4.12 The Role of Accounting and Finance

Future Trends in Cost Accounting

Societal pressure and trends have arisen to demand that organizations account for the real cost of materials production, supply chain impacts, and end-of-life management. Organizations and consumers do not pay the ultimate costs for goods and services. Conservation groups are advocating for prices to reflect environmental degradation from raw material extraction; to the air, land, and sea; pollution of transportation; waste to landfill of packaging materials; and consumer discard. None of these costs are accounted for in activity-based costing.

Environmental accounting metrics are becoming more status quo. However, Generally Accepted Accounting Principles (GAAP) do not allow for emissions and social equity metrics to be included in financial statements. Thus, two sets of balance sheets are being prepared for those organizations that report carbon emissions. The future goal of the United Nations Environment Program (UNEP) is to integrate environmental and social metrics into GAAP. The UNEP advocates that environmental and social metrics should be included with financial accounting methods to show the true costs of a product or service.

The Role of Accounting and Finance

The accounting and finance departments play a key role in aligning business systems by measuring, tracking, and compiling TBL metrics for reporting purposes. Some organizational structures centralize all sustainable reporting in the accounting department. Other organizations choose to track and measure progress by unit or departmental function. Whichever method of decentralization or centralization makes sense for the organizational structure would be the best method to choose.

Tracking and Measuring Performance

Sustainability reporting is reliant on data and metrics. If each department tracks and measures environmental, social, and economic performance, the organizational impact can be communicated to internal and external stakeholders. Progressing toward achieving the strategic goals of the organization should be celebrated so sustainability management is not just a tool but a strong motivator and performance indicator. (Refer to Chapter 8—Communications and Sustainability Reporting.)

The accounting department has multiple tools to help departments track sustainability:

1. Establish a system of reporting quantifiable TBL key performance indicators
2. Track intrinsic and extrinsic value of TBL impacts
3. Centralize departmental communication so a project in one department does not create a problem for another. All departments should communicate projects and progress to reduce costs across all business units
4. Activity Based Costing (ABC) is the process of analyzing the costs of a product or service as compared to a similar alternative
5. Life Cycle Costing (LCC) is ABC, but also creates projections based on the longevity of the product and considers price, quality, features, and benefits of a product or service. LCC moves far beyond ABC as it considers LCA impacts to the environment, compares features and benefits of products and services regarding TBL, and makes the final product choice based on cost benefit analysis, features, attributes to TBL, and benefits
6. Life Cycle Assessment (LCA) is the environmental impact of a product or service. The organization can analyze the life cycle of a product or good. LCA assists organizations in identifying major impacts in which to set target goals and objectives to reimagine the system

7. Carbon footprinting—tracks emissions from fleet and employee travel, air pollution from direct and indirect energy consumption, and manufacturing. The United States did not sign the Kyoto Protocol Treaty, and does not participate in the involuntary cap and trade market. Yet, many multinational American companies have to report carbon as their subsidiaries are in Kyoto countries. The accounting department maintains a separate balance sheet to record carbon emission assets and liabilities for the involuntary market and may also choose to report emission to voluntary reporting companies such as the Carbon Fund or CA Climate Action Registry

The Role of Finance

The finance department's role in sustainability is to analyze capital investments, invest in other sustainable organizations, and ensure that sustainable projects are feasible and viable. When requesting budget approval for upgrades, retrofits, etc., sustainable projects oftentimes have longer payback periods. Investing in long-term solutions will require acceptance of longer returns on investment. Senior management support is needed to accept longer payback periods and higher risks in proposing longer returns on investment.

The finance department also has a major role in collaborating with investors and creditors to obtain working capital or equipment financing for upgrades and sustainability management initiatives.

In addition, many large corporations are listed on the Dow Jones Sustainability Index based on rating scales that assess risk and liquidity.

Summary

Both departments play a major role in calculating, compiling, and reporting sustainability metrics to internal and external stakeholders. The details in Chapter 2—Systems Thinking Approaches and Environmental Metrics—and Chapter 8—Communications and Sustainability Reporting—are the primary concern of the accounting and finance departments. Both departments will play an integral role in internal auditing and compiling reports for the organization to monitor, evaluate, and develop planning for continuous improvement.

4.13 The Role of Marketing

The term "sustainable marketing" is the processes of creating, communicating, and delivering value to customers that respect natural and human resources.[12]

The role of marketing in sustainability management is to follow "truth in advertising." Marketers should responsibly build awareness through marketing messages that build consumer awareness of the following:

- Raw material or ingredient disclosure
- Usage features and benefits
- Discharge to water, landfill, or air

Seventh Generation pioneered the naturally-derived cleaning products industry in 1988, with a mission to revolutionize the next seven generations.[13] The company is founded on the belief that collaborative efforts through the supply chain create healthier solutions for people, pets, air, surfaces, sewage, and partnerships. The marketing messages on the packaging are well-crafted to address all of the above ways to build consumer awareness. Seventh Generation uses a double label that peels back to reveal more information and details. On the outside label, they clearly outline that raw materials are plant derived and how the product is effective for cleaning. It also clearly states "Chlorine free, Phosphate free, non-toxic, biodegradable." This satisfies discharge questions. Customers are able to download the MSDS sheets directly from the website for each product to show transparency and backup marketing claims with facts. When you peel the label back, the ingredients are listed and translated into plain English that anyone can understand.

The following is a quick sample of how to disclose raw material ingredients. Ingredients of Seventh Generation's Automatic Dishwasher Gel:

- Water
- Sodium citrate = plant derived water softener
- Sodium silicate = mineral protection agent and alkaline booster
- Protease and amylase = plant-derived enzyme soil remover
- Medicalimonum peel = lemon[14]

Seventh Generation appeals to consumers that are searching for products that are mutually beneficial, environmentally friendly, and healthy due to low-toxicity and chemically-derived ingredients. Seventh Generation creates marketing labels to answer consumer questions, while comparing product A to B, to provide customers with information to select the best choice that suits their needs.

On the other hand, Green Works by Clorox, uses a simpler marketing message. The label simply states that the product is natural, biodegradable, works well, never tested on animals, and is made from plant- and mineral-based ingredients. The ingredients on the Natural Dilutable Cleaner just lists coconut-based cleaning agents, corn-based ethanol, filtered water, and lemon oil. That's sure easy to understand and determine if the "natural" is really natural. Their products are marketed to the general public that is loyal to Clorox Bleach products that might be willing to go with a household brand they recognize instead of trying a new brand.

Another important role is to be both internally and externally focused. As the function of marketing spans from research and development, to developing marketing strategies, to communicating with both internal and external stakeholders, their role in achieving the strategic goals of the company are critical to building brand reputation. Sustainable marketing strategies should build employee plus public awareness.

Target Markets

Truly "green" consumers vary in the causes they care about, which makes target marketing them challenging. Therefore, it is best to stick with the traditional segments of demographic, psychographic, behavioristic, and geographic. Embedded within all traditional market segments are the green consumers. These are a small percentage of consumers who will actually pay more for a green product or make a purchasing decision based solely on sustainable attributes. Green consumers are reading the packaging, reading the ingredient and nutrition labels, evaluating life cycle costing of the product, and considering end-of-life solutions. To reach this market, more is better. If marketing provides the details so a consumer can make an informed decision it is the best option. Society is still building awareness of environmentally friendly products, how to use them, why they are beneficial, and why they are better choices. Providing that information is helpful to consumers in order to inform and educate. Responsibly only providing the facts is sustainable marketing.

The hotel industry and The Green Hotel Association worked together to develop the marketing messages for reusing towels and bedding. The effort was not based on just targeting green consumers, it was an appeal to the general public to collaborate with the hotel to reduce natural resources. Many hotels display the card in the restroom to educate consumers that towels and bedding can be reused. To satisfy green consumers, the hotel should ensure the cleaning crews are trained to actually leave the towels if they are left hanging. Thereby the marketing message is backed up by the action.

Conventional marketing strategy methodologies should absolutely be used for sustainable initiatives as the traditional market segments all have varying degrees of target consumers that care about sustainability. It is important to remember that the product and service must still continue to sell on price, quality, and satisfy a need or want. Marketing a product on just its sustainable attributes and features will not sell the product. Yet, there are emerging methodologies in consumer trends that may very well create a "green target market" in the future.

Trends

This section on marketing will focus on emerging trends and methodologies that are utilized broadly in marketing for sustainability. Many consumers argue that sustainability is just a trend. Due to this perception, it then becomes a marketing imperative to sustain "truth in advertising" to responsibly communicate a message that portrays the true attributes of a product or service with both integrity and transparency in order to build trust and respect.

The opposite of transparency in sustainability management is called greenwashing. Greenwashing is where organizations may tout sustainable practices, but have very little to back up those claims. Greenwashing actually hurts the sustainability management field and is irresponsible. Whether it is a first impression of a green product, or thinking that green is trendy and popular, these perceptions are long lasting in the minds of consumers.

To avoid greenwashing, companies can use the Federal Trade Commission's Green Guide or the ISO 14020 Environmental Labels and Declarations: General Principles. Both of these guides will assist organizations in self-declaring marketing messages that are meaningful to consumers and using them in the right context.

Consumers are becoming more concerned about health and the environmental benefits of products. This trend will continue to support companies with a sustainability management strategy to appeal to consumers and communicate what and how they are making a difference. This trend will also spur entrepreneurship and innovation.

Another marketing ploy that hurts sustainable marketing is unclear labeling that is self-declared, not always explained well, and/or difficult to verify. There are currently no laws regulating when a company can use labeling, such as organic or natural. Labeling products irresponsibly severs the trust of consumers if the terminology is found to be untrue. On the other hand, self-declared labels can be absolutely true. Frito Lay's Potato Chip is labeled "All Natural". The ingredients simply state potatoes and salt. Simple, true, and easy to verify.

To distinguish themselves, many companies are certifying products for a competitive advantage. Some widely recognized certifications are USDA Organic, Green Seal, Energy Star, Marine Stewardship Council, Forest Stewardship Council, NSF International, and UL, etc. The distinction between a certified product or process is that it has been audited by a third party accredited certifying body that is separate and unbiased from the certifying agency. The company pays for the cost of the audit and then is able to pay an annual fee to use the label on packaging materials. Therefore, consumers can choose to support the supply chain that is participating in collaborating on sustainability management by purchasing a product that is certified by a third party. (See more about certified product labels in Chapters 6 and 7.)

Another reason why labels are confusing is that the company may not be able to afford certification, but the products attributes are absolutely true and verifiable. For instance, in the grocery store it is common to see fruits and vegetables in the "organic" section in the produce aisle. Most do not display the USDA Organic label. The grocers, such as Safeway or Trader Joe's, will vet the supply chain to ensure the farmer is using organic farming practices. Also the product may have been imported. The label organic is indeed true and verifiable by the retailer.

Finally, labels are confusing as consumers have no idea what they mean. Starbucks and many coffee shops have been selling Fair Trade coffee for more than a decade. Most consumers are now just becoming aware that the label attests to fair wages and working conditions to foster economic development of the farmers that grow the coffee beans.

Marketing can take the opportunity to include more details to build consumer awareness, label recognition, and brand loyalty. These efforts will reduce confusion as consumers learn about the meaning behind the label.

4.14 Aligning Business Systems—Putting the Pieces Together

When each department rallies behind the strategic future state of the organization, systemic change can occur. A culture can be built based on responsibility and stewardship by each department actively pursuing strategic goals. The only roadblock to sustainability is our own inhibitions and barriers to overcome. Making smarter choices and informed decisions is managing for sustainability. Creating value for employees and stakeholders through values and integrity is just smart management. Innovating new products and services that meet the needs of future generations will be the next technology boom. Future generations depend on the choices that we make today. Humankind has passed the point of overshoot; sustainable development is the necessary revolution.[15]

4.15 Experiential Exercises

I. SWOT Analyses

The SWOT Analyses is a tool that you can use to evaluate internal strengths and weaknesses and external environment opportunities and threats. SWOT can be used to research internal operation's current state and to prepare the organization for future upcoming trends. It can then be used as a tool to create a strategic plan. This exercise will practice using SWOT Analyses to devise strategic plans, the tactics to align business systems, and operational change management to ensure a successful implementation of the plan.

To evaluate sustainability management using SWOT, assess each room in the facility for TBL positive and negative impacts List positives as strengths and negatives as weaknesses. Refer to the exercises completed in Chapters 1 and 2 and integrate your ideas.

Next, research the trends in the external environment that are outside your span of control. Trends should be evaluated concerning customers, suppliers, competitors, regulatory requirements, economic conditions, technology and innovation.

Strengths	Weaknesses
Go room by room within the facility and exterior of the building and list all current practices focused on TBL	Go room by room within the facility and exterior of the building and list ways to improve TBL
Opportunities	**Threats**
Research the competitive environment to identify partnerships and ways to open new markets. Research the macro environment to prepare for compliance, preparing for social trends, economic conditions, technology changes, etc.	Research the competitive environment to determine if leading or lagging. Study competitors who are respected in sustainability management Research the macro environment to prepare for compliance, preparing for social trends, economic conditions, technology changes, etc.

II. Strategy Worksheet

Evaluate the SWOT. From the strengths and weakness sections, identify what employees need to learn in order to make suggestions and take action. In what areas does the organization need to build awareness?

Analyzing the external environment will identify ways to reposition the organization for the future. Based on data and trends, envision how your organization can meet the needs and operate within the constraints of the future:

- Is the organization leading or lagging?
- How can the organization differentiate and capitalize on a competitive advantage by managing for sustainability?
- What new markets present opportunities to increase revenues?
- Do we face obsolescence or high costs of essential raw materials or even our own business model?
- Are we innovating ahead of consumer trends?

- Are we responding to consumer and industry trends?
- What are strategic priorities?

III. Tactical Planning Worksheet

Develop the process of change management with tactical plans to execute the strategic plan. In order to develop tactics, ask yourself the following questions:

- What programs should be planned?
- What partnerships need to be formed?
- What are key areas in which more expertise is needed?
- Who should we collaborate with externally?
- What key performance indicators would be meaningful?
- How much funding will be allocated?
- What timelines are expected for short-, medium-, and long-range goals?
- What is needed from employees?
- What are the responsibilities of employees?
- Who should participate and in what capacity?
- Who will lead the effort?
- How and when will the organization implement goals?
- How will the frontline communicate metrics and progress?
- When should progress reports be communicated and to whom?
- How will employees receive feedback on how the organization is progressing?
- How will employees be recognized formally and informally?

IV. Implementing into Operations Worksheet

Program management focuses on the major priorities of the organization, such as an environmental plan, social responsibility, risk management, brand management, and increasing revenues and reducing costs. Use this worksheet to draw up a program management plan to use for implementation of key target goals.

Those programs are then managed as multiple projects to accomplish the strategic priorities. Following are key project management tools that must be in place:

- Capital and budget approval for programs
- Senior management support to empower employees to take action
- Collaborative efforts with internal and external stakeholders
- Known barriers to implementation
- Timelines to achieve incremental target goals
- Budget allocations for programs and projects
- Key personnel for change management
- Accountability and responsibility structure
- Monitoring and evaluating implementation
- Continuous improvement process
- Communicating results internally and externally
- Aligning departments to achieve organizational strategy

SAMPLE QUESTIONS

Senior Management

1. The role of senior managers in sustainability management is to position the organization to meet the future needs of stakeholders and the environment, while maintaining a profitable business.

   A. True
   B. False

2. Stakeholders are demanding that organizations take responsibility for all actions that occur throughout the value chain?

   A. True
   B. False

3. Why is it important to create terms and frameworks for managing sustainability?

   A. Creates a common language in an organization
   B. Embraces a framework (i.e., Triple Bottom Line, Cradle to Cradle)
   C. Motivates, inspires, and gives direction to employees
   D. All of the above are important

Middle-Level Management

4. What is the role of middle-level managers in sustainability management?

   A. Develop strategic priorities
   B. Creating plans that implement the strategic goals of the organization
   C. Implementing plans
   D. Sustainability reporting

5. Middle-level managers also play in important role by doing which of the following?

   A. Anticipating barriers
   B. Eliminating barriers
   C. Reducing resistance to change
   D. All of the above
   E. None of the above

6. _____ is a key tactic to engage stakeholders to achieve the organization's strategy.

   A. Operational planning
   B. Change management
   C. Time management
   D. Organizational structure

Operations Management

7. Employees need to understand basic concepts in order to make TBL decisions. Which of the following is not an imperative?

    A. Understanding that both society and the economy cannot thrive without a healthy ecosystem
    B. Strain on natural resources created by the industry
    C. How the organization already manages for sustainability
    D. Rely on directives from senior management
    E. All of the above are needed to make decisions

8. _____ is defined as all departments are working together to achieve strategic goals

    A. Operations management
    B. Change management
    C. Tactical management
    D. Aligning business systems

9. Finding the emotional appeal to engage employees is a key aspect in successful program management.

    A. True
    B. False

Human Resource Management

10. Which one is not a major role human resource managers play in sustainability management?

    A. Change agents
    B. Public relations
    C. Unbiased management authority
    D. Job function focusing on quality of life and people

11. Key performance indicators will focus on all but which one?

    A. Training and development
    B. Communication of progress
    C. Accountability
    D. Reliability

12. The job function of human resources focuses on the people realm of TBL.

    A. True
    B. False

Facilities Management

13. When conducting an assessment, what is the most important aspect to improve energy efficiency?

    A. Building integrity
    B. Lighting
    C. Router equipment
    D. Reduce phantom loads

14. Facilities managers assess inputs, throughput, and output to manage material resources.

    A. True
    B. False

15. Water management should focus on all but which one of the following?

    A. Indoor and outdoor usage
    B. Ways to reuse
    C. Discharge
    D. Diversion

Equipment, Health, and Safety

16. The role of the equipment, health, and safety manager should be to manage the organization's strategic priorities as a centralized function.

    A. True
    B. False

17. Before disposing of equipment, what should the EHS manager try to do?

    A. Find a buyer
    B. Repair and reuse
    C. Sell parts for new revenue streams
    D. All of the above
    E. None of the above

18. Why does the Equipment, Health, and Safety Manager become responsible for sustainable initiatives?

    A. Manager is familiar with toxic chemicals
    B. Manager is familiar with Material Safety Data Sheets
    C. Knowledgeable about environmental regulations
    D. Knowledgeable about safety regulations
    E. All of the above

Information Technology

19. The role of IT managers is to improve efficiency in business processes.

    A. True
    B. False

20. Which of the following is not one of the 7 major functions of sustainability in the IT department?

    A. Data center management
    B. Personnel security
    C. Client desktop and mobile solutions
    D. Virtual technology tools

21. Environmentally Preferable Purchasing is a key policy for IT professionals that achieve all but which one?

    A. Reduce material usage of hardware
    B. Toxicity reduction of equipment
    C. Procure equipment with end-of-life solutions
    D. Codes of conduct

Accounting and Finance

22. What is driving the push to account for the environmental costs of products?

    A. Environmental degradation
    B. Societal pressure
    C. Lack of public trust in businesses
    D. Lack of public trust in governmental entities

23. Generally Accepted Accounting Principles (GAAP), allow social and emissions metrics to be included on balance sheets.

    A. True
    B. False

24. Which of the following is most closely related to Activity Based Costing?

    A. Life cycle assessment
    B. Life cycle costing
    C. Life cycle loops
    D. Life cycle principles of accounting

Marketing

25. Touting sustainability with little actions or results to back claims is called?

    A. Sustainability management
    B. Greenwashing
    C. Green practices
    D. Labels

26. Marketing strategies should directly target the "green" consumer as they will pay premium prices.

    A. True
    B. False

27. Sustainable marketing is a term that targets consumers that are mainly focused on the environment.

    A. True
    B. False

ENDNOTES

[1] *Our Basic Beliefs.* n.d. J.M. Smuckers. Retrieved June 5, 2011 from: http://www.smuckers.com /family_company/join_our_company/our_basic_beliefs.aspx

[2] *Performance with Purpose.* 2010. PepsiCo. Retrieved June 5, 2011 from: http://www.pepsico.com/Purpose.html

[3] *Supplier Engagement.* 2011. Proctor and Gamble. Retrieved June 5, 2011 from: http://www.pg.com/en_US /sustainability/environmental_sustainability/operations_suppliers/supplier_engagement.shtml

[4] *EICC Code.* 2009. Retrieved May 24, 2011 from: http://www.eicc.info/EICC%20CODE.htm

[5] What is a Smarter Planet? Retrieved June 27, 2011 from: http://www.ibm.com/smarterplanet/us/en/overview /ideas/index.html?re=CS1

[6] Nattrass, B. & Altomare, M. (1999). *The natural step for business: Wealth, ecology and the evolutionary corporation.* Canada: New Society Publishers. (p. 25).

[7] *SAP Solutions for Sustainability.* Retrieved June 22, 2011 from: http://www.sap.com/solutions/sustainability /index.epx

[8] Nattrass, B. & Altomare, M. (1999). *The natural step for business: Wealth, ecology and the evolutionary corporation.* Canada: New Society Publishers. (p. 23).

[9] Esty, D. & Winston, A. (2009). *Green to gold: How smart companies use environmental strategy to innovate, create value, and build competitive advantage.* New Jersey: Yale University Press, Inc.

[10] Hitchcock, D. & Willard, M. (2009). *The business guide to sustainability: Practical strategies and tools for organizations.* Sterling, VT: Earthscan. (p. 172).

[11] Hitchcock, D. & Willard, M. (2009). *The business guide to sustainability: Practical strategies and tools for organizations.* Sterling, VT: Earthscan. (p. 222).

[12] Martin, D. & Schouten, J. (2012). *Sustainable marketing.* Upper Saddle River, NJ: Pearson Education, Inc. (p. 10).

[13] *Our Mission.* (2011). Retrieved on April 21, 2012 from: http://www.seventhgeneration.com /seventh-generation-mission

[14] *Automatic Dishwasher Gel.* (2011). Retrieved on April 21, 2012 from: http://www.seventhgeneration.com /Dishwasher-Gel

[15] Senge. P, Kruschwitz, N. Laur, J. & Schley, S. (2008). *The necessary revolution: How individuals and organizations are working together to create a sustainable world.* NY: Doubleday.

Chapter 5

Supply Chain Management

Phase II of the senior management process to manage sustainability relies on the collaboration of the supply chain. This chapter will discuss the major terms and frameworks associated with professionals in supply chain management. Collaborating in today's global market is a necessity to solve regional issues with regional partners.

5.1 Part I: Strategic Approaches

Supply Chain Vision

A corporate vision is normally a short statement defining the way an organization will look in the future, or what it intends to become or achieve. It is usually a relatively broad statement of intentions and seeks to take a long-term view of the organization's aspirations. A well-structured vision is one which is clear and realistic, while remaining aligned with organizational values and culture, and while providing an optimistic view of the future. A clear, well-structured corporate vision provides direction so that the organization can achieve its strategy.

Similarly, a strong supply chain vision (which is clearly aligned with the organization's vision) provides direction for the supply chain strategy as well as providing a useful basis for the evaluation of the success of the supply chain. For a supply chain vision to be successful, it requires buy-in at the highest levels of management and support throughout the organization. To do this, it is important to have consulted with and obtained support from the organization's leadership structures.

Sustainability in a supply chain requires commitment to the concept from management and support throughout the organization. To achieve a sustainable supply chain, sustainability needs to be addressed within the supply chain vision, which in turn needs to be aligned with the corporate sustainability strategy and the overall business strategy.

To develop a sustainable supply chain vision, the organization's leadership needs to determine how they view the business and its supply chain in terms of all the issues and challenges associated with environmental, social, and economic concerns. The sustainable supply chain vision must incorporate these views in terms of growth, values, employees, communities, customers, partners, and society. A successful sustainable supply chain vision statement will give a sense of the future envisioned for the supply chain, and will concisely describe the outcome.

Thus, it guides decision making and strategy, as well as performance measurement. The visions should be clear and inspire emotion and in turn creates a shared purpose.

Supply professionals play an integral role in achieving the vision of the supply chain. The Institute for Supply Management™ (ISM) encourages supply professionals to serve on appropriate committees, boards, nongovernmental partnerships, and governmental panels to promote social responsibility and environmental management. Actively participating creates the ability to align standards within a global supply chain. It is also important to consider regional social issues, environmental challenges, laws, trade agreements, and customs when developing and implementing strategies and policies. ISM considers the following nine principles to align the supply chain:

ISM Principles

1. **Community**
   Provide resources for community support where the company operates
2. **Diversity and Inclusiveness—Supply Base**
   Make the effort to engage suppliers in sourcing processes and decisions.
3. **Diversity and Inclusiveness—Workforce**
   Attract and retain a workforce that reflects the demographics within the community.
4. **Environment**
   Take actions and make decisions that protect and preserve the vitality of the environment.
5. **Ethics and Business Conduct**
   Ensure all parties are acting with high ethical behavior and conduct business with governance.
6. **Financial Responsibility**
   Make decisions regarding capital, reporting, and risk management with responsible business practices.
7. **Human Rights**
   Human beings have universal natural rights, or status, regardless of legal jurisdiction or other localizing factors.
8. **Health and Safety**
   Actively manage risks of injury, danger, failure, error, accident, harm, or loss.
9. **Sustainable Development**
   Actively meet current needs without hindering future generations in terms of economic, environmental, and social challenges.[1]

Codes of Conduct for Sustainability

A code of conduct is critical to the sustainability of the supply chain. Codes of conduct frequently focus on social issues, but may be extended to include environmental and even economic issues. The purpose of the code of conduct is to ensure that acceptable levels of behaviors within the supply chain are adequately defined so that the organization can control what happens throughout its supply chain. It also ensures that there is no unethical behavior anywhere throughout the supply chain. Therefore, organizations can respond to stakeholders that expect high ethical standards. The rise in headlines pertaining to the use of child labor in suppliers' businesses, sweatshop conditions in factories, the lack of compliance with wage and hour standards, etc. has led to creating codes of conduct that are critical to meeting stakeholder expectations.

Codes of conduct are necessary:

- to define accepted/unacceptable behaviors;
- to promote high standards of practice;
- to provide a benchmark for members to use for self-evaluation;
- to establish a framework for professional behavior and responsibilities;
- as a vehicle for occupational identity; and
- as a mark of occupational maturity.[2]

The code of conduct could set out general principles about the organization's principles regarding quality, privacy, employment standards, working conditions, environmental issues, etc. There is considerable debate about what the extent of the code of conduct for the supply chain should be, whether it should be short and succinct or extensive, or cover all possibilities. This will largely be dependent on the purpose of the code; whether it intends to guide, inspire, or regulate behavior. The code of conduct could also define the procedures to decide whether standards have been violated. Then penalties or remedies may need to be imposed.

An effective code of conduct will, just as the vision, be dependent on obtaining support from management. If a code of conduct is well designed, it can assist in enhancing productivity, credibility, and profitability. ISM's code of conduct clearly outlines guidelines that are widely accepted.

ISM's Standards

1. **Impropriety**
   Unethical or compromising conduct in relationships, actions, and communications should be avoided.
2. **Conflict of Interest**
   Protect the interests of your employer and avoid conflicts of interest in any personal, business, or other activity.
3. **Issues of Influence**
   Avoid actions and behaviors that may negatively influence, or appear to influence, decisions.
4. **Responsibilities to Your Employer**
   Uphold standards of your employer by following fiduciary responsibilities.
5. **Supplier and Customer Relationships**
   Promote positive customer and supplier relationships.
6. **Sustainability and Social Responsibility**
   Champion social responsibility and sustainability practices.
7. **Confidential and Proprietary Information**
   Confidentiality and proprietary information must be protected.
8. **Reciprocity**
   Avoid improper reciprocal agreements or favoring suppliers.
9. **Applicable Laws, Regulations, and Trade Agreements**
   Comply with applicable laws, regulations, and trade agreements.
10. **Professional Competence**
    Promote the supply management profession with professional competence.[3]

The Institute for Supply Management™ clearly guides supply management professionals to conduct business operations with a clear code of conduct. The standards are for decision making based on integrity, valuing your employer, and displaying loyalty to the supply management profession. Supply professionals can also obtain professional certification on two levels:

1. The Certified Professional in Supply Management® (CPSM®). This credential certifies professionals in areas such as supplier relationships, finance, global strategy, and risk compliance.
2. The Certified in Supply Management™ (CSM™). This credential certifies a broad-based knowledge of the major concepts and methodologies of supply management.[4]

Supply Chain Integration

Typically, supply chain elements consist of purchasing, operations, and logistics process activities which occur between the organization and its suppliers and customers; there may be a number of tiers of each. Supply chain integration implies the coordination of these practices amongst all the role-players in the supply chain. The activities in the supply chain are said to be integrated when all members work together when making decisions that impact on the profitability of the supply chain, regardless of whether the decisions are related to delivery, production, inventory, or purchasing. If any of these decisions are made in isolation and they fail, this can result in disruptions throughout the supply chain. In essence, integration occurs when the members of the supply chain incorporate supply chain management into the organization's strategic planning and management process; the supply chain practices are in accordance with customer requirements, as well as the requirements of the supply chain as a whole.

Integrating the supply chain can be a complex task. It requires better internal integration of all functions within each supply chain member's organization, so that the supply chain functions as a single unit rather than as a fragmented collection of individuals. First, this requires that the supply chain is properly aligned and appropriate linkages are built between member organizations. Alignment refers to the establishment of common vision, objectives, and strategies for the supply chain. This implies that the vision is shared by all organizations in the supply chain; and the direction of the supply chain is thus established. The second aspect of supply chain integration is the development of appropriate linkages between member organizations. This pertains to how information is shared within the supply chain so that decisions made within the supply chain are based on the same information.

Because of the high levels of alignment and information sharing required to enable real supply chain integration, there are a number of challenges that are typically encountered in these endeavours. These typically relate to issues of systems and exposure. To enable supply chain integration, a number of features are critical, although it should be noted that the existence of these features are not a guarantee of real supply chain integration or success. The first of these is trust between member organizations. In order to share a single vision and strategy for the supply chain, real information sharing can only materialize if the members are confident that the information that they share will not be abused or used for individual gain. The information sharing required for supply chain integration also necessitates information technology that is capable of providing critical information as and when it is required. Additionally, the organizational structures throughout the supply chain need to be aligned to the strategy so that the structure and people are all moving in the same direction.

Figure 1: Workflow Diagram: Packaging Design

Product Stewardship	Identify goals

• Consider sources of raw materials and sinks for end-of-life

End-of-Life Considerations	Identify destination of the package

• What are end-of-life disposal options in region: landfill, recycling, incineration?
• Identify regional shipping, storage, disposal
• Identify tax of fees of region for environmental impacts

Regulatory Considerations	Packaging guidelines and regulations of the region and

• Environmental regulations
• Will the package need to be tailored for multiple regions or is single-use option available?

Modes of Shipping	Packaging considerations based on shipping modes and costs

• Will shipping method impact the footprint of product?
• How are costs determined—by truckload, volume, weight, etc.?
• Mode increases risks of high temperatures, moisture, etc.

Internal Requirements	Company-specific policies and procedures

• Product protection requirements to reduce physical or other harm
• Is the packaging alternative viable?
• Will the packaging perform well throughout its life cycle?

Raw Material Selection	Closed loop design

• Consider applicable material options and new innovations to market
• Consider renewable sources and end-of-life options by region

Packaging Design	Resource efficiency

• Design for minimal resource usage, recycled content, reduce overpackaging, and disassembly
• Reduce toxic substances
• Design for reuse, recyclability, disassembly

Environmental Characteristics	Communicating value

• Labels and marketing accurately portrayed
• Build consumer awareness by communicating design

The final feature of supply chain integration is an appropriate supply chain performance measurement system. It is essential that performance measures are agreed on and used throughout the supply chain to ensure that the supply chain strategies and targets meet expectations and, if not, that they are adjusted accordingly. Performance measurement assists the members in deciding on the value of certain tactics and how to mutually direct supply chain efforts in the future.

An excellent example of supply chain integration is the Environmental Packaging Certification issued by the Institute of Packaging Professionals (IoPP). University of California, Santa Barbara's Donald Bren School collaborated with Hewlett Packard, IBM, and AMD to create the *Environmental Packaging Guideline for the Electronics Industry.* The guidelines for the packaging industry establish procedures, life cycle costing, performance measurements, and impact reduction strategies based on life cycle assessment impacts. The guidelines focus on the environmental impact and alternative materials to consider for packaging design for the following.

- Corrugated cardboard
- Paperboard
- Wood
- Solid plastics
- Expanded plastics
- Printing inks

The IoPP guideline has three objectives:

1. Decrease the negative impacts on the environment and society;
2. Increase financial benefits by reducing costs of materials and shipping; and
3. Reduce risks as well as increase brand value through social responsibility.[5]

The procedures provide guidelines for packaging professionals to make considerations before designing and choosing packaging materials. The workflow process aligns decisions around the supply chain strategy.[6]

Collaborative, Meaningful Partnerships

At the turn of the twentieth century, many organizations were vertically-integrated organizations, providing manufacturing, distribution, and warehousing, etc. services in-house. However, by the end of the century, vertical integration had almost disappeared and most organizations contracted external organizations to assist them in non-core functions. Outsourcing is oftentimes the norm. However, one of the key problems with outsourced relationships is the so-called "bullwhip" effect, whereby uncertainty in demand and lead times causes order quantities and lead times to be inflated the further upstream and the further away from the end consumer. This leads to large quantities of excess goods and a great risk of obsolete stock. To counteract this, organizations have recognized the need for much higher levels of coordination in the supply chain so that information on final customer demand is shared timeously throughout the entire supply chain.

Supply chain integration thus implies that information flows are improved through all the links in the supply chain. However, if the supply chain is coordinated by a dominant party, this implies that information could be shared selectively resulting in a skewed distribution of information, inventory, and power. To optimize the entire supply chain, and not just one or two key role players, coordination has to go much further than sharing information. Strategic partnerships evolve where supply and demand decisions are made together to ensure the creation of sustainable value for all parties.

Collaborative partnerships require strong trust relationships, integrated technology systems, process integration, and appropriate performance measures. Over and above these aspects, these partnerships require a shared vision, goals, and objectives.

Effective collaborative partnerships can reduce inventory levels, cut transport costs, reduce warehousing costs, shorten lead times, and improve customer service levels. Meaningful collaborative relationships can also result in benefits unrelated to cost reduction such as increased sales, better decision-making, higher levels of operational effectiveness, stronger strategic relationships, top line growth, better market intelligence, etc.

There are, of course, a number of barriers to achieving meaningful collaborative relationships, not least of which are technology difficulties and trust issues. In addition, barriers include incorrect partner selection, corporate cultural issues and lack of a strategic approach to the relationship. Despite this, evidence suggests that truly open and meaningful collaborative supply chain relationships can result in far more successful supply chains.

One of the earliest examples of supply chain collaboration was within Walmart's supply chain. Walmart realized that the in-stock averages of one of their suppliers did not meet their vendor performance standards. To address this issue, Walmart plus the vendor and two software companies collaborated to identify a process that would ensure that customer demands were communicated throughout the supply chain. The goal was to ensure replenishment could materialize when required. The team collaborated by choosing one product to test as a pilot project. Within the test period, the vendor's in-stock averages of the selected product rose from 87% to 98%, lead times dropped from 21 to 11 days, and sales increased by $8.5 million. These results occurred despite only including a single manufacturing plant and three Walmart distribution centers.[7]

Supply Chain Risk Management

Risk management is critical to the sustainability of the supply chain. Issues that affect sustainability need to be clearly articulated plus the risks associated with each issue identified. The risks are rated according to the magnitude and the likelihood of the impact. Key risk areas are highlighted and mitigation actions and plans defined. There are a number of issues that may place the sustainability of the supply chain at risk.

1. Procurement
The source of raw materials may not be sustainable, implying uncertainty in the chain of custody which may, in turn, result in customer concerns, ineligibility for tenders, etc. Similarly sustainability risks in the procurement function may arise from the use of hazardous substances, various animal husbandry, breeding and feeding practices, long term supply issues, waste and packaging, labor practices, supplier viability, fair pay, geographical sourcing practices, and the escalating cost of supply.

2. Operations
The sustainability of internal operations may be at risk as a result of issues such as water, air or soil pollution, health emissions from local emissions, waste management, employee work/life balance, labor practices, inefficient operations, and poor productivity.

3. Distribution
Distribution issues may arise from suboptimal modal choices, increased fuel and petrol costs, route planning and scheduling choices, delivery times increased due to congestion, etc.

4. Product Development and Stewardship
Sustainability issues in this area may be associated with end-of-life disposal, raw material price increases and the need for substitutes, product traceability, changing customer demand,

cost increases, investor appeal, packaging and raw materials, impact, and efficiency of product in use.

Supply chain risks pose a serious threat to short-term revenue, profit, brand reputation, and the health and safety of employees, customers, and supply chain partners. Despite this, it is often underestimated and under-emphasized in supply chain management. In developing supply chain risk plans, consideration needs to be given to each step, and the inter-relationships between steps and the corresponding business processes.[8]

Planning for risk can certainly achieve quick wins under uncertainty. A number of years ago, a Philips microchip plant was struck by lightning, resulting in a fire that ruined millions of mobile phone chips. Two of Philips' major customers, Nokia and Erikson, were affected by the disaster. Because Nokia had a relatively flexible supply chain, this strategy allowed them to quickly switch to an alternative supplier, and re-engineer the phones to accept American and Japanese chips. As a result, the production line was not significantly affected by the disaster. Philips had promised its customers that production would be resumed within a week. Erikson accepted this and decided to do nothing. This cost them approximately $400 million in annual earnings as well as a significant loss of their market share. Nokia's risk management strategy allowed them to be flexible when faced with disaster, and their profits grew by 42% that year.[9]

Supply Chain Synchronization

Supply chain synchronization has been written about extensively, but is difficult to achieve in operation. Synchronization of the supply chain can result in reduced time to market, decreased costs, and effectively more managed inventory turns. Synchronization is a building block in sustainable supply chain management, enabling true integration. This generally relies on excellent communication (EDI, web-based), better information (real time data, collaborative planning, forecasting, and replenishment), and a willingness to work together coupled with trust. Communication (data sharing), management commitment, and demand visibility are the keys to the success of true synchronization.

The real challenge is to present real-time information concurrently so that all supply chain partners can receive and utilize it at the same time. The benefits are obvious. Synchronization of demand/supply information minimizes work-in-process and finished goods inventories up and down the channel, dampens the "bullwhip effect" as products are pulled through the distribution pipeline, reduces costs overall, and matches customer requirements with available products. To be of value, supply chain synchronization requires all members of the ecosystem to engage in partnerships that collectively optimize resources and reduce costs. A synchronized supply chain will consist of the following key components: a unified business strategy, common measurements for product and performance excellence, and the selection of enabling technologies.[10]

Supply Chain Optimization/Rightsizing the Supply Chain

Optimizing, or rightsizing, the supply chain relates to the use of various processes to achieve the optimum supply chain. This implies that inventory needs to be positioned optimally in the supply chain, but also requires that manufacturing, transport, and distribution costs are optimized. Optimizing, or rightsizing, does not imply cost minimization, but rather considers process and system redesign, including the possible addition or reduction of certain supply chain activities. This could include human resources, finance, assets, or the entire supply chain. In essence, the entire supply chain is restructured to achieve the optimum cost service mix for the organization.

Often, practitioners regard rightsizing as the optimization of inventory within the supply chain. Too much, too little, or inappropriately positioned inventory can result in unnecessarily high inventory costs and risks, as well as potential cash flow problems. Rightsizing inventory implies that the organization tries to achieve efficiencies in the market place with as little inventory as possible. This means that the organization needs a thorough understanding of its market and the demand patterns within that market: 1) how inventory is positioned within the supply chain to respond to changing market demand, and 2) how to respond to supply chain disruptions.

However, supply chain optimization, or rightsizing, goes beyond inventory decisions. These other decisions are also critical:

- What inventory to carry
- Decisions on inventory levels, positioning, and inventory costs
- Developing optimal purchasing
- Transport and distribution processes to ensure that stock is readily available
- Ensure customers receive appropriate levels of in-store service
- Introducing new products or product variations at appropriate times
- Ensuring that store design stays aligned with changing consumer trends
- Communication of changes in products or service levels to the customer

Ultimately, rightsizing the supply chain requires continuous process optimization, and ensuring that the entire supply chain stays responsive to the changing demands in the modern business environment. Excellent information technology systems, redesigning the network as required, and a business strategy that supports this will ensure that the supply chain is able to adapt and respond to market demands by making and delivering products when they are required.

5.2 Part II: Operations and Terminology

The next section discusses supply chain management terminology and operational imperatives relating to sustainability management.

Carrier Selection

Selecting the correct carrier can be critical to the sustainability of an organization. When selecting a carrier, the organization needs to consider a number of critical features that will influence the level of service provided to the customer as well as the costs. Because transportation has such a major impact on customer service, inventories, reliability, time-in-transit, warehousing, packaging, and the environment, any decisions that are made regarding carriers will influence the entire supply chain as well as its sustainability.

When selecting a carrier, the first aspect most commonly considered is freight costs. Organizations typically look for the lowest freight costs within a predefined service specification. However, freight costs need to be considered in the context of other costs, which may be incurred as a result of the selection of a particular carrier. These may include aspects such as inventory carrying costs of inventory in the pipeline, safety stock and cycle stock at the receiving location, as well as the investment costs associated with producing inventory to fill the pipeline. In addition to the monetary costs, each decision about transport, inventory, and investment has associated social and environmental consequences, which must be factored into the carrier selection process.

Other factors that must be taken into account are aspects such as the reliability of the service, total transit times, claims handling, tracking and tracing capabilities and availability of real time information, accuracy of invoicing, EDI capabilities, cargo capacity, insurance claims history, personnel, complaints handling, response time to queries, complaints and claims, market coverage, expediting of shipments, financial stability of the carrier, scheduling flexibility, and flexibility of freight rates. Each of these factors could influence the sustainability of the supply chain and the decision on the correct carrier will be dependent on the carrier's ability to deliver a service which lowers the total cost (resource, environmental, and social) in the supply chain while still delivering an acceptable service to the customer.

Centralized versus Decentralized Warehouses

One of the key decisions that must be made in the supply chain is whether to service markets from a single centralized location or whether to place a warehouse in each market. This decision is critical as it has an effect on costs as well as on customer service, thus significantly impacting supply chain sustainability.

When comparing a decentralized to a centralized inventory system, a number of key features need to be taken into account. First, a decentralized system will require higher safety stock levels than a centralized system. Service levels differ between the two systems, overhead costs are greater in a decentralized system, lead times are faster in a decentralized system, and transport costs differ. Notably, in a centralized system, outbound transport costs are higher as warehouses are far from the markets. However, in a decentralized system, inbound transport costs are higher. Each of these decisions affects not only costs and customer service levels but also has associated environmental and social impacts.

When inventories are centralized, this also implies that order processing is simplified. There is a smaller requirement for working capital as well as actual inventory and the need for nationally-based warehouse operations is eliminated. A centralized warehouse may also be a bigger and more sophisticated facility in order to handle multiple markets or countries. The bundling of available knowledge, product flows, and production factors also add to the attractiveness of a centralized inventory system. Finally, overhead costs are usually reduced in a centralized system due to the economies of scale that is achievable in having fewer facilities. However, these advantages need to be traded off against the disadvantages.

Aside from higher outbound transportation costs, the centralized system can negatively affect the supply chain by offering longer lead times to the customer. There could also potentially be issues relating to the diverse customer base and the divergent needs of the various markets. A bigger, single facility could also imply greater bureaucracy resulting in slower decision-making processes and lower levels of flexibility. Finally, a centralized facility can have a negative impact on both customers and staff perceptions. Customers and staff may not like goods shipped from countries other than their own. Customers and staff may also react negatively to the longer lead times and loss in flexibility. They may also feel that a centralized facility is not capable of meeting their specific market needs unless a definite mechanism is created to address this. Local staff may also feel that they have lost control of their inventories. A decision on centralization or decentralization needs to be carefully weighed to consider customer service, costs, as well as long term sustainability impacts.

Cross-Docking

Cross-docking refers to the practice whereby items received into a warehouse are not kept in storage (or are kept in storage for a very short period) but rather readied for shipment to another location. Inbound goods from suppliers are transferred (almost) directly to outbound flows destined to go to customers with little, if any, warehousing. Shipments usually spend less than 24 hours in the distribution center. This differs from a traditional system where goods are stored in a warehouse or in a similar fashion until a customer orders them. Typically, cross-docking is performed to change the form of transport, to sort products intended for different destinations or to combine products from different origins into vehicles bound for the same or similar destinations.

The purpose of cross-docking is to minimize or eliminate the storage in the supply chain. Goods are received from a number of suppliers. Within a short period, they are sorted to be shipped out as a consolidated load (with goods from other suppliers) to customers.

Cross-docking supports better timing of freight distribution and better synchronization with demand. The distribution center acts as a sorting facility rather than as a warehouse. Throughput in the distribution center should be relatively high. Cross-docking is used primarily in the retail sector, but it is also used frequently in manufacturing and distribution. Cross-docking relies heavily on effective transportation, without which the high throughput rates that are required for this type of operation are not possible.

The primary advantages of cross-docking practices are reduction of warehousing space and the realization of economies of scale in outbound distribution. As inventory in storage is leveraged, significant cost reductions are possible in this area, while still achieving all of the benefits of consolidation.

In a conventional distribution system, it is difficult to achieve full truckload (FTL) shipments. Cross-docking batches sorted and consolidated goods from different suppliers to maximize FTLs.

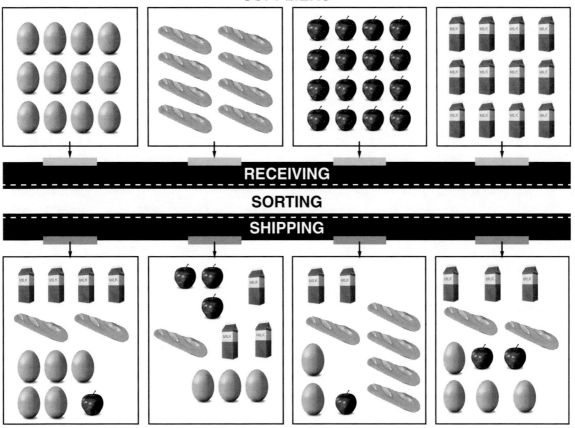

Figure © Kendall Hunt Publishing Company; Food images © 2012. Used under license from Shutterstock, Inc.

Aside from the benefits inherent to FTL shipments, cross-docking can result in reduced labor costs due to the reduction in picking and put-away activities, and reduced lead times in the total supply chain. Therefore, FTL achieves enhanced customer satisfaction levels, reduced warehousing space handling costs, storage costs, operating costs, and could increase available retail space.

A major Tier 1 (main contractor), automotive supplier was concerned about its network, which was regarded as suboptimal and inefficient. In their network, they considered daily and weekly direct routes, plus weekly deliveries from suppliers to one of their plants. Transfreight, a third-party logistics service provider (3PL), analyzed the suppliers operations and recommended the use of a dedicated cross-docking operation. Also included in this solution were sub and direct routes, sequenced delivery to the Original Equipment Manufacturer (OEM), traffic management, and on-site logistics support. Freight was consolidated at the cross-dock facility and shipped via daily main routes to the Tier 1 plant. Daily direct routes were also used to send directly to the OEM. The benefits achieved by the customer included improved cube efficiency, process design and inventory management, reduced logistics miles, space requirements, and double handling. Cross-docking incurred a significant savings.[11]

Facility Layout

After an organization has made the decision on where to place its facilities, the layout of the facility is critical to the success of the facility. An appropriate facility layout requires that equipment, materials, people, infrastructure, and data collection points are optimally located.

Good facility layout design requires a clear understanding of the product flows within the facility as well as the process flows. The requirements in terms of data transfer, equipment, and inventory levels need to be clearly specified. Conducting an audit of the facility will determine appropriate next steps.

Facility layout is influenced by a number of critical factors. The first of these is the flow of movement. It is essential in a warehouse that the facility is designed in such a way as to facilitate the easy movement of goods, equipment, and people through the facility. This does not necessarily imply a straight line. Flow could be parallel lines, u-shapes, etc. as long as the flow does not cross itself, go against or back on itself, and confuse movement in any other way. Good flow will enable quick movement through the warehouse, smooth transition from the receiving stage to the shipment stage, and effective coordination while in the facility.

A second critical feature to be considered is materials handling. The facility should be designed to accommodate a materials handling system which enables the simple, logical, and effective movement of goods through the premises. Facility design, selection of materials handling equipment, and product flow should be considered simultaneously in the facility decision-making process.

Future expansion or growth should also be taken into account. Facilities need to be flexible enough to be adjusted to changing demands and manufacturing requirements. The facility should be designed in a way that is conducive to helping the business meet its production needs.

Other factors that must be taken into consideration in facility layout and design are space utilization, shipping and receiving, communication, employee satisfaction, and safety and brand reputation. Sufficient space is required for shipping and receiving as this must be performed efficiently and effectively. Communication must be facilitated through the warehouse so that interactions between operational areas and interactions with suppliers and customers are easy. The facility should also be a place where employees are happy to work; a badly designed facility will impact on wellness and morale. The facility must be aligned with the requirements of any occupational health and safety legislation. Finally, the facility should be designed in such a way that brand image is enhanced.

A well laid-out facility can increase throughput and output, enhance the flow of products through the facility, reduce costs, provide better working conditions for employees, and improve overall levels of services to customers.

Facilities Location

Location decisions have a major impact on the total cost and sustainability of the entire supply chain. Where plants, warehouses, distribution centers, and other facilities are located determines distribution costs, customer service levels, and the speed of service. When organizations make decisions on facility locations, they typically need to look at the number of facilities they require as well as their network. Decisions also need to be made regarding centralized or decentralized systems, hub-and-spoke arrangements, and the countries within which facilities will be located.

All decisions will have an impact on the ability to serve the customer efficiently and effectively. From a strategic perspective, location could influence the firm's competitive position, current facility arrangements, market size, and penetration and expansion capabilities. These decisions however, need to be balanced against issues related to accessibility, communities, business climate, labor, utility, risk, plant site, and financial factors.

There are a number of different points of view on the factors that should influence the location of facilities. Some practitioners locate warehouses at places which are most likely to reduce product costs or improve customer service. This implies that warehouses can be located close to sources or close to customers or at some point in-between. Location could also be dependent on the range of products carried by the organization, the demand for the product, labor costs or availability, profitability, land costs, tax laws, etc. The decision on the optimal location will finally be based on the location where costs are minimized, profits are maximized, and/or customer service is maximized.

Camelot Management Consulting performed a network redesign on behalf of one of its clients, a leading chemical company with multi-billion euro/dollar revenue figures. The company had a highly dispersed distribution network within the European region, implying high inventory levels and costs as well as high transportation and warehousing costs. The consultancy was tasked with reducing bottlenecks in one plant while optimizing idle capacity in other plants. Simultaneously, it had to address the company's expansion plans as well as ensure an early payback period. Before the project, the company's network consisted of four manufacturing plants, two central distribution centers, and twelve local warehouses. The consultancy used a network optimization tool to optimize warehouse locations, reallocate products to plants, and design cost-optimized materials flows. A number of alternatives were evaluated by the various functions within the organization (e.g., logistics, manufacturing, customer service) especially in regards to availability of logistics service providers, lead times, and differences in demand growth across countries. The result was a change in the network to four plants, one central distribution center, and six local warehouses with one satellite. The real value however, was the reduction in complexity and costs achieved through the redesign. This included less primary transport, a more equal distribution of capacity within the plants, elimination of bottlenecks, an 11% reduction in supply chain costs, and an 18% reduction in inventories.[12]

Facilities Management

The supply chain is the network of retailers, distributors, transporters, storage facilities, and suppliers, all of which make a contribution to the production, sale, and distribution of a product. Thus, the supply chain typically comprises a number of facilities which can have a considerable impact on the overall sustainability of the supply chain.

It is the role of the facility management function to ensure the safe, secure, and environmentally-sound operations and maintenance of these assets in a cost effective manner aimed at long-term preservation of the asset value. This ensures the sustainability of the facilities and contributing to the overall sustainability of the supply chain.

Sustainable facilities management practices can include aspects such as:

- Ensuring Indoor Environmental Quality (IEQ): inclusive of appropriate air quality, lighting, temperature, and sound levels to ensure that the health and productivity of the building's tenants is adequately considered.
- Energy Efficiency: critical to the sustainability of a facility. Most modern buildings have considerable challenges in ensuring that the demands for heating, cooling, ventilation, lighting, etc. are balanced against the requirement of minimizing energy consumption. New efficient technologies and methodologies such as occupancy sensors, automatic air conditioning control, and the use of natural light and ventilation can make a big difference to the facility's energy consumption.
- Resource efficiency: another key component of sustainable facilities management, comprising methodologies to ensure that upstream waste (associated with inbound products, e.g., unnecessary packaging), operational waste (paper, tins, glass, etc.), and outbound waste is minimized. Resource efficiency should also include minimizing water consumption.
- Refurbishment or renovation: a method of attaining better building efficiencies. This can include aspects such as incorporating natural design features, such as better use of natural light, ventilation or installation of systems designed to conserve energy, and resources, such as water treatment systems.

Sustainable facilities management practices can result in improved efficiencies, lower costs, higher productivity, and better allocation of resources, streamlined operations, reduced liability, and quality assurance.

Inventory Management

Inventory management is primarily concerned with the decisions on how much stock to keep and where and how to position that stock. Inventory management requires that the balance is found between achieving appropriate replenishment lead times, minimizing the carrying costs of inventory, managing assets appropriately for the supply chain, forecasting of inventory requirements, inventory valuation, managing quality of inventory, price forecasting of inventory, space planning and network design for inventory, etc. The correct balance between all of these requirements will result in the optimal levels of inventory within the supply chain. However, if these are not balanced correctly, there are wide ranging consequences for the supply chain. In essence, inventory management requires that inventory levels do not become too high as this implies escalating costs, or too low as this could result in stock-outs and placing the businesses operations in jeopardy. Inventory management means ensuring that no negative effects of incorrect stock levels are incurred anywhere in the supply chain.

Inventory represents cash that has been converted into goods which have not yet been sold. Inventory can be seen as an opportunity cost. If inventory levels are too high, cash is tied up in goods that are at risk of not being able to be converted into cash if sales do not happen or if inventory cannot be returned to the supplier. The organization can therefore not afford to have too much cash tied up in inventory as it could affect the long-term profitability and sustainability of the organization due to cash flow problems. On the other hand, the organization needs enough inventory to meet sales or face reducing or losing its customer base.

Inventory management essentially seeks to make the correct decisions on how much stock to order and when to order the stock. Well managed inventory can add value to the supply chain by ensuring appropriate quality levels. The location of inventories affects speed and flexibility of service while reducing costs. Conversely, inventories tie up cash, represent opportunity costs, can be non-value adding costs, and incur considerable risks.

Managing inventory is therefore primarily a task that is focused on achieving efficiencies. Traditionally this has meant that inventories should be managed in such a way as to save costs throughout the supply chain. The implication is that inventory levels be kept as low as possible, whilst maintaining a specified customer service level. Realistically, zero inventories are not really possible because of forecasting inaccuracies in complex markets, so inventory cost savings efforts are the norm in manufacturing, distribution, and warehousing. In modern supply chains, where the emphasis is placed on sustainability, the cost savings efforts in inventory management are extended to include savings in carbon, water, energy, and raw and other materials to ensure that inventory has a minimum financial, social, and environmental cost to the supply chain.

McDonalds used a just-in-time inventory management system to reduce overall inventory costs. Prior to implementation of the system, McDonalds would pre-cook their burgers and allow them to sit under heat-lamps until they were either sold or had to be disposed of. Implementing a JIT system means that burgers are produced on demand. Aside from better customer service, in terms of supplying a fresher, higher quality product, the system has impacted inventory holding costs. The holding costs for burger parts are high because of their high spoilage rates. Frozen burger patties can be kept for several months at a time; however cooked patties have a shelf life of approximately 15 minutes. The result of implementing a JIT system has dramatically reduced the costs of holding and scrapping inventory.[13]

Inventory Put Away

To ensure success of the supply chain, inventory needs to be accurately recorded in the warehouse management system throughout all entities. The lack of accurate data on inventory can have far-reaching consequences ranging from incorrect order quantities to overstocking, under stocking, or obsolete inventories. Ensuring inventory accuracy is largely dependent on the warehousing system, and in particular, the receiving and put away functions. Having accurate information at this stage of the warehousing process leads to quicker order fulfillment, greater control of the order filling process, and fewer errors in order fulfillment.

Ideally, an effective inventory put away system will be part of an integrated warehousing management system that allows for quick identification of available and appropriate stock locations and full integration with all the other warehouse functions. Part of ensuring that the put away system is effective is recognizing that the put away system entails not only receiving from the docks and putting away into an available location, but also relocation within the warehouse as well as replenishment from reserves, where applicable.

Ensuring that the put away process is efficient and effective requires that inventory is put into locations that are aligned with its stock turnover levels, picking frequencies, size, etc. Stock should be easily and quickly located, and in a logical sequence to enhance the picking process. A good inventory put away system follows storage rules that are designed to enhance space utilization. The put away system should allow for effective picking later on and stock should be located in accordance with velocity, storage requirements such as refrigeration, and usage requirements.

An effective inventory put away system will enhance productivity in the warehouse, eliminate unnecessary labor movements and labor intensity, ensure that goods move through the warehouse faster and with lower costs. It will also be fully aligned with all other warehousing processes and facilitate the total warehousing value chain, ensure inventory accuracy, and enable faster and more accurate order fulfillment.

Maximizing Space

Warehousing plays a critical role in the supply chain as it stores crucial inventories, allows for the achievement of transportation and production economies, facilitates the critical linkages in the supply chain, enables the flow of product through the supply chain, enhances customer service, etc. However, the warehouse plays a considerable role in adding value within the supply chain. Unless managed exceptionally well, it can result in a considerable drain on resources. It is therefore essential that warehouses be used optimally, as warehousing space is generally regarded as expensive. Part of the solution is to ensure that warehousing space is used to its maximum capacity.

The first step in utilizing warehousing space is to maximize capacity to ensure that obsolete and excess inventory is eliminated from the inventory list. Any inventory that cannot be converted into cash within a relatively short time period is wasting space within the warehouse and thus adding to costs. Secondly, increasing turnover rather than increasing warehouse space is a possible solution to space issues. Warehousing space is more effectively utilized when inventory only spends a short time within the facility. This will not only reduce on-hand inventory, but also enable more productive stock and therefore optimize costs. A third step is to consider warehouse procedures. Procedures such as inventory control methods, put away procedures, pallet utilization, etc. can all be used to optimize warehouse space. Physical warehouse space adjustments can also assist in maximizing space utilization. Better layout, flow design, materials handling equipment, rack configuration, etc. can all impact on how well space is used. Finally, the warehouse management system can have a considerable influence on space utilization. The warehouse management system should provide accurate, real-time information on the current status of the stock, inventory locations, etc. It should also allow for quicker picking and packing; which in turn enables faster stock turnaround and better facility productivity.

Making the best use of warehousing space enables better use of resources, quicker inventory turns, better lead times, lower total logistics costs, higher productivity, and higher levels of customer service. In essence, warehousing and other facility space is expensive in the supply chain and without effectively managing the space and using it to its maximum capacity, a facility can become a drain on resources. Effective space utilization ensures that the facility adds value to the total supply chain.[14,15]

Modal choice

The selection of the mode of transport can have major implications for the sustainability of the supply chain. The five modes of transportation are: road, rail, air, water, and pipeline. Each of the modes have their own unique characteristics and consequently have major implications for the supply chain.

1. Road

Road transport, for example, is a highly flexible mode of transport. Although bound to the way, the routes on which it can travel are extensive, with a very wide range of geographical coverage. The entry into the market place is also relatively cheap, which makes this a highly competitive market, with many role players. The result is that road transport is a highly utilized mode of transport, particularly over short distances where this can provide an excellent and flexible service to customers.

2. Rail

Rail transport, in contrast, is well positioned to carry bulk products at a very low cost. Where low-value products are being transported, rail provides a low-cost service, ensuring that the final landed cost of the product is not negatively impacted by high logistics costs. Rail is also an effective mode for general freight over long distances, although it may have to cooperate effectively with other modes so as to provide the customer with a more flexible service. Rail is restricted to pre-determined routes. On the other hand, its unit costs tend to be lower than road, and its environmental impacts are lower. Entry into this market can be limited.

3. Water

Water transport can be divided into a number of areas, i.e., inland transport and sea transport. Inland water transport is usually used in countries where the geography allows for it. Many countries in Europe, for example, have navigable waterways, which allow for these types of logistics activities. Africa, on the other hand, has almost no navigable rivers and trade is therefore restricted to inland rivers. Sea transport is more flexible and is mostly used for bulk low-value products, and long distance transport. There are few barriers to entry for this mode, although the way itself is restricted by the necessity of specialized terminal ports.

4. Air

Air transport is characterized by its higher unit costs. Similar to water transport, its way is restricted by the need for specific terminal points. Air transport tends to be restricted to time-sensitive products or high-value, low-weight products. Air transport is a fast mode of transport, but also bears high unit costs. To provide door to door services to customers, air, like rail, requires intermodal solutions.

5. Pipelines

Pipelines are a unique mode of transport, but responsible for a considerable portion of freight traffic. Pipelines are limited in the products that can be carried. Examples of these are natural gas, crude oil, petroleum products, water, chemicals, and slurry products. The mode is unique in that product losses and damages are extremely rare, climatic conditions have minimal impact, and pipelines are not labor intensive. This mode tends to carry low unit costs, but is capital intensive in its set up.

The selection of mode can affect sustainability in terms of unit costs, customer service characteristics (such as speed, availability, and reliability), losses and damages, flexibility, etc. Modal choice can also have major environmental consequences such as carbon emissions. The decision on the mode or combination of modes is dependent on the product that is being transported, the distances over which it needs to be transported, and the level of service required by the customer.

In an effort to reduce CO_2 emissions, Colgate Palmolive (CP) embarked on a program to convert a significant amount of its transport from road to rail and short-sea by selecting a specific route from their Anzio plant in Italy to their distribution center in Unna, Germany. The alternative route required that the same service level be maintained. The route that was selected comprised a road section of approximately 40 kilometers (km) from Anzio to Pomezia. Pomezia to Bonen has a rail section of just over 1,580 km. The final section from Bonen to Unna is approximately 10 km by road. This new system meant that 97% of the total distance was covered by rail. The result of the switch was that the same transit times by rail as road were achieved. Emissions were reduced by 786 tons CO_2E (53%) for the route, fuel consumption and travel distances were reduced, and payload was improved from 25 tons by road to 29 tons by intermodal solution.[16]

Packaging

Packaging is one of the central issues in supply chain sustainability, but its role is frequently underestimated. Packaging serves two basic functions: 1) product protection, and 2) marketing. Product protection is a key feature in supply chain sustainability, ensuring the right product reaches the customer in the right quality, quantity, and condition, thereby enhancing customer service and the associated profitability. The marketing aspect of packaging also plays a role in ensuring the correct product reaches the desired customer.

The role of packaging, however, extends beyond these basic functions to further support the sustainability of the supply chain and the organization. The materials used for packaging are critical. Many retail organizations are focusing on innovative materials that are either biodegradable or reusable, thereby ensuring a minimized landfill impact and an optimized use of scarce resources. Organizations seek to minimize packaging, where possible, and ensure that the use of hazardous materials, non-recyclable plastics, etc. are minimized.

The role of packaging can be extended to include assisting the optimization of some of the other logistics functions. Standardized and minimized packaging, for example, may increase space utilization in warehousing and transport, thereby optimizing the use of these resources. Similarly, better packaging may streamline the materials handling function. Good packaging can potentially provide further benefits, such as facilitating the reverse logistics function or being reused in the refurbishing/remanufacturing process.

In 2006, Walmart and Sam's Club stores committed to a 5% reduction in supply chain packaging by 2012. In order to achieve this, a scorecard was developed to evaluate suppliers' packaging performance which is inclusive of several key metrics:

- Greenhouse gas emissions and target reduction goals
- Product-to-package ratio
- Space utilization
- Innovation
- Solid waste generated and reduction targets
- Water usage and reduction targets
- Establishment of public purchasing guidelines for direct suppliers
- Social responsibility

At the conception of the scorecard, it was anticipated that carbon dioxide emissions could be reduced by 667,000 metric tons with a cost savings of $10.98 billion achieved.[17]

Hewlett-Packard redesigned their LaserJet toner cartridge package to reduce packaging material by 45% in weight. This resulted in reducing shipping volumes by a massive 30% due to the fact that a standard shipping pallet that previously held 1444 cartridges now holds 203.[18]

Reverse Logistics

Reverse logistics is an essential component of the total logistics function, which aims to move goods from the point of consumption to the point of origin. Typical reverse logistics activities would be the processes a company uses to collect used, damaged, unwanted (stock balancing returns), or outdated products, as well as packaging and shipping materials from the end user or the reseller.

Organizations utilize reverse logistics processes for a number of reasons, in particular customer service, environmental considerations, product stewardship, and the optimization of resources. These can be summarized as one of the two primary purposes of reverse logistics, such as proper disposal or recapturing value. From an operational perspective, reverse logistics is used for the handling of returned goods, recycling, refurbishing, remanufacturing or reusing of products, and disposal of salvage and scrap.

The reverse logistics function also fulfills a major strategic role. Reverse logistics activities can impact the firm's competitive position, be indicative of a clean supply chain, minimize legal disposal issues, assist in recapturing value and recovering assets, as well as protecting margins.

E.ON is a major generator and supplier of gas and electricity in the United Kingdom. As part of its responsibility to treat domestic properties with energy efficient measures, retro-fitting external wall insulation is a key part of their strategy. E.ON began returning phenolic board off-cuts to the supplier for use as a fuel replacement in cement kilns. These boards were historically sent to landfill as a mixed waste. This required that off-cut boards were separated from other waste and placed in specially marked bags at the point of fitting, transported via forklift to a central storage area at the end of each day, checking for contaminants, and transferred to the supplier at the point of new delivery. The project found that the take-back operation delivered a 75% cost saving over landfill charges and carbon emissions of 9.9 tons avoided by the take back option (calculated by including transport of off-cut board from site to its end use, preparation of the board for its end use, and end use and abated fossil fuel).[19]

Routing and Scheduling

Vehicle routing can be defined as the problem of designing routes for delivery vehicles (of known capacities) which are to operate from a single depot to supply a set of customers with known locations and known demands for a certain commodity. Routes for the vehicles are designed to minimize:

- The number of vehicles used (vehicles, and their associated drivers, are often a fixed cost)
- The total distance (or time) traveled (this typically corresponds to variable cost)
- Some combination of number of vehicles used and total distance (or time) traveled

These objectives can however, be extended to include aspects such as:

- Minimizing labor
- Satisfying customer service requirements
- Maximizing orders
- Maximizing volumes delivered per unit of distance/increase load factors (and minimize empty return legs or deadheading)

From a sustainability perspective, achieving these objectives could result in fuel consumption and therefore lower emissions and costs. Better routing can generally be accomplished through increased computerization and coordination among distributors.

Routing is often considered together with scheduling, although these are separate fleet management tasks. While routing requires the optimum selection of the routes that vehicles should take to achieve the objectives, as described above, scheduling requires consideration of when vehicles should depart on their routes. As the best route may differ according to the time of day, these tasks are usually considered together. The economic, environmental, and social costs of road freight transport vary by time of day and day of the week. Sustainability could be enhanced if the planning of delivery operations took more account of the variability of external costs over daily, weekly and seasonal cycles.

It is important, however, when considering the optimal routing and scheduling system for an organization, to ensure that the trade-offs in the system are appropriately managed. Deliveries made outside peak hours (e.g., very early in the morning), could result in major cost savings as a result of better driving conditions and lessened congestion. The efficiencies achieved in fuel consumption must however, be balanced against the costs and social impacts of requiring drivers and destination laborers to work outside of normal working hours, all of which must be considered together to ensure the most sustainable solution.

Virtual Integration

Virtual integration can be defined in several ways; however, the most common definitions include the use of the World Wide Web to replace physical elements of the business with information sharing. The business itself can be a completely virtual business. This implies that, while owning the brand and the customer, the design, system development, sourcing, logistics, manufacturing, and assembly can all be outsourced to other role-players in the supply chain. Another way of looking at virtual integration is that individual supply chain organizations each focus on their core competencies or areas of specialization. Each organization is then integrated into a linked supply chain in such a way that each organization benefits. The core competencies are linked together by means of cost and risk sharing agreements. The implication is that these organizations will function together as a larger entity.

The principle underlying virtual integration is sharing of knowledge. Physical assets are of less importance in the supply chain than the efficiencies and output that can be achieved through virtual integration. The goal is to replace physical assets with information in such a way that every member of the supply chain will benefit and the supply chain becomes a flexible network. Outsourcing and close collaborative relationships should be used as much as possible to achieve efficiencies. Virtual integration is based on value-adding relationships and the recognition that all role players are working towards the same goal.

In a traditional supply chain, transactions between each layer of the supply chain tend to be arm's length transactions. Through virtual integration, it is frequently possible to eliminate some role players in the supply chain by facilitating much tighter supply chain collaboration. Virtual integration allows the organization to interact with customers, suppliers, and trading partners amongst others.

Effective virtual integration will promote a more flexible supply chain that is more closely aligned with customer requirements and normally associated with a comparative cost advantage. To achieve effective virtual integration, a high level of information sharing is required, which implies effective information technology as well as a considerable level of trust in the relationships in the supply chain. This is achieved through a shared vision in the supply chain, common objectives, and shared risks and rewards.

GreenSCOR

The Supply Chain Operations Reference (SCOR®) model is a process model developed by the Supply Chain Council in an effort to develop a standard tool for evaluating, measuring, and improving supply chain performance. The SCOR® model is based on breaking down the supply chain into six basic processes. These can be described as follows:

- **Plan:**
  Processes associated with planning, scheduling, and coordinating supply chain activities
- **Source:**
  Processes associated with procuring material, physically receiving material, and storing raw materials
- **Make:**
  Processes associated with transforming raw material into a finished product. In defense maintenance, repair, and overhaul operations, the Make category is used to model maintenance activities
- **Deliver:**
  Processes associated with storing, packaging, and delivering finished products to the customer
- **Return:**
  Processes associated with delivering and receiving material from a customer to a supplier, commonly called reverse logistics
- **Enable:**
  Processes that facilitate the movement of materials (e.g., business rules, data management, performance management, contract management, asset management, and compliance management)

These processes are further broken down to form three process levels. Level 1 defines the scope of the supply chain and is used to evaluate the competitive performance of the entire chain. Level 2 configures the supply chain into three primary types: make to stock, make to order, and engineer to order. Level 3 defines the processes that compose a supply chain's operations. These levels define a company's ability to perform via the application of best practices and the use of performance metrics.[20]

The goal of GreenSCOR is to create an analytical tool that provides a clear view of the connection between supply chain functions and environmental issues; thereby, improving organizational management of both.

Each process within the SCOR® model needs to be reviewed to determine the impact that each one has on the environment. Table 1 is an example of the impact each process has on the environment.

SCOR® Process Environmental Impacts

SCOR® Example Process	Potential Impact
Plan	Plan to minimize energy consumption and hazardous material usage: • Plan the handling and storage of hazardous materials • Plan for the disposal of ordinary and hazardous waste • Plan compliance of all supply chain activities
Source	• Select suppliers with positive environmental records • Select materials with environmentally friendly content • Specify packaging requirements • Specify delivery requirements to minimize transportation and handling requirements
Make	• Schedule production to minimize energy consumption • Manage waste generated during the Make process • Manage emissions (air and water) from the Make process
Deliver	• Minimize use of packaging materials • Schedule shipments to minimize fuel consumption
Return	• Schedule transportation and aggregate shipments to minimize fuel consumption; prepare returns to prevent spills of hazardous materials (oils, fuels, etc.) from damaged products

Table 1: Example of SCOR®

Following top-level processes and process element revisions, the SCOR® best practices and metrics are revised along the same lines, to assess the environmental integration opportunities associated with each element.[21]

5.3 Part III: Sourcing and Purchasing

Sustainable Sourcing

Sustainable sourcing is the procurement of products and services with environmental, social, ethical, and economic issues in mind. This is essentially an extension of the green purchasing policy to include social and economic aspects into the acquisition decision. The environmental decisions that need to be taken into account in the acquisition decision were described in the section on Green Purchasing Policies.

Sustainable sourcing should also address social issues such as inclusiveness, equality, diversity, integration, and regeneration. Additionally, economic considerations in purchasing are essential in the sustainability equation. In addition to the economic benefits that derive from efficiency gains, it is argued that the creation of sustainable markets is critical to the long-term success of the organization. Other targets such as job and wealth creation can be included. Often, social and economic sourcing practices are amalgamated as socio-economic considerations. Typical examples of these are assistance for small businesses or affirmative action policies.

For sourcing to be sustainable, every sourcing decision should take into account all three pillars of sustainability. The Chartered Institute of Purchasing and Supply (CIPS) has segmented the areas as follows:

- Economic impact of sustainability: corporate governance, ethics followed in all trading, timely payment of suppliers
- Environmental impact of sustainability: are issues such as biodiversity, and climate change
- Social impact of sustainability: diversity in the workplace, worker's welfare, and human rights[22]

Although integrating all three pillars into the sourcing decision can be complex, there are a number of benefits that can be achieved from sustainable sourcing practices. These include achieving cost savings through reducing use as well as waste, achieving more efficient use of resources through reuse and recycling, enhancing corporate or brand image through the promotion of the organization's values in sourcing processes, reducing risks of non-compliance with legal requirements, reducing the risks associated with supplier non-compliance, creating new markets by being an early adopter, controlling costs by adopting a wider approach to whole life costing, improving internal and external standards, and building a sustainable supply chain.

Global versus Local Sourcing

One of the most critical decisions in the supply chain is the decision regarding whether to source goods, materials, or services locally or globally. Global sourcing implies that goods or services are sourced from other geographical areas, usually referring to sourcing across geopolitical or national boundaries. The purpose of global sourcing is to make the most of global efficiencies in the supply chain. These efficiencies are diverse and range from low cost labor to low cost raw materials, and from aspects such as tax incentives or breaks to lower trade tariffs.

In contrast, local sourcing refers to sourcing within the national borders of a particular country, or within the geographical proximity of their intended use. There are a number of definitions for local sourcing that imply a more immediate proximity than the national borders. However, for the purposes of contrast with global sourcing, local sourcing is considered to be sourcing within the national boundaries of the country of the intended use.

There are a number of reasons for global sourcing pertaining to costs and achieving efficiencies such as reduced total costs, lower labor costs, reduced taxation effects, and lower land and facility costs. Other reasons could include strategic and value creation opportunities such as enhancing vendor competition, improving environmental performance and compliance, improved quality, improved delivery and reliability, and increased total supply capacity. Similarly, there are many arguments for local sourcing such as supporting local businesses, greater control, flexible delivery, and smaller lot quantities.

Although global sourcing can enable high levels of efficiency and cost savings within an organization, there are a number of risks associated with global sourcing. These include, but are not limited to:

- Loss of knowledge
- Environmental concerns such as longer distances

- Language and cultural issues
- Time differences and time delays
- Bureaucracy
- Customs requirements
- Legislation
- Currency fluctuations
- Competition regulation
- Labor standards and productivity
- Hidden costs such as those associated with delays, corruption and legal fees

The decision to source globally should be taken with careful consideration of the cost savings and efficiency gains in balance with the potential pitfalls that may result in supply chain disruptions or other negative consequences.

Roclin Global Sourcing is a company which seeks to find global sourcing solutions, primarily in China, on behalf of its clients. Roclin was approached by a pumping systems company to seek suppliers of pumps and related components in China. By speaking to local experts, contacting industry associations, using industry catalogues, etc., Roclin found all the qualified suppliers as well as discovered all the sourcing OEM relationships between them. Based on their findings, the client could buy directly from the manufacturer, thereby achieving the lowest possible sourcing cost. In the end, the company selected for the client's purposes had previously produced goods for the client, which had been sold to the client by an importer at a much higher cost. The client was able to achieve significant savings through its direct global sourcing arrangement and eliminating the middleman.[23]

Green Purchasing Policies

Green purchasing, or Environmentally Preferable Purchasing (EPP), pertains to addressing environmental impacts of buying decisions. A green purchasing policy is one of the cornerstones of a sustainable purchasing policy, but relates specifically to the environmental impact of the purchasing decision. The other two cornerstones are ensuring the economic case of the business decision and addressing the social impact of the buying decision. Having a green purchasing policy in place is part of a wider agenda to promote sustainability within the overall supply chain.

Green purchasing is the deliberate selection and procurement of products and services that aims at most successfully minimizing the adverse environmental impacts over their life cycle. This life cycle is inclusive of all aspects such as manufacturing, transportation, use, and recycling or disposal. Typically, reducing adverse environmental impacts will include considering products and services that do any or all of the following:

- Conserve energy
- Conserve water
- Minimize waste
- Minimize pollutants
- Made from recycled material
- Can be reused or recycled
- Are made with energy from renewable resources
- Do not use hazardous or toxic materials

When considering including environmental aspects into the sourcing decision, the following product features should be taken into account: the composition of the materials used in the product; the transport used during the supply, manufacturing, and distribution process; manufacturing processes; packaging; product use; and end-of-life solutions.

Purchasing typically requires that price and performance criteria are considered when making decisions to acquire goods or services. Green purchasing implies that environmental aspects are added to the criteria. The ultimate intention of a green purchasing policy is to reduce the environmental impacts of the organization's sourcing decisions and to increase resource efficiency.

The City of Palo Alto embarked on a green purchasing project to replace traditional street lighting with LED technology. The purpose was to determine whether the high initial set-up costs would be offset over time by energy savings, reduced maintenance costs, reduced greenhouse gas emissions, and reduced hazardous waste disposal. In a study conducted in collaboration with students from Stanford University, it was determined that a $1.3 million return on investment could be expected just from the city's 70W LED street lighting inventory, which constituted 45% of the city's total inventory of a variety of different lighting.[24]

Vendor Evaluation/Certification

Vendor or supplier evaluation is a continuous purchasing task. Existing vendors require continual monitoring to ensure that they are still on target to meet expectation. New vendors require screening to determine whether they potentially meet the business' requirements and whether they should be considered for future business.

There are a number of methods to evaluate vendors. However, the most important aspect of the evaluation is to understand and clearly define what the business requires. With most vendor markets being highly competitive, it is essential that the business selects vendors that are the best match in terms of relationships as well as products that they intend to supply.

Typically, suppliers will be evaluated according to cost, delivery, and quality; however, this may be extended to include aspects as diverse as production facility and capacity, information technology, financial status, innovation and R&D, geographical location, attitude and strategic fit, terrorism risk, etc.

To incorporate sustainability elements into the vendor evaluation requires that the organization has clearly defined its sustainability strategy and requirements. These are then incorporated into the vendor evaluation under headings which can be generic, such as environmental and social responsibility, or under more specific targets such as total CO_2 emissions.

The vendor evaluation process can be an informal process performed by the procurement officer or similar position, whereby discussions are held with user groups within the organization to assess the vendor's fit and performance. Alternatively, the process can be formal where vendors are evaluated in terms of specific criteria which are normally weighted to determine the vendor which is most appropriate to perform a specific task.

The formal vendor evaluation process can be extended to certify vendors. This process may vary from organization to organization. Some organizations require that an industry-accredited certificate is required in order to perform a specific task. These could be as diverse as being ISO 14001 certified, being a Microsoft Certified Systems Developer (MCSD), or certified by the Association for Proposal Management Professionals (APMP). Other organizations require that vendors are certified in accordance with their own terms and conditions. Many states, hospitals, and large retailers have used their own certification as a means of evaluating potential and current suppliers.

Sustainability Certification/Directives

Lead companies in a supply chain need to ensure that their suppliers comply with the company's vision, mission, and objectives in terms of sustainability. Companies that do not understand their supply chains or the practices within their supply chains may have problems later on when they are asked to account for these practices to their customers. There are many examples of companies having to account for their supply chain practices, where second- or third-tier suppliers' practices have been questionable. In these instances, the lead company has typically been affected from a financial, as well as from a reputational perspective and has had to adjust their suppliers' standards very quickly to comply with market requirements.

The companies that have been through these processes have generally learned that practices in the supply chain will be scrutinized and the organization will be held responsible for unscrupulous practices. Similarly, other companies observing such processes have been able to draw on the same lessons. As a result, companies have devised methods of ensuring that suppliers comply with their supply chain standards. Typically companies may ensure supplier compliance by setting codes of conduct with which suppliers must comply in order to remain an approved supplier. The benefit of this is that approved suppliers will be 100% compliant with the company's requirements. This method can, however, have disadvantages as it requires a considerable administrative burden to ensure all suppliers are consistently compliant. It is also cumbersome from a supplier's perspective, particularly if the supplier needs to comply with a number of customer's codes of conducts. Because of this, many organizations have opted for standardized practices, requiring that their suppliers become compliant with norms set by the industry. Some of these are described below. Note however, that these are just some of a number of similar examples which may be used:

- **WEEE:**
  The WEEE (Waste Electrical and Electronic Equipment) directive is an European Community directive for electrical and electronic equipment and sets collection, recycling, and recovery targets for all types of electrical goods. It also obligates member states to establish and maintain a registry of producers putting electrical and electronic equipment onto the market. Without the WEEE registration a product cannot be placed on the EU market.[25]
- **REACH:**
  This term stands for the Regulation on Registration, Evaluation, Authorization and Restriction of Chemicals. The main aims of REACH are to ensure a high level of protection of human health and the environment from the risks that can be posed by chemicals, the promotion of alternative test methods, free circulation of substances on the internal market, and enhancing competitiveness and innovation. All manufacturers and importers of chemicals must identify and manage risks linked to the substances they manufacture and market. For substances manufactured or imported in quantities of one ton or more per year per company, manufacturers and importers need to demonstrate that they have appropriately done so by means of a registration dossier, which must be submitted to the European Chemicals Agency (ECHA).[26]
- **RoHS:**
  The Restriction of Hazardous Substances directive is another EC directive and restricts the use of six hazardous materials in the manufacture of various types of electronic and electrical equipment. It is closely linked with the WEEE.[27]

- **Packaging and Packaging Waste Directive:**
  An EC directive which aims at limiting the weight and volume of packaging to a minimum in order meet the required level of safety, hygiene, and acceptability for consumers; reducing the content of hazardous substances and materials in the packaging material and its components; and designing reusable or recoverable packaging.[28]

5.4 Part IV: Sustainable Supply Chain Metrics

Supply Chain measurements or metrics are measures such as inventory turnover rate, cycle time, Defects per Million Opportunities (DPMO), and fill rate, which are used to track supply chain sustainability performance.[29] Commonly used by supply chain management, metrics can assist in understanding the business' operational performance over a given period of time. Supply chain measurements can cover many areas including procurement, production, distribution, warehousing, inventory, transportation, and customer service—any area of logistics. However, good performance in one part of the supply chain is not sufficient. A supply chain is only as strong as its weakest link and the solution is to focus on the key metrics in each area of the supply chain.

Supply chain metrics are not universally accepted; however, below is a limited list of some examples of sustainable supply chain metrics:

- Disposal and waste management policies and practices
- Water conservation and consumption
- Green House Gas (GHG) footprint (Aggregate CO_2 number)
- Paper and paper product consumption
- Packaging reduction initiatives
- Energy consumption (power, gas, electric)
- Use of sustainability criteria in procurement decisions
- Processes in place to embed sustainability and social responsibility into supplier qualifications and certification decisions
- Processes in place to embed sustainability and social responsibility into product design, redesign, and statements of work
- Developing processes/knowledge to ensure understanding of sourcing and recycling

Lean Six Sigma

Six Sigma is a management strategy that aims at eliminating defects in any process, regardless of whether it is manufacturing, distribution, product, service or transaction, etc. Six sigma is a data-driven approach which strives for quality that is close to perfect.

Essentially, Six Sigma seeks to provide a quantitative measurement of how well a process is performing. To achieve Six Sigma, a process cannot produce more than 3.4 defects per million opportunities. A Six Sigma defect is defined as anything that does not meet the customer's specified requirements. The underlying principles of Six Sigma are thus that processes need to be measured. What gets measured gets done. If a process is to be improved, the current process needs to be measured to determine the status quo and a clear understanding is required of where the organization intends to be in the future. The principle is management based on measured facts and the reduction of variations and exceptions.

One of the key focus areas in Six Sigma is the customer. As defects are measured in terms of variations from customer specifications, this forms the basis of the system. A clear understanding is also required of the processes that are followed to get the work done. As the system is based on reducing defects in the value stream's processes, this is critical to the success of the system.

In Six Sigma, problems are identified one by one and each problem is solved as a project. Customer involvement is crucial to the process, as it is the customers that will identify the problems that require solutions. The selection and prioritization of the problems that need to be addressed are based on the problems that are causing the greatest concern (i.e., those problems that are costing the organization the most money). Aside from identifying the problems that are resulting in the biggest levels of customer dissatisfaction, key questions to be addressed are why errors are committed and what can be done to resolve them.

Six Sigma businesses can realize considerable savings in terms of improving quality due to decreased discarded products and less refunds or warranty refunds. Effective Six Sigma should have commitment from top management and people dedicated to driving the process. It also requires a large level of involvement and buy-in from all the people involved in the process. Six Sigma should be a systematic approach to reducing all defects in all processes.

Lean Six Sigma is an extension of the Six Sigma strategy and essentially combines the principles of lean manufacturing with those of Six Sigma. Lean approaches focus on identifying waste within existing processes in order to reduce costs. Six Sigma focuses on meeting customers' expectations by reducing and eliminating errors in existing processes. Six Sigma also considers new processes or process redesign. Combining Lean and Six Sigma enables the removal of non-value-adding steps and waste. Lean Six Sigma focuses first on the use of lean techniques to identify and remove waste and then follows with Six Sigma to identify and reduce process variations. As IBM states—the goal is to do better things, not just do better.[30]

Six Sigma has been used extensively by many organizations, most of whom reported remarkable savings through the implementation thereof. Albertsons®, together with its parent company Supervalu®, achieved hundreds of millions of dollars in savings by using the Six Sigma quality control processes. One of the projects was to improve bakery margins in one of their areas of operations. The project started with the weighing of cakes over a predetermined period from a number of their outlets. The conclusion was that the workers were making cakes which were far larger than the organization had intended. Through a process of adjusting recipes and ensuring that bakers used scales in the baking process, Albertsons® saved 900,000 pounds of icing, translating to $700,000 in savings. Albertsons undertook 556 projects between 2002 and 2008 and achieved an average of $500,000 per project.[31]

5.5 Summary

Reducing risks in the supply chain and managing inefficiencies improve supply chain management strategies. Managing up or down the supply chain is always a business imperative. Sustainability management brings together suppliers, manufacturers, transportation companies, distributors, and retailers to work together to help one another reduce waste or achieve better supply chain management efficiencies.

5.6 Experiential Exercises

I. Collaborating Upstream and Downstream

Many waste streams exist. Refer back to Chapter 2 to evaluate the sources and sinks of your organization and how risks exist from raw material extraction to end-of-life management. Collaboration within the supply chain is the key to success to creating closed loop management systems to mitigate negative impacts.

This exercise will evaluate the waste streams and inefficiencies throughout the supply chain. The outcome will be finding solutions to operational inefficiencies that are outside the span of control, as well as create goals and objectives to work together as partners to solve mutual inefficiencies.

From the previous chapters you have already identified inefficiencies and developed policies needed to continuously improve. Some ways to identify supply chain collaborative needs are to evaluate the following:

- What materials do we pay for twice as inputs and outputs?
- What packaging solutions could be collaborated on to reduce packaging waste?
- What chemicals or hazardous materials do not have an end-of-life solution?
- What end-of-life problems do we create throughout the supply chain?
- What natural resources are used for products and services? What risks are posed to supply in the future of those resources? What cost implications will be encountered?
- What are the human resource management practices of vendors upstream?
- What volatile political risks or hostile markets do we do business in?
- What is the market's perception of the supplier's reputation?

Use the above questions to identify your major impacts and formulate priorities. Create a process map by working through systems thinking to identify feedback loops that can reimagine the current system to redesign the future state. Drawing process maps can mitigate overwhelming analyses of the supply chain.

II. Supply Chain Scorecards

Scorecards are valuable tools for vetting existing and new suppliers. Selecting suppliers that align with the organization's values is the goal. Refer to the worksheets on values and strategic priorities to develop a system to rate suppliers. Criterion will depend on the complexity of the supply chain, but as a general rule, evaluate TBL practices of suppliers and then collaborate with suppliers to achieve expectations. Many governmental entities and large corporations have minimum standards and established scorecards for vendors. Therefore, being closed out of markets is a high risk that can be turned into an opportunity.

Research existing scorecards and develop a methodology that works best for your organizational structure. Keep in mind the following key performance indicators.

Expectation	Supplier A	Supplier B	Supplier C
Labor practices			
Human rights			
Fair wages			
Employee benefits			
SMS policy			
EMS policy - Energy conservation - Water use/waste - Emission reduction - GHG reduction - Solid waste diversion			
EPP policy			
Fines and penalties			
Lawsuits			
Ethical code of conduct			
Philanthropy			
Investment in sustainability			
Third-party inspections or certification			

Take a moment to jot down additional criteria for supplier vetting. The above criterion is just a short list of priorities to consider. Finally, develop a process to track and monitor supplier progress.

III. Collaborative Solutions

Sustainability management solutions cannot be achieved alone. Collaboration is a necessity to achieve supply chain strategies. Many industries have successfully collaborated together to work with numerous suppliers. The ripple effects are far-reaching. If the industry is collaborating, the industry proactively reaches beyond compliance. Suppliers also have one set of standards to follow; this also opens new markets for suppliers that have already met those criterions to do business with more industry partners. Collaboration is a win-win!

In the previous exercises you have identified your priorities and written out supplier expectations. The next step is to engage in collaboration. There are multiple nonprofits, governmental entities, academia, and industries already highly engaged. You do not have to start from scratch. Research the following to align your organization with existing efforts:

- What alliances or associations already exist within your profession? Which ones align with your values?
- Are there existing third-party certifications for the products and services used?
- Are there already physical inspections of products and labor available?
- Are there existing scorecards already available?
- What software solutions exist to manage collaboration?
- What competitors are also on the journey of sustainability management?
- What stakeholder groups would make excellent partners?

SAMPLE QUESTIONS

1. The purpose of the balanced scorecard is:

   A. To achieve a balance between financial and nonfinancial results
   B. To align business, industry, government, and non-profit organizations
   C. To align strategic objectives with non-strategic objectives
   D. To achieve a balance between a customer and a business perspective

2. When selecting a carrier, which of the following would be taken into account in the selection process?

   A. EDI capabilities
   B. Market coverage
   C. Complaints and claims history
   D. All of the above

3. The following is considered a benefit of centralized warehousing:

   A. Higher safety stock levels
   B. Longer lead times
   C. Lower inbound costs
   D. Lower outbound costs

4. The code of conduct aims at:

   A. Ensuring acceptable levels of behavior within the supply chain
   B. Surveying employees attitudes
   C. Legally regulating supply chain attitude
   D. None of the above

5. One of the main benefits of establishing collaborative meaningful partnerships is:

   A. Cultural interchange
   B. Reduced inventory costs
   C. Bottom line growth
   D. More supply chain role players

6. Cross-docking is a form of:

   A. Warehousing
   B. Sorting and consolidation
   C. Inbound transport
   D. Outbound distribution

7. Identify which one of the following was not identified as one of the three top distribution risks:

   A. Regulation
   B. Management
   C. Security
   D. Costs

8. Facility layout should take into account:

   A. Future growth, occupational health and safety, and retail space
   B. Employee wellness, retail space, and cost reduction
   C. Space Utilization, communication, and employee wellness
   D. Materials handling and transport distances from warehouse to customer

9. From a strategic perspective, facility location could affect the organization's:

   A. Competitive position
   B. Accessibility
   C. Product selection
   D. Life cycle costing

10. The goal of GreenSCOR is to:

   A. Create an analytical tool that provides a view between supply chain functions and sustainability
   B. Create a process to ensure the that the supply chain complies with environmental directives and legislation
   C. Create an analytical tool that provides a view between supply chain functions and environmental issues
   D. None of the above

Answers: 1A, 2D, 3C, 4A, 5B, 6B, 7B, 8C, 9A, 10C

ENDNOTES

[1] *ISM Principles of Sustainability and Social Responsibility.* (2012). Retrieved on April 6, 2012 from: http://www.ism.ws/SR/content.cfm?ItemNumber=18497&navItemNumber=18499

[2] *Life Skill Coaches Association of BC: Code of Ethics.* Retrieved on June 1, 2011 from: http://www.calsca.com/ethics_lscabc.htm

[3] *Principles and Standards of Ethical Supply Management.* (2012). Retrieved on April 6, 2012 from: http://www.ism.ws/tools/content.cfm?ItemNumber=4740&navItemNumber=15959

[4] *Professional credentials.* (2012). Retrieved on April 14, 2012 from: http://www.ism.ws/certification/

[5] Crumrine, B, Decker, S, Loughman, E. and McMullan, R. (April 2005). *Environmental packaging guideline version 2.* The Donald Bren School of Environmental Science and Management, University of CA, Santa Barbara. (p. 9).

[6] Crumrine, B, Decker, S, Loughman, E. and McMullan, R. (April 2005). *Environmental packaging guideline version 2.* The Donald Bren School of Environmental Science and Management, University of CA, Santa Barbara. (pp. 15–24).

[7] *Close Encounters of the Best Kind.* Retrieved on March 3, 2012 from: http://www.businessweek.com/adsections/chain/2.1/chain_index.html

[8] *Supply Chain Risk Management.* Retrieved on May 20, 2011 from: http://www.shipperscouncil.co.nz/SupplyChainRiskManagement.htm

[9] *Economist Intelligence Unit: Managing supply-chain risk for reward.* (2009). Retrieved on March 26, 2012 from: http://www.acegroup.com/eu-en/assets/ace-supply-chain-web.pdf

[10] *Warehouse Procedure Manual.* (1999). Lawson. Retrieved on May 29, 2011 from: http://support.nabs.com/lawson/manuals/Warehouse_manual.pdf

[11] *Cross docking case study.* Retrieved on March 29, 2012 from: http://www.transfreight.com/About_Us/Case_Studies/Crossdocking_Case_Study.aspx

[12] *Strategic network design: Focus topic paper.* (2011). Retrieved on March 26, 2012 from: http://www.camelot-mc.com/fileadmin/user_upload/Flyer/camelot-strategic-network-design-focus-topic-paper.pdf

[13] *McDonald's, a guide to the benefits of JIT.* Retrieved on March 26, 2012 from: http://www.google.co.za/#hl=en&sclient=psy-ab&q=cost+savings+from+better+inventory+management+case+studies&oq=cost+savings+from+better+inventory+management+case+studies&aq=f&aqi=q-w1&aql=&gs_l=hp.3..33i21.36667l38740l1l39057l13l12l0l0l0l0l436l3146l2-2j6j1l9l0.frgbld.&pbx=1&bav=on.2,or.r_gc.r_pw.r_qf.,cf.osb&fp=8f2f0c1151d3c15e&biw=1280&bih=843

[14] *Distribution Group.* (2012). Alexander Communications Group. Retrieved on June 10, 2011 from: http://www.distributiongroup.com

[15] *Warehouse Procedure Manual.* (1999). Lawson. Retrieved on May 29, 2011 from: http://support.nabs.com/lawson/manuals/Warehouse_manual.pdf

[16] Rail case study: Colgate - Road to Rail. Retrieved on March 26, 2012 from: http://www.igd.com/index.asp?id=1&fid=5&sid=43&tid=59&foid=128&cid=1769

[17] *Packaging gets renewed attention as sustainability initiatives take hold.* (2008). Retrieved on March 26, 2012 from: http://www.supplychainbrain.com/content/headline-news/single-article/article/packaging-gets-renewed-attention-as-sustainability-initiatives-take-hold/

[18] *Green packaging: waste not, want not.* (2008). Retrieved on March 26, 2012 from: http://www.inboundlogistics.com/cms/article/green-packaging-waste-not-want-not/

[19] *External wall insulation take back trial.* Retrieved on March 26, 2012 from: http://www.wrap.org.uk/sites/files/wrap/EON_Kingspan_case_study.pdf

[20] *GreenSCOR.* Retrieved on June 13, 2011 from: http://supply-chain.org/about

[21] *GREENSCOR.* (2003). Retrieved on May 28, 2011 from: http://postconflict.unep.ch/humanitarianaction/documents/02_08-04_05-11.pdf

[22] *Guide to Sustainable Procurement.* Chartered Institute of Purchasing and Supply. Retrieved on June 11, 2011 from: http://www.ekobai.com/analysis/details/1

[23] *Reducing costs through direct China sourcing.* Retrieved on March 27, 2012 from: http://www.roclin.com/reducing_costs_through_direct_china_sourcing.html

[24] *Green purchasing benefits.* Retrieved on March 27, 2012 from: http://www.stopwaste.org/home/index.asp?page=1154

[25] *WEEE.* Retrieved on November 4, 2011 from: http://www.weeeregistration.com/index.html

26 *What is Reach?* European Commission Environment. Retrieved on November 4, 2011 from: http://ec.europa .eu/environment/chemicals/reach/reach_intro.htm

27 *Working with EEE producers to ensure RoHS compliance through the European Union.* Retrieved on November 4, 2011 from: http://www.bis.gov.uk/nmo/enforcement

28 *Packaging and Packaging Waste.* (2011). Retrieved on November 4, 2011 from: http://europa.eu/legislation _summaries/environment/waste_management/l21207_en.htm

29 *Supply Chain Metric.com.* Retrieved on June 11, 2011 from: http://www.supplychainmetric.com/

30 *Driving Operational Innovations Through Lean Six-Sigma.* (2007). IBM Global Business Services. Retrieved on May 22, 2011 from: http://www-935.ibm.com/services/at/bcs/pdf/br-stragchan-driving-inno.pdf

31 *Supervalu Sees Savings in Six Sigma.* (2010). Retrieved on March 26, 2012 from: http://supermarketnews .com/latest-news/supervalu-sees-savings-six-sigma

Chapter 6

Certifications: Built Environment and Products

Consumers are looking for alternative products on the market to reduce environmental impacts, to live a lifestyle as stewards of the environment, and make purchasing decisions based on social values and moral beliefs. Across all industries, certifications and labels are establishing clear standards to create products and services that satisfy consumer choices. On the other hand, labels are oftentimes used as marketing messages that can blur consumer confidence. One example is the "Organic" label. "Organic" implies that the product was grown without pesticides, herbicides, insecticides, or antibiotics. As of 2012, there are no packaging regulations on when a label, such as organic, can be used. The confusion lies in whether the label is absolutely true, or if the label is being used as a marketing ploy in order to charge a premium price or attract the green consumer niche. Therefore, certifications are more trustworthy than a label as the product has successfully met the standards and criterion of a third party certifying body, such as the difference between the label "Organic" and the certification by USDA Organic.

Certifications are prevalent today for major systems and programs. Certifications are a valuable competitive advantage to open new markets, create new opportunities, partnerships, and foster relationships.

The main benefit is that certifications create standards and consistent reporting processes. The most highly respected certifications are audited by an unbiased third party to ensure transparency. Thus, auditing the process or procedure by an independent auditor brings greater value to all stakeholders by establishing trust throughout the value chain.

There are few accepted standards on how and when to use a label, and an even greater lack of regulations. The Federal Trade Commission has issued the FTC Green Guides and the International Standards Organization has issued ISO 14020—Environmental Labels and Declarations. These two standards will help industries streamline when and how to use labels responsibly.

Third party certifications foster consumer trust and collaboration across the supply chain. Scientific Certification Systems (SCS), a firm of consultants that certifies over 4800 clients in 38 countries, performs on-site audits of chain of custody for multiple certifications. A chain of custody is the audit paperwork trail of the supply chain from raw material to finished good. According to SCS, a certification should be validated by a third party to ensure unbiased verification. SCS also recommends asking the following questions when deciding to obtain certification or use a certification:

- Which is the best certifying body to choose?
- What are the components of the certification program?
- Which program is more substantive or rigorous?
- What is the cost structure of the certification, hidden fees, and threats to credibility that could create risks?

Choosing a certification can be a daunting task. Certification can be a long process and increase costs to obtain and retain certification. Therefore, the benefits must outweigh the consequences to ensure it is indeed a competitive advantage. Making an informed decision will take time and effort. The goal of Chapters 6 and 7 is to provide an overview of just a few well-respected certifications for certain industries, processes, or systems.

6.1 LEED Certification/USGBC Green Associate

Introduction

Standards and consistency are meaningful ways to build awareness and create industry collaboration. The construction industry and all the professionals that work within the built environment, from real estate to property owners, as well as general contractors to architects, have worked together to create a standard that is highly respected called Leadership in Energy and Environmental Design (LEED). LEED certification accredits professionals as well as new and renovated buildings.

Background

The U.S. Green Building Council (USGBC) is a non-profit organization that was co-founded by Mike Italiano, David Gottfried, and Rick Fedrizzi in 1993. The USGBC is dedicated to a prosperous and sustainable future for our nation through cost-efficient and energy-saving buildings. The USGBC is prominently known for developing the Leadership in Energy and Environmental Design (LEED) rating system. Shortly after the formation of the USGBC, the members realized that the construction industry needed a rating system for "green buildings." LEED version 1.0 was created in 1993, with the collaboration of an environmentalist, real estate professional, architect, lawyer, and industry representatives.[1]

Overview of LEED

LEED is an internationally recognized green building certification program for the built environment and also certifies professionals accredited in "green building". Green building is essentially the process and practice to create structures that are environmentally- and resource-efficient throughout a building's life cycle. The life cycle of the building includes: siting to design, construction, operation, maintenance, renovation and deconstruction.

LEED uses a third-party verification system for buildings and communities to ensure that green building practices are implemented. Third-party verification is the process of attaining an independent organization to verify industry standards in a particular project. This allows a project manager to hire an outside, independent organization to perform an assessment to ensure that the building meets LEED requirements and also avoids any falsifications so that the building can be a certified project. Third party certification bodies are utilized to ensure transparency and an unbiased verification.

The following information for this chapter is an overview from the USGBC's website: http://www.usgbc.org/Default.aspx.

Objective

The USGBC established LEED to provide building owners and operators a concise framework for identifying and implementing practical and measurable green building design, construction, operations, and maintenance solutions.

LEED is a structured system that can be applied to all building types—both commercial and residential. LEED can also be implemented at any time during the building life cycle; for example, design and construction, operations and maintenance, renovations and retrofits.[2]

LEED Metrics and Criteria

There are five metrics and criteria categories for LEED:

1. Energy Savings
2. Water Consumption
3. CO_2 Emissions
4. Indoor Environmental Quality
5. Stewardship of Resources and Sensitivity to their Impacts

These metrics are the environmental components of Zero Waste. The building will conserve and reduce usage for the end user by reducing energy, water, and resource materials throughout the building's life cycle. The building will also be designed with particular attention to air quality and reducing harmful greenhouse gases.

Overview of LEED Professional

LEED Professional accreditation asserts a person's knowledge and skills in the built environment. The objective of accreditation is to acquire and retain the skills and knowledge necessary to provide verification services on LEED projects. Certificates are administered to those individuals who meet the minimum requirements and pass a certification exam.

The LEED Professionals examination is administered by a third-party called the Green Building Certification Institute, just as LEED for buildings or communities is verified through the U.S. Green Building Council. This ensures that industry standards are met and each candidate is fairly tested through an unbiased entity. In-depth details on each different certificate are further explained later[3] (LEED Professional Credentials, 2011).

How to Register

Visit the Green Building Certification Institute website: http://www.gbci.org/Homepage.aspx to register a project or apply to take the professional certification examination.

LEED Rating System

The Leadership in Energy and Environmental Design developed rating systems for the following building types.

1. New Construction
2. Existing Buildings: Operations and Maintenance
3. Commercial Interiors
4. Core and Shell
5. Schools, Healthcare, and Retail
6. Homes
7. Neighborhood Development

Each rating system uses credit categories that measure energy savings, water consumption, CO_2E emissions, indoor environmental quality, and stewardship of natural resources, as well as environmental sensitivity impacts. Each rating system is based on a 100 point scale with the potential of earning 110 points. Of the extra 10 points, six points can be obtained through innovation and design and an additional four points through regional priority. The only exception is the LEED for Homes Rating System, which is based on 136 points.

The LEED certification scale is broken down into four categories:

1. Certified—40 points
2. Silver—50+ points
3. Gold—60+ points
4. Platinum—80+ points

The California Environmental Protection Agency, located in Sacramento, CA, is a certified LEED Platinum building. The 950,000 square foot headquarters office is a strong morale booster for employees. Being awarded the platinum rating gives employees a sense of pride, and also enables the agency to lead by example. During the certification process, one of the initial drawbacks was the concern that a LEED certified building would be expensive to construct. It was important to the EPA to meet stakeholder expectations and keep costs low while constructing the new building. It turns out the actual costs were lower than a conventional building. Buildings that are designed to conserve energy, water, waste water, and sewage are important in the design stage, but even more important during the usage stage. The energy efficient appliances and environmentally friendly materials achieve efficiency and low cost utility bills. The CA EPA building used recycled materials from tiles to carpets, applied zero Volatile Organic Compound (VOC) paints, low-flow toilets and aerators, fan rooms to control air quality, and installed solar panels. The EPA now enjoys a lifetime of low-cost utilities, and can proudly boast making a positive impact.

Description of LEED Measurements

LEED measures the following credit categories to certify a building or community on a point system:

1. Sustainable Sites
2. Water Efficiency
3. Energy and Atmosphere

   4. Materials and Resources
   5. Indoor Environmental Quality

LEED for Homes Only

   6. Locations and Linkages
   7. Awareness and Education

Extra Credit Categories (10 points available)

   8. Innovation and Design
   9. Regional Priority

The credit categories express the effort to reduce environmental impacts and improve human benefit as a result of the life cycle of the project. Projects are evaluated on these credit categories:

- Measuring how well they have fulfilled each credit category upon completion of the prerequisites
- Third party certifying bodies sign off on the chain of custody and verifies points

For a complete "New Construction" checklist access: http://www.usgbc.org/ under the "LEED Rating Systems" tab.

Description of Credit Categories

1. Sustainable Sites
When choosing a building site and deciding how to manage it, it is crucial to consider the impact of each step in the building process through the end of the building's life cycle. Some factors to consider are: avoid developing on undeveloped land, protect the ecosystems, waterways, minimize impact, choose regionally appropriate landscaping to assist in conserving water, implement incentive plans for cleaner transportation choices during construction for employees and tenants, manage storm water runoff, and minimize all pollution aspects (i.e., light pollution, heat island effect, and construction pollution).

2. Water Efficiency
Buildings and users consume a lot of potable water supply throughout the life cycle. The Water Efficiency credit category focuses on water conservation inside and outside of the building. Generally, this can be done by using more efficient appliances, such as low-flow faucets or toilets, as well as changing fixtures and fittings in addition to making better landscaping choices for water tolerance.

3. Energy and Atmosphere
The Energy and Atmosphere credit category encourages a wide variety of energy strategies such as: commissioning, energy use monitoring, efficient design and construction, installing efficient appliances, systems as well as lighting, the use of renewable and clean sources of energy, generated on-site or off-site, and other innovative strategies.[4]

4. Materials and Resources

Buildings produce solid waste throughout their entire life cycle. The materials and resources credit category emphasizes managing resources efficiently. Ways to reduce waste can be achieved by managing inputs and outputs. Reducing what you use in the first place, reusing materials to end-of-life, or recycling materials all reduce a buildings solid waste to landfill. One way this can be achieved is to work through the entire supply chain and procure sustainable product choices, such as products that are sustainably grown, harvested, produced, and transported.

5. Indoor Environmental Quality

Indoor Environmental Quality refers to any factor that may affect the comfort or health of the building occupants; this could range from availability of natural light, acoustics, air quality, or even glare on computers. The Indoor Environmental Quality credit category stresses the importance of implementing strategies that can improve the health or comfort for those that utilize the area. Implementing strategies such as placing real plants within the building, keeping surfaces clean, or utilizing natural daylight are all beneficial ways to start improving indoor environmental quality. Implementing such strategies as mentioned above will result in energy savings and increases in productivity.

6. Locations and Linkages (Only applicable to LEED for Homes Rating System)

The locations and linkages credit category is only required for the LEED for homes rating system. Builders should choose sites that are on previously developed land and encourage that the land surrounding the project be developed for at least five years. If the home is located in a new development than the term "development site" includes all the homes in the development in order for it to be certified. Buildings are rewarded points for construction near existing infrastructures, community resources, and public transit.

7. Awareness and Education (Only applicable to LEED for Homes Rating System)

The Awareness and Education category encourages the builder or real estate professionals to provide the proper information so that the tenants, homeowners or building managers are aware of how to make their building green and get the most out of the green features. Awareness is targeted through open house functions or participating in expos, creating webpages displaying information regarding LEED homes, newspaper coverage, or signage. Tenants can request a hard copy of the operations and maintenance manual if they are unable to receive it electronically. The project team must have a planned training program and it must focus on the actual buyer or occupant. The education transfer to home owners is critical because only they can implement sustainable living practices and utilize the full function of the home as its intended.

8. Innovation in Design

The Innovation in Design category measures the projects demonstration of innovative technologies and strategies to improve a building's performance beyond what is initially required by other LEED credits or other green building considerations. Bonus points for implementing such strategies are awarded in this category. Points are also awarded if a LEED Accredited Professional is working on the team.

9. Regional Priority

The U.S. Green Building Council (USGBC), chapters and affiliates have identified the environmental concerns that are locally most important for each region of the country. (To view the specific regional priority credits by zip code simply visit the www.usgbc.org and follow the

LEED tab to the new LEED v3 section and click regional priority credits. Choose the desired state and use the excel spreadsheet to find the applicable zip code(s).) There are six LEED credits available through regional priority. A project that earns a regional priority credit will earn one bonus point in addition to any points awarded for that credit.

California State University, Chico was an early adopter of the LEED Certification. As an early adopter, there were several challenges. First, the campus community had to understand the value of building a certified LEED building. The director of the Institute of Sustainable Development played a major role in building awareness within the campus community about the benefits of a certified building all throughout the design, construction, usage, and deconstruction phases. Another challenge was selecting a knowledgeable team of architects, a general contractor, subcontractors, and certified inspectors, which was difficult to find in the local region. Yet in the end, the University benefited a great deal. The old structure was reused by another school and the trees from the site were also relocated. The new building has many benefits that reduce costs with energy efficient building design, utilizing natural daylighting, energy efficient lighting and appliances, and materials that are made from recycled material. Today, all new construction at the CSU, Chico campus has been built and certified as LEED Silver or above.

LEED Accredited Professional

LEED Professional Credentials

LEED Professionals demonstrate a thorough understanding of green building practices, principles, and familiarity with LEED requirements, resources, and processes. Achieving certification in this field demonstrates expertise and gives the individual a competitive advantage. The Green Building Certificate Institute (GBCI) provides a professional credentialing program, third-party administration, and verification of the LEED Professional Credentials in three categories:

1. LEED Green Associate
2. LEED AP
3. LEED Fellow

The LEED Green Associate credential is intended for professionals who want to demonstrate green building expertise in non-technical fields of practice. This credential covers the basic knowledge of green design, construction, and operations. The LEED Green Associate is required to have been in, or is currently involved, in a LEED certified project, sustainable employment position, or has completed an educational program in green building. Upon providing proof of meeting the requirement, passing the LEED Green Associate exam, the new LEED Green Associate is required to maintain credentials by earning 15 continuing education hours in every two year period.

LEED Accredited Professional credentials are awarded to individuals who meet the minimum prerequisites and have passed the appropriate credentialing exam. The LEED AP credential is a mark of professional excellence and is recognized throughout the industry. The LEED AP credential is awarded based on the professional's expertise in the following categories.

- LEED AP Building Design and Construction
- LEED AP Interior Design and Construction

- LEED AP Homes
- LEED AP Operations and Maintenance
- LEED AP Neighborhood Development
- LEED Fellow[5]

LEED Accredited Professional candidates must have experience within three years of application on certified LEED rating systems. The candidate must have documented proof of experience in a registered or LEED certified project, pass the LEED AP exam within their specialty, and maintain credentials by earning 30 continuing education hours every two-year reporting period. On successful completion of the LEED AP exam, the newly certified professional demonstrates competency of the LEED rating system and has the ability to facilitate LEED building certifications.

Description of LEED Accredited Professional Emphasis

LEED AP Building Design and Construction: to be eligible for the LEED AP BD+C exam, candidates must have documented experience on a project registered or certified for LEED and agree to the credentialing maintenance. This exam is designed to measure the knowledge and skills in understanding the LEED rating system and project certification process. Candidates who passed the LEED AP BD+C demonstrate understanding of the Green Building Design and Construction LEED rating systems which includes LEED for New Construction, LEED for Schools, and LEED for Core and Shell. The LEED AP BD+C provides a standard for professionals participating in the design and construction phases of high-performance, healthy, durable, affordable, and environmentally sound commercial, institutional, and high-rise residential buildings. LEED APs must maintain their credential with 30 continuing education hours for every two year reporting period.

LEED AP Interior Design and Construction: to be eligible for the LEED AP ID+C exam, candidates must have documented experience on a project registered or certified for LEED and agree to the credentialing maintenance. This exam is designed to measure the knowledge and skills in understanding the LEED rating system and project certification process. The LEED AP ID+C certification denotes practical knowledge of the Green Interior Design + Construction LEED rating system: LEED for Commercial Interiors. The LEED ID+C credential provides a standard for professionals participating in the design and construction of environmentally responsible, high-performance commercial spaces and tenant improvements.

LEED AP Homes: Certification denotes practical knowledge of the LEED for Homes rating system. The LEED AP Homes provides a standard for professionals participating in design and construction of high-performance green homes.

LEED AP Operations and Maintenance: Certification denotes practical knowledge of the Green Building Operations + Maintenance LEED rating system, and LEED for Existing Buildings: Operations and Maintenance. The LEED AP O+M credential provides a standard for professionals participating in the operation and maintenance of existing buildings that implement sustainable practices and reduce the environmental impact of a building over its functional life cycle.

LEED AP Neighborhood Development: Certification denotes practical knowledge of the LEED for Neighborhood Development rating system. The LEED AP ND credential provides a standard for professionals participating in the design and development of neighborhoods that meet accepted high levels of environmental responsibility and sustainable development.

LEED Fellow: the LEED Accredited Professional must be a certified LEED AP for a minimum of eight years, show documented experience of 10-years in the green building field and complete the application package provided by the Green Building Certification Institute. The LEED AP can be awarded this title by nomination only. The LEED AP nominee is evaluated on five criteria: technical proficiency, education and mentoring, leadership, commitment and service, and advocacy. The LEED Fellow is the most prestigious designation awarded and was developed to honor and recognize distinguished LEED APs who have made a significant contribution in the green building industry.[6]

What are the Benefits and Detriments of LEED Certification? An Inside Look at Roebbelen Construction

At the onset of LEED certification, Roebbelen Construction sent its employees to training. Roebbelen's engineers, project managers, and architects are now all certified LEED APs. The company was an early adopter as most of their contracts are in the commercial built environment. The company knew that LEED would open new markets and accredited professionals would differentiate the company while submitting new bids.

Indeed this has been the case. They were able to survive the contraction of construction in state of California throughout the subprime mortgage housing market crash. They have also been able to obtain larger contracts with companies that value sustainability and have been awarded government contracts for new construction requiring LEED silver as a minimum standard within the state.

LEED AP is a highly respected certification. The company has been able to develop marketing materials that target new markets. In addition, the state of California issued new codes for Title 24 in January 2011. Roebbelen was already positioned to consult with companies on the new requirements and construct to code when the requirements went into effect. This was also another benefit to the company—as an early adopter of LEED AP they had already positioned themselves to meet the standards of the future.

Throughout their experience, there have been some detriments. Consumers did not understand that the new requirements might be more expensive during construction, but that the conservation methods would save a tremendous amount of money for the user of the building. The Roebbelen team spent a tremendous amount of time educating clients on LEED benefits and costing out projects to show the long-term benefit.

As an early adopter, another pitfall for general contractors was helping subcontractors responsibly dispose of waste materials or byproducts, such as wood and drywall. The infrastructure in reclaiming and remanufacturing construction site material was also in its infancy except in established areas. In urban areas, Zero Waste to Landfill is much more manageable. Finding partners willing to keep waste out of the landfill was not a problem, it was finding a location for the materials. The subcontractor was responsible for finding the buyer or vendor to send the waste materials to. The subcontractor was also responsible to sort and weigh the waste before the buyer would transport materials. This was also a very new process for subcontractors, yet if the subcontractors did not dispose of materials correctly, the entire project would be disqualified from certification.

Another area of concern was that products or appliances for energy or water efficiency had longer arrival times as the shipping was not from a local source. In some instances, the product was only available from the east coast or from an overseas supplier. This actually increased the carbon footprint in some cases.

It was also a steep learning curve to learn how to evaluate life cycle assessment and the environmental impacts the project had. Life cycle assessment of the product from raw material extraction to arrival at the job site was time consuming. The chain of custody was also a learning curve. Forest Stewardship Council's chain of custody certifies that the wood was harvested without clear cutting or rainforest destruction by a certified logger, the wood was processed at a manufacturing company at a certified mill, and then the distributor sold the wood to a certified fabricator. This entire process has a tracking number so the paper trail can be verified. The paper trail is called chain of custody. This process is verified by the auditor, but the general contractor must be aware of the requirements to ensure that the client will receive points in the rating system.

Constructing new buildings for LEED Certification also required additional manpower. The company was required to have four managers on the jobsite, with 25% of the personnel as LEED AP. The LEED AP on the jobsite was also the liaison between the customer and the U.S. Green Building Council. In addition, the owner of the project had to hire a consultant from Green Building Services to verify the chain of custody. The LEED certification is highly respected due to the process inclusion of an unbiased audit that reviews the chain of custody and point rating system. The consultant verifies chain of custody and then sends verification to the owner, general contractor, and USGBC. The USGBC then awards the certification if the project meets the criterion.

Overcoming these challenges was a transition for the company at the onset. Now the company has a solid foundation in LEED certification requirements and is able to attract new business from domestic and overseas markets. The LEED APs at the company have a deep understanding of life cycle assessment and are able to inform the client of the benefits of building green, such as the building's air quality is healthier for the people who will use it, the ecosystem is preserved through conservation and land planning, and finally there are substantial cost savings for the user.

Roebbelen Construction now fully embodies expertise in green building, not because they had to, but because they believe it is the right thing to do. Since then, they have been training and developing their staff on new certifications, such as ISO 14040—life cycle assessment, ISO 18000 for safety, and ISO 9000 for quality management. This certification gives them further reach into international markets that require these standards. Looking toward the future, positioning the company for new standards and stakeholder expectations is just smart business. LEED Certification has become a core competitive advantage for Roebbelen Construction.

Summary

The USGBC continues to evolve LEED certification as the program becomes more defined and members are calling for differentiation between generalized knowledge and expertise. Consistent standards ensure that green building can become mainstream as the industry has a clear guide to follow. LEED certification is a competitive advantage in so many ways. Buildings built to LEED standards significantly reduce costs during usage and conserve precious natural resources. Certified buildings have also ensured waste does not go to landfill. From upstream certified suppliers and manufacturers to the downstream users of the building, LEED certification is a competitive advantage for society, the environment, and economy.

6.2 Energy Star Certification

Source www.energystar.gov

Introduction

In the home, the average homeowner spends $2,200 on energy costs in the following ways:[7]

- 29% Heating
- 17% Cooling
- 14% Water heating
- 13% Appliance usage
- 12% Lighting
- 4% Electronics
- 11% Other

It is quite easy to reduce expenses with building integrity, such as awnings, which create shade and adequate insulation. Innovative products are being brought to market to help customers make choices regarding products that reduce energy usage and reduce costs. Manufacturers who design innovative products to reduce energy during the usage stage of the product life cycle are also creating many TBL benefits, such as reducing and reusing byproducts and reducing environmental impacts of pollutants to soil, water, air, and emissions. By making choices to manufacture and purchase products that reduce energy, the entire value chain wins.

Background

The U.S. Environmental Protection Agency (EPA) initiated the voluntary program of ENERGY STAR in 1992. Products are evaluated for energy efficiency and receive a certification. Computers were the first certified product of this certification, which was soon followed by office equipment, and then heating and cooling appliances.[8] (Since 2011, the ENERGY STAR is third party verified to be even more transparent.)

In 1996, the EPA and the U.S. Department of Energy (DOE) teamed up to create standards for consumers and businesses alike to use the certifications as a basis for energy efficiency. The partnership expanded the rating system to include more than just product testing. The ENERGY STAR certification program is currently available in four different categories:

1. Products
2. Home Improvement
3. New Homes
4. Building and Plants

Overview

The ENERGY STAR label was created to meet two goals in order to protect the environment:

1. Reduce emissions and pollutants
2. Enable customers to easily recognize products that offer savings on energy reduction without sacrificing performance, comfort, or features[9]

Certification Criterion

Product specifications are determined by key guiding principles:

- Nationwide energy savings for product categories
- Meet customer expectation in features and performance
- If charging a price premium, consumers will recover costs through reduced energy costs during the usage stage
- Technology is offered by more than one manufacturer
- Energy consumption and performance is quantifiable and verified through testing
- Labeling visible to consumers to differentiate products

Product standards can be revised when a product reaches 50% market share, or there are changes in regulatory guidelines, technology, availability, significant consumer complaints, performance or quality issues, or issues with testing procedures.[10]

1. Products

ENERGY STAR products are divided into three categories:

1a. Home
1b. Business/government
1c. In-development

Appliances such as microwave ovens, ovens, ranges, solar, and space heaters are not rated under this certification.[11]

The next section will briefly describe the three categories of products. The ENERGY STAR website has multiple tools for consumers to calculate current energy usage and compare savings over the lifetime of a new product. See *Save Energy at Home*: http://www .energystar.gov/index.cfm?c=products.pr_save_energy_at_home

1a. Home Products

Appliances
Appliances include many product types, such as dishwashers, clothes washers, air purifiers, and water coolers to refrigerators. Consumers can save money on utility bills by using less energy and water. For example, ENERGY STAR refrigerators can save consumers 20% compared to non-rated models.[12]

Building Products
Building products help to improve the efficiency of a home's ability to retain heat in the winter and reduce heat gain in the summer. Building products include seal and insulate materials, roofing materials, windows, doors, and skylights.

Computers, Electronics, and Batteries

From computers, laptops, telephones, televisions, power tools, and yard care, this category has a wide range of products. With 230 million products in use in American homes today, these categories make a significant impact on the environmental and economic footprint.[13]

Heating and Cooling

Effective as of January 1, 2009, ENERGY STAR-labeled central air conditioners must have a score of 14 or below in regards to the Seasonal Energy Efficiency Ratio (SEER) and a score of 11 or below for Energy Efficiency Ratio (EER). These two ratios represent a quick way to determine the efficiency of equipment for cooling and heating. With these standards, the units are 14% more efficient as compared to standard units.[14]

Lighting and Fans

This category covers products from light strings to light bulbs, to fixtures, and ceiling fans. The average single family home spends 17% of their utility bill paying for cooling. By utilizing fans in lieu of air conditioning, the homeowner will reduce expenses and use less energy from the electricity grid. Modern fans take advantage of improved technologies in motor design and blade design.[15]

Plumbing

Water heaters are available using many technologies: gas, heat pump, solar thermal, and tankless. Savings on efficient systems can reduce energy by up to 30%. There are three main requirements water heaters must follow. First, ENERGY STAR labeled product must use 75,000 BTU/hour or less for units holding between 20–100 gallons. Second, the energy factor (simply the amount of energy necessary to run the equipment) must be .8 or higher. Lastly, the first-hour rating (the amount of water that can be heated per hour) must be 67 gallons per hour.[16]

1b. Business and Government Products

Building Products

This area is used in remodels of homes and for developers. Currently, standards for windows and skylights vary depending on the region and climate in which the particular product will be used due to variations in regional weather. The product categories are exactly the same as the Home Products, but additionally include categories in commercial appliances and food service equipment.

Windows and doors must be independently tested and certified according to the National Fenestration Rating Council (NFRC). The NFRC is a non-profit organization that's purpose is to help consumers compare performance. NFRC rates windows and doors in five categories:

Figure 1: National Fenestration Rating Council (NFRC)

1. The U-factor measures how well the window is insulated with a range of .25 to 1.25. The lower the number the better the efficiency.
2. Solar heat gain coefficient demonstrates how well the window blocks heat from entering, rated on a scale of 0–1. The lower the number, the less heat allowed to pass through.
3. Visible transmittance evaluates the amount of light allowed through the window, measured on a scale of 0–1 with the lower number representing more light.
4. Air leakage represents the amount of air allowed to pass through the window.
5. Condensation resistance measures resistance to condensation on a scale of 0 to 100. The higher the number represents less condensation.[17]

1c. New Product Specifications in Development

Products with ENERGY STAR certification provide the consumer with an easily recognizable seal that represents the most efficient products in a category.

Figure 2: Source www.energystar.gov

ENERGY STAR is most well-known for certifying products. The next section is an overview of the other three services offered: home improvement, new homes, and building and plants.

2. Home Improvement

The category of home improvement offers tips to consumers and contractors on upgrading energy efficiency. Checklists for finding ENERGY STAR-certified contractors and product details are all displayed on a helpful weblink: http://www.energystar.gov/index.cfm?c=home_improvement.hm_improvement_index.

3. New Homes

In addition to the certification of products, ENERGY STAR also provides homeowners with an opportunity to purchase certified homes. This program began in 1995, and today there are over one million homes labeled with this prestigious recognition. Certified homeowners save 15%[18] on utility bills.

ENERGY STAR Homes are certified based on the following:

• Effective insulation systems
• High-performance windows

- Tight construction and ducts
- Efficient heating and cooling equipment
- ENERGY STAR-qualified lighting and appliances[19]

A third party Energy Rater is required to work closely with the general contractor to verify installation of equipment and conduct inspections.

To become a partner with ENERGY STAR for home certification, there are four main steps:

Step 1

The process begins with the builder partnering with ENERGY STAR. With this partnership, the builder agrees to build a qualified home at least every 12 months. In addition to agreeing to produce houses every 12 months, partners also choose a Home Energy Rater to work with the properties to assist with standards of qualifications. Note: Builders with ENERGY STAR partnerships are not obligated to only build ENERGY STAR homes.

Step 2

The second step is the process of design and finding the best features for energy efficiency to be used in construction.

Step 3

In step three, the builder constructs the home and the rater ensures standards are upheld and followed. During the entire construction phase, the rater evaluates the processes being used through diagnostic tests and verifies the installation meets standards.

Step 4

The last step of the certification process entails the rater qualifying the entire process and the ENERGY STAR label is displayed on the circuit box at the home.

*Source: http://www.energystar.gov/index
.cfm?c=new_homes.h_verification_process*

Figure 3: ENERGY STAR Label displayed on circuit box.

4. Building and Plants

ENERGY STAR certification of buildings and plants is becoming very popular in metropolitan areas. As of 2012, Los Angeles, CA has the most ENERGY STAR certified buildings. 510 buildings have earned the label. As a combined total, the savings have amounted to

$117.9 million in reduced energy costs. Washington DC is currently second with 301 buildings and San Francisco is in third place with 248 buildings as of 2012.[20]

Figure 4: www.energystar.gov

ENERGY STAR certification of buildings and plants began in 1999. The EPA began a competition in 2010 called the "Battle of the Buildings" to reduce energy. In 2010, the winner was the Morrison Residence Hall at UNC at Chapel Hill. Through the reduction of 35.7% of its energy use, this building was able to prevent 733 metric tons of greenhouse emissions from being emitted and saved over $250,000 on the energy bills.[21]

To earn the ENERGY STAR certification for buildings and plants, the owners must take specific steps in order to receive this prestigious recognition. For commercial properties, the following facilities can be certified: bank branches, courthouses, data centers, dormitories, financial centers, hospitals, hotels, houses of worship, K–12 schools, medical offices, offices, retailers, supermarkets, and warehouses, etc.[22]

Summary

The ENERGY STAR program was a collaboration between business and government to engage consumers, building contractors, and building owners to reduce energy and greenhouse gas emissions. As the certification continues to evolve, the certification program has created new jobs in the energy rater field, has reduced significant energy usage nationally, motivated innovation and design, and constructed countless facilities designed for efficient energy usage.

6.3. WaterSense

http://www.epa.gov/watersense /product_search.html

Introduction

The Environmental Protection Agency (EPA) states there is just one percent of fresh drinking water available on the planet, even though 70% of the surface is covered in water.[23] Water is a regional resource, plentiful in some regions and scarce in others. Water supply relies on weather. Potable drinking water is either sourced from surface water—ponds and lakes, or underground sources—aquifers.

Background

WaterSense was launched in 2006, as a voluntary partnership between the EPA and the private sector. The mission is to protect the nation's future water supply by promoting water-efficient products and services. The purpose is to help consumers make choices that will reduce water usage and help save money, all while not sacrificing product performance quality. In order to do this, the EPA gathered many stakeholders to form a partnership in order to:

- Promote water efficiency as a value
- Provide consumers with information on easy ways to save water
- Create a label for products to promote water efficient products
- Encourage manufacturing innovation
- Decrease water use in order to reduce the strain on water resources and infrastructure[24]

Overview

The WaterSense program has two types of certifications:

1. Product certification for water efficiency
2. Irrigation and landscaping professionals

1. Product Certification

The WaterSense product label is third party certified by an approved certifying agency, such as NSF International. The product will be tested according to EPA standards for water efficiency and performance for the following product categories

- Bathroom sink faucets and accessories
- New homes
- Showerheads
- Toilets
- Urinals
- Weather-based irrigation controllers

2. Irrigation and Landscaping Professionals

The second program certifies professional knowledge of irrigation system design, installation and maintenance, and auditing of water efficient irrigation systems.

Product Certification Process

Manufacturers can apply for a partnership agreement with the EPA for products produced or carried. The company has 12- months to meet the standards. The next step is to have the product certified by a licensed certifying body. Once these steps are achieved, the manufacturer can use the WaterSense label.[25]

Mark	WaterSense Labels Explained
Label 	Certifies product is independently tested and certified to meet EPA WaterSense criteria for efficiency and performance.
Promotional Label 	Advertises the availability of WaterSense labeled products.
Partner Logo 	Partnership agreement, signed with EPA, designating which organizations can display the logo to demonstrate a commitment to promoting water efficiency.
Promotional Logo 	Used in promotional materials to educate the public on the WaterSense program.

Source: http://www.epa.gov/watersense/about_us/product_certification_labeling.html

Product Specifications and Metrics

WaterSense certifies products that meet the following standards:

- Products are 20% more water efficient than average products
- Product is available on a national level to create widespread savings
- Results are measurable
- Water efficiency is achieved through several technology options
- Certified by an independent third-party certifying body[26]

Annually, the EPA estimates savings from labeled products. The EPA reports estimated savings in dollars, energy, water, and greenhouse gas emissions.

The following are some of the assumptions used to quantify metrics for reporting:

1. Energy Savings
   a. Water delivered in the public supply. These metrics account for pumping, transport, filtration, treatment, and distribution. The assumption uses 1.5 kilowatt hours of electricity per 1,000 gallons of water
   b. Water treatment plant assumption is 1.8 kilowatt hours per 1,000 gallons of residential
   c. Assumptions for household water heating use the formula 1 British thermal unit (BTU) per one pound of water raised by 1 degree
      i. 90% efficiency for electric hot water heater = .18 kWh per gallon
      ii. 60% efficiency for a natural gas water heater = .9 cubic feet of gas per gallon of water
         1. 1 Mcf of natural gas = 10.307 therms
         2. 1 therm = 29.3 kWh

     iii.   Water temperature is raised from 55 degrees to 120 degrees Fahrenheit
     vi.   Water used in lavatories is 27% cold and 73% hot

2. Assumptions used for water reduction are based on the American Water Works Association (AWWA) rate survey: www.awwa.org

3. Assumptions for reducing greenhouse gases are calculated using the EPAs Clean Energy Calculations Reference: www.epa.gov/cleanenergy[27]

Since 2006, the EPA estimates that the WaterSense certification's impact has resulted in a savings of $2 billion on energy and water, plus 125 billion gallons of water.[28]

Summary

The WaterSense label is another example of how business and government can work together to reach out to the public to encourage reducing and conserving water resources.

6.4 NSF International

www.nsf.org

Introduction

Consumer trends expect the highest standards and companies can deliver products to meet those expectations. Third party certification delivers consumers unbiased lab and product testing to build trust between the end consumer and manufacturer. NSF International conducts testing and certification for various products: food safety and equipment, genetically modified food testing, safe drinking water treatment, beverage and dietary supplements, and energy and water efficient appliances.

Background

NSF International was founded in 1994, and was formerly known as the National Sanitation Foundation. NSF International's focus is to protect and improve human health and the environment internationally. NSF International serves companies in more than 150 countries and is a not-for-profit organization that creates standards, conducts third party product testing and certification, conducts auditing, and focuses on public health education and risk management.

    Its origins began with the University of Michigan's School of Public Health that founded the National Sanitation Foundation to standardize sanitation and food safety requirements. The mission of NSF International today is to be the leading international provider of risk management for public health and safety that serves the interests of stakeholders to include business, government, and the public.[29]

    NSF International is accredited through the American National Standards Institute (ANSI), and has developed over 50 standards for public health and safety. NSF/ANSI Standards are developed through collaboration of users, manufacturers, and government officials.[30]

Overview of NSF International Programs

NSF International offers seven major programs spanning from food, water, health sciences, consumer products, sustainability, and management systems registration:

1. **The NSF Food Safety Division** is responsible for:
   a. NSF Foodservice Equipment certification
   b. Food safety and quality auditing and certification through NSF Agriculture
   c. NSF Cook & Thurber and NSF-CMi; Global Food Safety Standards Certification (Safe Quality Food (SQF), British Retail Consortium (BRC), GlobalGAP (Global Good Agricultural Practice), Food Safety System Certification (FSSC), International Food Standard (IFS), Dutch HACCP)
   d. NSF Restaurant and Supermarket Food Safety programs
   e. Marine Stewardship Council (MSC)
   f. Aquaculture Certification Council (ACC)
   g. Hazard Analysis and Critical Control Points (HACCP) validation and inspection through NSF Surefish Seafood Safety
   h. Bottled water/flavored beverage quality certification
   i. Organic and gluten-free certification through Quality Assurance International (QAI)
2. **The NSF Water Division** is responsible for certifying products that come into contact with drinking water in residential and commercial buildings, such as plumbing components, water treatment chemicals and drinking water filters, as well as pool and spa equipment.
3. **The NSF Health Sciences Division** offers industries in pharmaceuticals, medical devices, and dietary supplements services such as certification, consulting and training, auditing, and manufacturing testing.
4. **The NSF Consumer Products Division** completes product tests and also certifies consumer products and appliances such as toys, dishwashers, washers and dryers, and kitchen items.
5. **NSF Sustainability** issues standards and certification for products such as carpet, flooring, fabrics and other building materials; and process verification services such as greenhouse gas inventory, carbon footprinting, and environmental management systems registrations with organizations such as the Climate Registry.
6. **NSF International Strategic Registrations (NSF-ISR)** offers quality assurance management systems for the automotive, aerospace, medical, and manufacturing industries (e.g., ISO 9001, ISO 14001, AS9100, etc.).
7. **NSF Education and Training** trains companies to meet regulations and standards.[31]

Summary

The diverse services offered by NSF International are a one stop shop to attaining standards, education, product testing, and certification. The organization continues to adapt to changing market trends and environmental regulations by creating services that will allow business, government, and society to continuously collaborate.

6.5 Green Seal

www.greenseal.org

Background

Green Seal is a nonprofit organization headquartered in Washington, D.C. that was founded in 1989. The organization uses life cycle-based standards to offer third party certification for products, services, communities, and companies. Green Seal is well known for creating a certification label that communicates to buyers and end consumers that a product or service is environmentally friendly. Their customers are household brands and the certification label builds trust between the consumer and the manufacturer. Green Seal works with responsible companies, such as: 3M, Kimberly Clark, Eco Green, Simple Green, Cintas, Staples, Office Depot, Mohawk Fine Papers, Akzo Nobel Canada, etc.[32]

With a mission to empower consumers and companies to utilize science to create a more sustainable world, it's Green Seal's vision to create a green economy that is renewable and creates minimal negative impacts so that all life and natural resources are not just protected, but honored.[33]

Overview

Green Seal offers multiple industry specific scientific standards that are accredited through the American National Standards Institute (ANSI). One of the most well-known service is lab testing of new products for no-VOCs, toxins and other chemicals in order to certify the product as environmentally friendly. Green Seal's standards certify the life cycle from raw materials to packaging that has an end-of-life disposal solution.

Green Seal offers many services to both business and government. Not only do they certify products, but they certify facilities, manufacturing facilities, and industries such as restaurants, food services, hotels, and cleaning service providers. Green Seal created the Green Mail program for the U.S. Postal Service (USPS). They also award community leader certification to governments and Chambers of Commerce, as in Los Angeles and Chicago. They also offer Institutional Greening programs for customers, such as Environmentally Preferable Purchasing policies.

Product Certification

Green Seal certifies many product categories, such as:

1. Household products
2. Construction material and equipment
3. Paint and coatings
4. Printing and writing paper
5. Paper towels, napkins, tissue paper
6. Food packaging
7. Institutional Cleaning Products
8. Hand Soaps
9. Personal care and cosmetics[34]

Figure 5: www.greenseal.org

They do not offer certification for products, such as:

- Air freshener or furniture polish
- Degreasers
- Oven cleaners and upholstery cleaners
- Disinfectants or sanitizers, dish cleaners, deck or outdoor products
- Laundry care
- Motor vehicles
- Paint removers and thinners[35]
- Artificial nails, glues, and removers
- Artificial eyelashes
- Bubble bath or soaps
- Fragranced products—perfumes, body spray
- Hair dye and relaxants
- Hand sanitizers
- Nail polish remover[36]

Procurement professionals and end consumers can easily identify the Green Seal label and know that the ingredients have been lab tested to ensure the products perform and deliver the expected usage. The nonprofit does reserve the right to test any product for follow up testing at any time.

Standards

The standards for certification vary from product to product and can also be industry specific. In general, standards for product certification will include most of the following criterion in the GS-37 Standard for Cleaning Products for Industrial and Institutional use:

1. Product Performance Category—Product must clean common surfaces and soils
   a. General purpose
   b. Restroom cleaners
   c. Carpet cleaners
   d. Glass cleaners
2. Health and Environmental Requirements
   a. Product shall not be toxic to humans either orally or when ingested
   b. Should not create skin corrosion or irritate eyes significantly, according to the Globally Harmonized System for Classification and Labeling Chemicals (GHS)
   c. Not contain carcinogens, reproductive toxins, or mutagens
   d. Ingredients should not cause asthma
   e. Product should not create an allergic reaction on the skin

    f. No more than one percent of ingredients can be listed on the American Conference of Governmental Industrial Hygienists Threshold Limit Value list

    g. Ingredients may not have heavy metals (lead, hexavalent chromium, selenium), 2-butoxyethanol, alkylphenol ethoxylates, or phthalates

    h. Product must meet strict VOC content standards that will not significantly create smog, ozone, or poor air quality

    i. Chronic inhalation toxicity levels cannot exceed 1 mm mercury at ambient pressure

    j. Not toxic to aquatic life, must not bioaccumulate and must biodegrade

    k. Fragrances must be disclosed and color must be natural or not have any toxins or metals

    l. Product is concentrated in the following ratios: General-purpose 1:32; and glass and others at 1:16

    m. To avoid animal testing, previous tests will meet criterion

    n. 99% of volume cannot combust over 150 degrees fahrenheit

3. Packaging

    a. Plastics must be recyclable, refillable, source reduced, or contain 25% post-consumer material

    b. Concentrated products cannot be sold with spray dispenser bottles

    c. Primary package must pass a drop test for durability

    d. Backflow prevention meets the American Society of Sanitary Engineering 1055B standard

    e. Aerosol cans are not permitted and heavy metals cannot exceed 100 parts per million

    f. Phthalates and chlorinated packaging cannot be used intentionally, but might occur as a post-consumer byproduct

4. Training and Labeling

    a. Material Safety Data Sheets are readily provided and declare fragrances and pH levels to employees

    b. Training materials on proper dilution, use, disposal, maintenance, and personal protection must be provided for each stage of the product's use

    c. Labeling must be in English plus one other language or be displayed with icons or pictures

        i. Contains dilution directions

        ii. Contains clear directions for disposal, recycling, reuse, and refill instructions

    d. Certification Mark can be displayed on both the packaging and product itself alongside the Green Seal standard GS number with a statement the product is safe for humans and environmental toxicity and also reduces volatile organic compounds[37]

Product Certification Process

The company should first submit an application to Green Seal to apply for certification. A project manager will then begin preliminary research on the product and request all details. To complete the process an on-site audit will be conducted. The company can take any corrective action within 120- days. Once the company meets the requirements, it is awarded certification. Periodic monitoring is then conducted and the company pays an annual fee to retain certification.[38]

Benefits of Certified Products

The benefits to certification should align with the organization's strategic priorities. Innovation and design of environmentally friendly products have many benefits, such as:

- Reduces negative impacts on the environment. To name just a few, environmentally products protect the health of the ecosystems from discharge of chemicals or toxins into air, land, or bodies of water.
- Environmentally friendly products protect worker safety. Oftentimes chemicals can absorb into skin with contact or create respiratory problems when using cleaners.
- Environmentally friendly products do not always have a price premium and are now available from major manufacturing companies such as 3M, SC Johnson, and GoJo, etc.
- Certification builds trust in consumers that the product will perform to the same or superior performance standards.
- Customers are searching for healthier alternatives. Environmentally friendly products increase brand recognition and perhaps loyalty.
- Certification opens new markets for an entire product line to reach a niche target market.
- Certification increases sales and fosters community relations.[39]

Green Seal's recognizable label will also aid in attracting consumer attention to a new product line. Finally, as competition increases, product innovation and quality will continue to improve environmentally friendly products and build consumer awareness.

Risks

There are also risks of manufacturing a green product. Manufacturers have invested large amounts of capital—both monetary and human resources, to create green products. Bringing these products to market requires building consumer awareness regarding why the product is better for the environment or human health. There are also perceptions that green products do not function or perform as well. There are also perceptions that green products always have a price premium. Another perception is that green is just a fad or a marketing ploy. Overcoming perceptions is a daunting and expensive barrier.

Company Certification

Green Seal also offers certification of industries and communities. Using life cycle assessment, a company's, or city's products and business practices are assessed. Thus far, Green Seal has been a catalyst of change in the following industries or programs:

- U.S. Postal Service (USPS) Green Mail program
- Restaurants and food services
- Cleaning services
- Hotels
- Manufacturing
- Vehicles and maintenance
- Green Buildings Operation and Maintenance
- Environmentally preferable purchasing
- Green cities and leaders

Sustainable communities rely on government, business, and members of society working together to achieve regional solutions. The certifications ask communities to assess their major impacts and then work toward reimagining a new system.

Green Seal's certification of industries and communities focuses on:

- Transparency and accountability
- Environmental management systems with clear roles of players
- Aggressive goals and achievements in social and environmental initiatives
- Life cycle assessment of key product lines
- Supplier management practices to work together to achieve goals that reduce impacts to the environment and society
- Collaborating with third Party Certifying bodies on social and environmental responsibility[40]

Summary

Product testing, on-site audits, and collaboration build trust throughout the value chain. Green Seal is a third party auditor that plays a vital role in working to bring science-based solutions for products and processes.

SAMPLE QUESTIONS

Questions from LEED Certification

1. What organization is the certifying body for LEED Certification?

   A. U.S. Spacial Association
   B. U.S. Green Building Council
   C. U.S. Automation Society
   D. U.S. Energy Department

2. What does the acronym LEED stand for?

   A. Leadership in Environmental and Energy Design
   B. Leadership in Energy and Environmental Design
   C. Leadership in Environmental Economic Design
   D. Leadership in Energy and Emissions Design

Questions from Energy Star

3. The U.S. Department of Energy created the Energy Star Certification.

   A. True
   B. False

4. The objective of the Energy Star certification is to certify products or buildings that are energy efficient.

   A. True
   B. False

Questions from WaterSense

5. The WaterSense program was founded by the U.S. Environmental Protection Agency.

   A. True
   B. False

6. The WaterSense program's objective is to focus on water quality.

   A. True
   B. False

Questions from NSF International

7. NSF International issues standards for public health and safety.

   A. True
   B. False

8. NSF International certifies products through lab testing.

   A. True
   B. False

Questions from Green Seal

9. Green Seal certifies products and facilities.

   A. True
   B. False

10. Product categories certified by Green Seal include all but which one of the following?

    A. Food packaging
    B. Cosmetics
    C. Hair dye
    D. Office copy paper

Answers: 1B, 2B, 3B, 4A, 5A, 6B, 7A, 8A, 9A, 10C

ENDNOTES

[1] *U.S. Green Building Council.* (2010). Retrieved January 13, 2011, from http://www.usgbc.org/Default.aspx

[2] *What is LEED.* (2011). U.S. Green Building Council. Retrieved on November 4, 2011 from: http://www.usgbc .org/DisplayPage.aspx?CMSPageID=1988

[3] *Green Building Certificate Institute.* (2011). Retrieved January 23, 2011, from: http://www.gbci.org/Homepage .aspx

[4] *What LEED Measured.* (2011). U.S. Green Building Council. Retrieved on November 4, 2011 from: http:// www.usgbc.org/

[5] *LEED Professional Credentials.* (2011). U.S. Green Building Council. Retrieved on November 4, 2011 from: http://www.usgbc.org/

[6] *LEED Professional Credentials.* (2011). U.S. Green Building Council. Retrieved on November 4, 2011 from: http://www.usgbc.org/

[7] *Where does my money go?* Retrieved on March 30, 2012 from: http://www.energystar.gov/index .cfm?c=products.pr_where_money

[8] *History of ENERGY STAR.* (2011). Retrieved on June 2, 2011, from: http://www.energystar.gov/index .cfm?c=about.ab_history

[9] *What is ENERGY STAR?* Retrieved on March 30, 2012 from: http://www.energystar.gov/index .cfm?c=products.pr_how_earn

[10] *How Does EPA decide when to Revise Specifications.* Retrieved on March 30, 2012 from: http:// www.energystar.gov/index.cfm?c=products.pr_how_earn

[11] *Find Energy Products.* Retrieved on March 30, 2012 from: http://www.energystar.gov/index.cfm?c=products .pr_find_es_products

[12] *Refrigerators.* Retrieved on March 30, 2012 from: http://www.energystar.gov/index.cfm?fuseaction=find_a _product.showProductGroup&pgw_code=RF

[13] *Products that Incorporate Battery Chargers.* Retrieved on June 2, 2011 from: http://www.energystar.gov /index.cfm?fuseaction=find_a_product.showProductGroup&pgw_code=BCH

[14] *Air-Source Heat Pumps and Central Air Conditioners Key Product Criteria.* Retrieved on June 2, 2011 from: http://www.energystar.gov/index.cfm?c=airsrc_heat.pr_crit_as_heat_pumps

[15] *Fans, Ceiling.* Retrieved on June 2, 2011 from: http://www.energystar.gov/index.cfm?fuseaction=find_a _product.showProductGroup&pgw_code=CF

[16] *Residential Water Heaters Key Product Criteria.* Retrieved on June 2, 2011 from: http://www.energystar.gov /index.cfm?c=water_heat.pr_crit_water_heaters

[17] *Independently Tested and Certified Energy Performance.* Retrieved on March 30, 201 from: http:// www.energystar.gov/index.cfm?c=windows_doors.pr_ind_tested

[18] *Qualified New Homes.* Retrieved on March 31, 2012 from: http://www.energystar.gov/index.cfm?c=new _homes.hm_index

[19] *How New Homes Earn ENERGY STAR.* Retrieved on March 31, 2012 from: http://www.energystar.gov /index.cfm?c=new_homes.nh_verification_process

[20] *Top Cities.* Retrieved on March 31, 2012 from: https://www.energystar.gov/ia/business/downloads/2010_Top _Cities_chart.pdf

[21] *The National Building Competition.* Retrieved June 2, 2011 from: https://www.energystar.gov/ia/business /buildingcontest/NBC_report_final.pdf. p. 19.

[22] *Business Buildings.* Retrieved on March 31, 2012 from: https://www.energystar.gov/index.cfm?c=business .bus_bldgs

[23] *Water Efficiency: Our Responsibility.* (February 14, 2012). Retrieved on April 7, 2012 from: http://www.epa .gov/watersense/about_us/index.html

[24] *About Us.* (February 14, 2012). Retrieved on April 7, 2012 from: http://www.epa.gov/watersense/about_us /what_is_ws.html

[25] *Produce Certification Labeling.* (February 14, 2012). Retrieved on April 7, 2012 from: http://www.epa.gov /watersense/about_us/product_certification_labeling.html

[26] *About Us.* (February 14, 2012). Retrieved on April 7, 2012 from: http://www.epa.gov/watersense/about_us /watersense_label.html

[27] *Methodology and Assumptions for Estimating WaterSense Annual Accomplishments.* (n.d.) Retrieved on April 7, 2012 from: http://www.epa.gov/watersense/docs/2010-accomplishments-methodology508.pdf

28 *Making a Difference.* (February 14, 2012). Retrieved on April 7, 2012 from: http://www.epa.gov/watersense /about_us/index.html

29 *What is NSF International?* (2004). Retrieved on April 7, 2012 from: http://www.nsf.org/business /about_NSF/

30 *Standards and Publications.* (2004). Retrieved on April 7, 2012 from: http://www.nsf.org/business /standards_and_publications/

31 *About NSF.* (2004). Retrieved on April 7, 2012 from: http://www.nsf.org/business/about_NSF/

32 *Find Green Products and Services.* (2012). Retrieved on March 31, 2012 from: http://www.greenseal.org /FindGreenSealProductsandServices/Products.aspx

33 *About Green Seal.* (2012). Retrieved on March 31, 2012 from: http://www.greenseal.org/AboutGreenSeal .aspx

34 *Find Green Products and Services.* (2012). Retrieved on March 31, 2012 from: http://www.greenseal.org /FindGreenSealProductsAndServices.aspx

35 *Cleaning Products for Industrial Use–GS-37.* (September 1, 2011). Retrieved on March 31, 2012 from: http:// www.greenseal.org/Portals/0/Documents/Standards/GS-37/GS-37_Cleaning_Products_for_Industrial _and_Institutional_Use_Standard.pdf. p. 20

36 *Personal Care and Cosmetic Products–GS-37.* (April 22, 2011). Retrieved on March 31, 2012 from: http:// www.greenseal.org/Portals/0/Documents/Standards/GS-50/GS-50_Standard_Personal_Care_and _Cosmetic_Products_First_Edition.pdf. p. 30

37 *Cleaning Products for Industrial Use–GS-37.* (September 1, 2011). Retrieved on March 31, 2012 from: http:// www.greenseal.org/Portals/0/Documents/Standards/GS-37/GS-37_Cleaning_Products_for_Industrial _and_Institutional_Use_Standard.pdf. pp. 6–15

38 *Get Certified.* (2012). Retrieved on March 31, 2012 from: http://www.greenseal.org/GreenBusiness /Certification/Getcertified.aspx

39 *Green Business.* (2012). Retrieved on March 31, 2012 from: http://www.greenseal.org/GreenBusiness /Certification/WhyCertification.aspx

40 *Institutional Greening Programs.* (2012). Retrieved on March 31, 2012 from: http://www.greenseal.org /GreenBusiness/InstitutionalGreeningPrograms.aspx

Chapter 7

Certifications—Triple Bottom Line Focus

7.1 Fair Trade USA

www.fairtradeusa.org

Introduction

The ingredients in foods and beverages are sourced from all over the world. Imagine a day in which the consumer is intimately connected with the farmer through the retailer. That day is fast approaching. Consumers are voting with their dollars to choose to shop with retailers who procure goods from farmers either through cooperatives or direct purchase. Retailers are benefitting because of this social trend. In 2012, sales of Fair Trade Certified™ products grew 75% over 2011 sales thanks to the efforts of mainstream grocers, such as Walmart, Sam's Club, Trader Joe's, Whole Foods, Ben & Jerry's, as well as a multitude of cafes and restaurants.[1] More and more, people care where their goods come from as well as if the farmers were paid fair wages and prices.

Fair Trade USA is a nonprofit organization that fosters economic development to improve the quality of life of communities through environmental and social responsibility. Oromia Coffee Farmers Cooperative Union of Ethiopia has over 180,000 members. The cooperative became Fair Trade certified in 2002. Over the last decade, the community has used Fair Trade premiums to make investments into education, clean water, building bridges, and flour mills. Today, the community no longer suffers with malaria infested water—people have potable drinking water from wells. The women no longer walk 20-miles to the nearest flour mill—they can now visit any one of five mills. Educational programs were expanded to include high school curricula, so now children can continue their education. Even the adults are going back to school. The community has worked together to invest in improvements.

Background

Fair Trade USA, formerly known as TransFair, can trace its roots back to 1998, but the global fair trade movement extends back to the 1940s, when a group of small organizations reached out to farmers in poverty to connect them to free trade markets. Fair Trade USA is a nonprofit that assists disadvantaged communities to take advantage of the free market and reinvest earnings into organic and natural farming practices or community improvements. The organization connects farmers and cooperatives to major brands to create long-term partnerships.[2]

Fair Trade USA envisions a future where poverty stricken communities are no longer reliant on aid, but dependent on their own innovation to create a living wage and garner a fair price for goods. The vision of the organization is to empower workers and family farmers worldwide and enrich the lives of those living in poverty.[3] The organization provides education for consumers; fosters relationships with retailers and manufacturers; and provides farming communities with tools, training, and resources to compete in the global marketplace.

The organization embarked on a mission to foster sustainable development, and economically empower communities to participate in global trade to benefit the entire value chain.[4]

The partnerships formed throughout the supply chain are built on a strong set of values.

- Empowerment: freedom of choice to create a better world
- Integrity: honesty, mutual respect, and trust
- Sustainability: solutions to global problems that affect the environment and society
- Excellence: quality of life, and excellence in performance of work
- Personal Development: reach our fullest potential
- Community: diversity of perspectives, collaboration, and partnerships mean success
- Fairness: create opportunities to all people worldwide
- Impact: positive solutions that are meaningful to change the world[5]

The economic impact of Fair Trade USA reaches far around the world. Alongside industry partners, donors, and NGOs, the investments span from Asia, Africa, and Latin America. Programs provide training and resources to market access, business capacity, and biodiversity. Coffee, tea, honey, sugar, cotton, mangoes, vegetables, and cocoa are all key ingredients to the beverage and food industries. Communities that produce those goods in Haiti, Rwanda, Costa Rico, Honduras, Guatemala, Mexico, and Peru, etc. are now learning about risk management, environmental management, capacity building, business management, accounting, and finance.[6]

Moreover, the impact of Fair Trade USA can also be very personal on an individual level. In America, Valentine's Day is celebrated with gifts of chocolate and roses. Who are the people that grow the roses? A 22-year-old flower worker on the Hoja Verde flower farm in Cayambe, Ecuador attests that Fair Trade USA actually saved her life. At the flower farm, which was certified in 2002, workers receive higher wages, overtime pay, free child care, access to eye exams, and routine medical screenings. At 22 years old, she was diagnosed with cervical cancer. Early detection was enabled by taking advantage of medical screenings. She is now a survivor that is investing in her future. She has been able to buy a plot of land for her new home through the loan program available from Fair Trade premiums. She grows the beautiful roses.[7]

Certification

Fair trade is just as the term implies: equitable or fair. Farmers are adequately compensated for their goods and the label builds consumer trust that the retailer supports fair trade.[8] Consumers and retailers can feel good by choosing Fair Trade certified products. The nonprofit improved the quality of life in disadvantaged communities. When consumers purchase Fair Trade products, they can feel good about the reinvestment in communities to open schools, educate children, open new health clinics, and farmer awareness of organic and natural farming practices. The certification aims to enable consumer participation in global economic, social, and environmental responsibility.

Source: http://www.fairtradeusa.org/
logo_download_confirmation?sid=4429

Figure 1: Certification Label as of 2012

Fair Trade USA teams up with Scientific Certification Systems (SCS) as an independent third party certifying body to audit products such as: coffee, tea, cocoa, fruits, vegetables, herbs, spices, sugar, honey, wine, flowers, grains, and rubber products.[9] The standards certify the following requirements:

1. Soil and water: irrigation uses water wisely and soil is enhanced with crop rotation
2. Biodiversity and Carbon Emissions
    a. Report methods to reduce carbon emissions and current ecosystem enhancements
    b. Report methods to improve biodiversity or limit carbon output
    c. Target goals
3. Prohibits use of genetically modified organisms (GMOs)
4. Agrochemicals: prohibits use of agrochemicals
    a. Agrochemicals cannot be used, sold, or distributed
    b. Handled safely
    c. Avoid spraying over bodies of water
5. Pests and Waste: control pests in a safe manner
    a. Education on approved pesticides
    b. Alternatives to chemicals explored
    c. Safe disposal plans for hazardous waste[10]

Although organic certification is not required, it is highly encouraged. Of all Fair Trade imports, 62% were organic and 52% of producers hold organic certificates.[11]

The certification upholds equitable trade practices throughout the entire supply chain. Companies can license the fair trade certification mark after completing and passing a rigorous supply chain audit. In order to obtain a license, companies must purchase goods from certified farms and organizations, as well as pay fair prices and premiums.[12]

Fair practices and equity can be subjectively interpreted. Pay disparity between genders, or even the right to earn a wage, impoverishes women around the world. In Peru, the first women-grown brand of coffee was founded in 2004 called Café Femenino. Central De Servicios Cafetaleros del Nor Oriente (CECANOR), a cooperative from the Lambayeque region of Peru, revolutionized gender inequality to include women in business. Women were encouraged to become leaders and get involved in the decision making process of all aspects of business. Fair Trade premiums were used to access funding for expansion plans, equipment, tools, and training. These programs allowed women to aspire to be leaders in business and achieve economic stability. There are now over 1,500 females working for Café Femenino in Bolivia, Colombia, Dominican Republic, Guatemala, Mexico, and Peru.[13]

Conclusion

Supply chain strategies are moving forward with sourcing ingredients and products from sustainable farmers. Supply chain strategies are also sourcing goods based on fair labor, fair wages, and fair practices. Collaboration across the entire chain will bring value to all partners, and offer consumers choices to vote with their dollars for companies that are doing the right thing. Although the farmer of the best chocolate bar in the world may be far away, purchasing chocolate with the Fair Trade mark is one way each person can make a difference in a big way.

7.2 USDA Organic

*http://www.usda.gov/wps/portal/usda/
usdahome?navid=ORGANIC_CERTIFICATIO*

Introduction

You are what you eat. This adage is still true today. The question is, what is in our food? The USDA Organic seal is a third party certification that answers this question with clear standards on how food is raised or grown. Organic is a term that an agricultural product has met the standards approved to integrate cultural, biological, and mechanical processes that foster ecosystem balance, conserve biodiversity, and resource reuse systems.

Background

The USDA Organic certification is an excellent example of partnerships. The organics industry worked together with the USDA to advocate for rulemaking and standards for labels that can be used for advertising. The Farm Bill of 2008, created a regulation that defined the meaning of terms such as organic, natural, wild fish vs. farm fish, and even beef. The Farm Bill assisted many industries to be able to label products with clear distinctions to build consumer awareness and consistent standards for fair competition.

Next, the organics industry approached the U.S. Department of Agriculture (USDA) to advocate for certification, resulting in the first certification created for agriculture. The certifying body for the USDA Organic label is the National Organic Program (NOP).

The NOP's mission is to uphold the integrity of the organic products sold worldwide. The NOP also certifies auditors worldwide who certify operations to the standards of the USDA program. The NOP also enforces compliance to protect the integrity of the seal.

The National Organic Standards Board (NOSB) is appointed by the Secretary of Agriculture and is a federal advisory board. The role of the NOSB is to advise the USDA on regulatory issues and/or national material listings. The Organic Foods Production Act names the NOSB as the sole authority to change the National List, either by recommending new additions or requesting deletions. As an example, the National List names specific materials that can or cannot be allowed during operations, such as synthetic substances are prohibited unless specified they can be used, and non-synthetic substances are allowed unless prohibited on the list. The National List can be found under regulation CFR Section 205.

The board has six committees:

1. Crops
2. Livestock
3. Handling

4. Materials
5. Compliance, Accreditation, and Certification
6. Policy[14]

The role of the board is to continuously improve the program, protect the label's integrity, and create taskforces to continuously grow. Board members have been represented from household brands, such as Smucker's, Campbell's, Engelbert Farms, Beechnut, Whole Foods Market, as well as Universities across the nation, consultants, chefs, and organic farmers.[15]

Organic Standards

Before a product can be labeled USDA Organic, an accredited auditor must verify the chain of custody. The chain of custody is a paper trail that shows how the product was sourced and then manufactured to a finished good.

There are three main product categories under the program:

1. Organic crops
2. Organic livestock
3. Organic multi-ingredient foods

1. Organic Crops
Crops that are certified were not grown with radiation exposure (irradiation), sewage sludge, pesticides that are prohibited, synthetic fertilizer, and not genetically modified during the past three-year period.

2. Organic Livestock
Standards of animal health and welfare must be met, to include the animal had access to free range conditions and was fed organic feed. In addition, the company is prohibited from using antibiotics and growth hormones.

3. Organic Multi-Ingredient Foods
95% of the ingredients must be organic in order to receive the seal.[16] The Smucker's brand Santa Cruz is a beverage that adopted the certification early on. Securing organic farmers and procuring fruits from around the world to meet the requirements of the program was not an easy task. Yet, manufacturers who supported organic farmers provided a value chain in which to grow the organic market and provide economies of scale in the market.

Accredited Agents

Accredited agents are independent auditors. The Organic Foods Production Act of 1990 allows for federal accreditation under the code of Federal Regulations Title 7, Part 205, NOP Regulations. Applications are reviewed by a committee, and an on-site assessment is conducted of the organization, filing system, and records. Corrective action can be taken in a given time frame; and the accredited professional can revoke certification at any time.[17]

The Certification Process

An accredited auditor will conduct an on-site audit to verify compliance with the NOP requirements. The NOP Accreditation Committee then makes a recommendation to approve or deny. If awarded certification, it is valid for a five-year period.[18] The cost of certification is paid for by the company who is applying for certification. Costs for certification include the application fee plus the audit—which includes labor and travel for the audit team. Not every company can afford certification, but may certainly be growing organically and/or treating animals with welfare.

Conclusion

You are what you eat. USDA Organic gives consumers options to choose foods that have been harvested without synthetic chemicals, as well as meats and poultry that have had access to free range or the outdoors. Organizations who obtain certification have gone far above and beyond to differentiate their products to build awareness and provide healthier foods, all while protecting the ecosystems and preserving land soil fertility. Partnerships and collaboration to form the USDA Organic certification are an excellent model to follow for other industries.

www.msc.org

7.3 Marine Stewardship Council

Introduction

Many populations around the world depend heavily on fish as their main source of protein for dietary needs. Protecting the health of the planet's water systems is vital to protecting and rejuvenating the fish population to sustain increasing demand.

The Marine Stewardship Council (MSC) has recognized the importance of sustaining life in the oceans' stock of fish. Unfortunately, the world has reached a point where the oceans' marine life is in danger. Important fish stocks are being depleted, the diversity of life in oceans is decreasing, and some have been damaged forever. The root of the problem is caused by overfishing, which has led to the endangerment of vital food sources for millions of people. Fish stocks and ecosystems are under more pressure than ever due to seafood demand.

MSC has developed a solution to approach the problem of overfishing.[19] The MSC solution has three goals:

1. Recognize fisheries that fish sustainably
2. Work with fisheries to build a market for sustainable seafood
3. Give buyers and consumers an easy way to find seafood from a sustainable fishery

MSC recognizes that the seafood economy is essential to supporting businesses and fishing livelihoods. It also recognizes that fishing communities need productive oceans and that fish are a healthy and renewable food source.[20]

MSC strives to promote sustainable fishing practices starting at the fishery all the way through the supply chain to the consumer. Their hope is that their efforts will have a domino effect and that oceans will once again be thriving with an abundance of marine life that can continue to sustain life for generations to come.

Many businesses and fisheries are achieving certification simply because it is the right thing to do. As of April 2012, there are more than 270 fisheries engaged in the MSC program with 148 certified fisheries and 126 fisheries in assessment. There are over 14,000 products worldwide that display the MSC Ecolabel. The MSC runs the only certification and eco-labeling program for wild-capture fisheries consistent with the International Social and Environmental Accreditation and Labeling Alliance (ISEAL) Code of Good Practice for Setting Social and Environmental Standards, and the United Nations Food and Agricultural Organization Guidelines for the Ecolabeling of Fish and Fishery Products from Marine Capture Fisheries. These guidelines are based upon the FAO Code of Conduct for Responsible Fishing.[21]

History of MSC

The MSC was founded in 1997, through a joint venture between World Wildlife Fund (WWF) and Unilever. Unilever is well-known for everyday household products. WWF is a well-respected NGO in wildlife conservation and also protects endangered species. These two organizations partnered due to the need to establish a global system that would ensure sustainable fisheries.[22]

MSC is an independent nonprofit organization that seeks to promote global sustainable fisheries. MSC collaborates with its partners to promote sustainable fishing practices and transform the world's seafood markets. The MSC is a collaborative effort towards achieving improvement and high standards in the fishing industry. It operates from many different offices throughout the world and has a staff of over 100 people. The headquarters office is located in London, UK and serves as the regional office for Europe, the Middle East, and Africa. In addition, MSC has two more regional offices serving the Americas and the Asian Pacific as well as local offices that support it throughout the world.

MSC Overview

Every fishery that is certified has demonstrated that it maintains sustainable fish stocks (subpopulations), reduces environmental impacts, and is properly managed.[23]

MSC does not issue certifications; they set standards in order for a fishery or business to achieve certification through a third party certification body.[24] MSC does offer supply chain participants Chain of Custody certification and licenses the MSC label on packaging and products. The label is used by restaurants, groups, and retailers to build consumer awareness and bring attention to the efforts of fisheries.

MSC's efforts have created a demand in the market for certified sustainable seafood and this has in turn, created an incentive to improve fisheries—the root of the problem. For example, the Germany North Sea Saithe Fishery is now winning contracts for frozen filets because consumers are demanding MSC-certified products.[25]

MSC Vision
MSC's vision aims to conserve ocean life and seafood supplies for current and future generations.

MSC Mission
The mission is to improve efforts towards sustainable fishing practices and setting respectable standards for the industry. The mission of the Marine Stewardship Council is to help conserve fisheries around the world by the use of the ecolabel. MSC also developed the standards to create a reward system that drives demand from consumers in order to build a reliable market for certified fisheries. Finally, the label is intended to market and promote environmentally conscious purchasing practices by consumers.[26] The goal is to build awareness throughout the entire value chain.

Mike DeCesare is MSC's Communications Director for the Americas Region that spans from North, Central, and South America, and also includes Russia. His role is to build awareness and represent MSC to members of the supply chain who are on their journey of sustainability management. He accomplishes his role by building partnerships and offering support.

His focus on involving the entire value chain is centered on the following key areas:

- Abating consumer confusion about the label
- Increasing the value chain's understanding of the value of sustainable fishing practices
- Encouraging fisheries to seek certification to increase the supply to meet demand
- Working with partners to place the MSC label on advertising and promotional materials through licensing
- Working with restaurants to use the MSC label on menus and printed materials

Mike believes that every person simply makes a difference by becoming aware of the problems and then committing to a shared vision and purpose to commit to the future. Companies that are awarded certification are committed to making a difference. While interacting with newly certified companies, he experiences the excitement and genuine pride of the awardees who know they are making a difference by becoming the solution. He also has been a catalyst of change to listen to feedback in order to streamline the certification process. Dining service managers at University of California, Berkeley exclaimed that certification was easier than expected.[27]

Examples from around the World

The MSC works to promote responsible fishing practices throughout our world. One way they have done this is through developing a program for children called "Fish and Kids." "Fish and Kids" is a project that promotes sustainable seafood products by working with the food industry. This project motivates schools and restaurants in England to serve MSC-labeled seafood. The program has been highly successful in gaining support from kids, parents, teachers, and caterers. In turn they learn about why choosing sustainable seafood is important for a healthy, thriving environment. The project focuses on teaching others about sustainable seafood issues as well as increasing the availability of MSC-Certified products on menus. The project even offers educational materials to promote schools to take a sustainable approach to their own operations.[28]

Another successful program to increase sustainability awareness by MSC has been "Sustainable Seafood Day" in Australia. Thousands of Australian consumers, and over 150 restaurants, took part in celebrating sustainable fishing practices by eating and serving MSC-Certified seafood products. Australia has three MSC-Certified fisheries and even offers over 60 different kinds of MSC-labeled seafood products for sale.[29]

Walmart initiated a seafood sustainability strategy in 2006, with a goal of promoting worldwide seafood sustainability as well as increasing the availability of sustainable seafood on the market. Walmart's strategy is to sell only fresh, frozen, farmed, or wild seafood that is certified by either the Marine Stewardship Council's standards or Best Aquaculture Practices' standards.[30] Fisheries that are not certified are required to develop plans to receive certification and report progress twice a year by June 2012. Walmart is offering incentives to promote sustainability in the seafood's value chain to increase the availability of sustainably-caught seafood products. As of January 28, 2011, 73% of seafood sold at Walmart stores was certified and the percent continues to increase.[31]

MSC Standards

In order to become MSC-Certified, there are three MSC environmental principles that every fishery in the program must achieve. These three principles are supported by 31 in-depth criteria, which can be found at www.msc.org.

> **Principle 1: Sustainable fish stocks (sub-populations).**
> Fishing activity must be sustainable for the fish population. Any certified fishery must operate so that fishing uses a sustainable amount of resources. For example, the fishery would need to provide accurate data regarding age and gender of the fish stocks in order to prevent too many young fish from being caught. In addition, the fishery would need to provide data of any other factors that could affect the health of the particular fish stock in question.
> **Principle 2: Reducing environmental impact.**
> Fishing activity must maintain integrity of the ecosystem within the fishery. For example, measures are put in place to limit by catch in order to prevent unintentional catching of other sea creatures, such as dolphins or sea turtles in the fishing gear.
> **Principle 3: Successful management for the fishery.**
> The fishery must meet all local, national, and international laws and maintain sustainable practices.[32]

Certification Process

The next section will discuss the process of obtaining certification for supply chain collaboration:

1. As a fishery
2. As a supply chain partner for Chain of Custody
3. License to use the Ecolabel for packaging, marketing, and retailers

Third Party Certification Process

The MSC Program assesses wild capture fisheries either freshwater or ocean, but does not include farmed fish.[33]

1. As a Fishery

The MSC does not issue certifications; certification is conducted by an independent third party assessment. Independent certifiers are also known as certification bodies. Certification bodies are auditors, or inspectors that are accredited through MSC and issue certifications. To ensure that MSC remains independent from the certification process, a third organization Accreditation Services International GmbH (ASI), manages the accreditation of certifiers to conduct MSC assessments. The third party is impartial and unbiased, but may be in consultation with MSC stakeholders.[34] More information regarding ASI can be found at http://www.accreditation-services.com/.

The first step is for the fishery to locate a third party certifier. A list can be found on the MSC website at: www.msc.org/get-certified/find-a-certifier.

Scientific Certification Systems (SCS), is an accredited third party certifying body that audits and issues a range of certifications. SCS certifies fisheries under MSC standards and have conducted over 400 assessments to fisheries all over the world.[35]

Methodologies of Third Party Certification

There are three different MSC methodologies that the independent certification bodies follow:

1. MSC Fisheries Assessment Methodology (FAM)
2. MSC Fisheries Certification Methodology (FCM)
3. MSC Chain of Custody Certification Methodology[36]

1. Fishery Assessment Methodology

The Fishery Assessment Methodology (FAM) is a formal guideline that accredited certifiers comply with when inspecting fisheries to ensure it is assessed correctly and effectively.

The Fisheries Assessment Methodology aims to:

Table 1: Fishery Assessment Methodology[37]

1. Simplify the assessment process and make it more transparent.
2. Reduce variability so that fisheries are assessed consistently.
3. Increase future certainty about reassessment for currently certified fisheries.
4. Improve credibility and streamline the assessment process.

2. Fishery Certification Methodology

The Fishery Certification Methodology provides the accredited certification bodies with the steps and measures it needs to take in order to certify fisheries.

These specific requirements are for the independent certification bodies and include:

Table 2: Steps to Certify a Fishery[38]

How to properly determine a fishery (unit of certification)
How relevant stakeholders will be contacted/alerted when a fishery enters full assessment
The process for inviting feedback from stakeholders at important stages of the assessment
What content should be covered in the certification report
How to direct a surveillance audit

The Fishery Certification Methodology (FCM) is a formal guideline and is often revised in order to keep up with a rapidly changing society; though the requirements stay the same.[39]

Overview of Assessment Process

The assessment is a multi-step process given by the accredited certification body. A company should select an independent certifier to begin the process.

Pre-Assessment

A confidential report by the certifier, which explains to the fishery whether or not it is ready for the full assessment. Certifier may give instructions on how to prepare for the assessment.

Preparation

To prepare for the full assessment, companies should communicate with appropriate colleagues, supply chain partners, and buyers. This process is necessary for all supply chain partners to apply for Chain of Custody certification.

Full Assessment

This seven-step process determines whether the fishery meets the MSC standard. The full assessment involves reviewing performance indicators, identifying strengths and weaknesses of the fishery, a peer review, and a final decision on whether the fishery meets the standard. After the fishery is assessed and has consulted with stakeholders, the certifiers gather the relevant information and then scores the fishery based on its compliance with the MSC standards.

The scoring requirements that constitute the MSC's minimum threshold for a sustainable fishery are:

Table 3: Scoring Requirements[40]

• The fishery must achieve at least a score of 80 for each of the three MSC Principles, based on the weighted aggregate scores for all performance indicators under each criterion in the principle.
• The fishery must achieve at least a score of 60 for each Performance Indicator.

After meeting these requirements, the fishery just needs to meet any areas for improvement noted in the audit and can then be certified. Once the full assessment and scoring is finished, the independent third party will make a decision on whether to certify. Stakeholders are involved in the decision making process and the information regarding the fishery is available to the general public.

Post-Assessment

The MSC certification is valid for five years. The certifier will conduct an annual audit to make sure that the fishery is continuing to be well-managed and sustainable. The certifier does have the right to conduct an unannounced audit at any given time. Each annual audit will examine the fishery thoroughly and will report any changes that would affect the achievement of the certification. After each audit, the certifier gives a detailed report to MSC about the fishery.[41]

Time and Costs

The average length of a fishery assessment is 18-months. The client is responsible for paying for the fishery assessment and certification costs to the third party certifier. The Marine Stewardship Council does not receive any payment for assessments or certifications. (MSC only receives payment when organizations choose to use the MSC Ecolabel on their products.)

The fees vary, but clients will be billed for labor to assess, communication with stakeholders, travel costs, and are also based on the complexity of the fishery and assessment. The cost of certification varies between $15,000 and $120,000 and even higher depending on the assessment's complexity. Costs can be significantly reduced if the fishery is adequately prepared prior to the pre-assessment.[42] More information regarding costs can be found on the Accreditation Services International website.

3. MSC Chain of Custody Standard for Seafood Traceability

Consumers are becoming more aware of the value of sustainable fishing practices and MSC-labeled products, which will continue to drive more companies to seek certification. The MSC Chain of Custody certification allows the use of the MSC Ecolabel.[43] Once a fishery has been certified, before it's seafood can carry the MSC label, all companies associated in the supply chain must have MSC Chain of Custody certification. This way, illegally-caught seafood can be kept out of the supply chain completely.

To earn this certification, every company involved in the supply chain must be MSC Chain of Custody certified. Processors, distributors, retailers, wholesalers, and restaurants are examples of those who would need to achieve the chain of custody certification in the supply chain.

The MSC Chain of Custody standard for seafood traceability guarantees that the MSC Ecolabel is only displayed on seafood that came from a MSC-Certified fishery. This ensures consumers that the seafood they are purchasing can be traced back to the original fishery that met the MSC environmental standards.[44]

There are four steps to obtain Chain of Custody Certification:

Table 4: Four Step Chain of Custody Certification Process[45]

1. Communicate internally:	Inform staff and appropriate colleagues about MSC and the certification being pursued.
2. Plan:	Develop a clear and strategic plan to make the process simple and effective.
3. Audit:	Select and contact an independent third party certifier and arrange a time for an inspection and audit. The independent certifier will align the business along the MSC Chain of Custody Standard for seafood traceability along with certifying the business against the MSC Chain of Custody methodology. If the audit is a success, certification will be awarded.
4. Maintain:	The MSC Chain of Custody certification is valid for three years and requires regular annual audits to make sure that the business is continuing to comply with the MSC standard.

Group Certification—Chain of Custody

Another way a business can become MSC Chain of Custody certified is through the MSC Group certification. This kind of certification is recommended to companies that can work together to become certified. To become group certified, the third party certifier inspects how the group ensures that each site is complying with the MSC Chain of Custody standard. Becoming certified as a group saves time and money. Groups that seek certification can typically be:

- Food service companies with individual catering sites
- Groups of local individual businesses
- Industrial corporations with multiple production sites

The following steps are taken for group certification:

- Select an MSC representative
- Implement the Chain of Custody standard in all sites
- Define and plan a system that explains how the sites meet the standard (e.g., who controls MSC-certified fish, etc.)
- Check regularly to make sure each site is complying with the MSC standard through internal audits
- The independent certification body will audit the group by inspecting group entities and random sites. If the audit is successful, the group will earn a certification for all sites, even if all sites were not visited by the auditor

Costs
The cost of becoming MSC Group Chain of Custody certified varies depending on the independent third party chosen as well as the complexity of the group's operations.[46]

4. License to Use the MSC Ecolabel
Bamboo Sushi, which is located in Portland, OR, was the first independent restaurant in the United States to earn a MSC Chain of Custody certification. Kristofor Lofgren, the owner of Bamboo Sushi, claimed that the certification was chosen so that the restaurant could prove traceability and accountability to their customers. Bamboo Sushi claims that their customers appreciate the sustainable seafood products on their menus by recognizing the MSC Ecolabel.[47]

The Ecolabel can be used on packaging, menus, and marketing materials. The MSC Ecolabel is a way of showing commitment to sustainable seafood to consumers.

There are six steps in gaining a license to use the MSC Ecolabel.

Table 5: Six Step Process to Use MSC Ecolabel[48]

1. Request a license to use the MSC Ecolabel. MSC will send the license agreement to sign and return, then email the MSC Ecolabel.
2. Create and design packaging or marketing materials using the MSC Ecolabel according to the rules. Rules can be found at www.msc.org.
3. Email the draft designs to ecolabel@msc.org for approval. Additional forms may be required depending on the materials (package or menu).
4. Once MSC approves designs, products may go on sale.
5. Product or menu item will be promoted on MSC's online "sustainable seafood product finder."
6. Once printed, send samples of the MSC-labeled materials to MSC's headquarters in London.

MSC Claim

In order for the MSC Ecolabel to be used on menus, packaging, price lists, etc. the appropriate MSC claim should be displayed in the appropriate language in addition to the Ecolabel. There is a different version of the MSC claim for consumer-ready products, bulk products, and menu use.[49]

Costs

In regards to the cost of using the MSC Ecolabel, there are two more costs involved: an annual fee and royalties. The cost depends on how the Ecolabel is used. Most supply chains, retail, and foodservice companies will need to pay an annual fee. The annual fee is calculated by the total value of the MSC-Certified seafood sold and purchased by the organization over the course of a UK financial year (April–March). For example, if the company sold between $0–$200,000 worth of MSC-Certified seafood; the annual fee would be $250. If the Ecolabel is being used on a restaurant menu, the business will need to pay royalties in addition to the annual fee. Royalties are calculated by taking 0.5% of the value of the seafood that is sold or purchased.[50]

Benefits

MSC seeks to provide many benefits to its partners and fisheries:

- The Ecolabel assures buyers that seafood comes from a MSC-Certified fishery
- Gives fisheries entrance to a global marketplace of sustainable products and secures contracts with existing companies that are committed to MSC
- The MSC environmental standard for fisheries allows the marine environment to flourish, helps seafood remain a global resource, and helps guarantee that fishing activities continue to grow for future generations
- There is a growing demand for MSC-Certified fish, and increasing commitments from retailers to source MSC-Certified fish[51]

Rock Lobster is a fishery located on the coast of Western Australia and was the first fishery to be certified through MSC in March of 2000. Dexter Davies, Executive Chairman of the Western Rock Lobster Council explains that the greatest benefit has been the access to new markets. After Rock Lobster had been certified, the Australian government developed the Environment Protection and Biodiversity Conservation Act (EPBC) which requires businesses to be audited and certified in order to export seafood. Dexter Davies claimed that the act was modeled on the MSC standard.[52] This was successful for the fishery, the community, and for MSC's reputation.

Another fishery that is experiencing benefits from becoming certified through MSC is the Pacific Halibut fishery in northern United States, which became certified in April 2006. One of the most important benefits is that chefs have been promoting and talking about MSC seafood products in their daytime TV shows and that Monterey Bay Aquarium promotes MSC products as well.[53] This has created more opportunities for Pacific Halibut, and in turn, supports the MSC organization.

Consumer Awareness

An important benefit of the Marine Stewardship Council is that consumers now have choices to dine in restaurants and purchase fish from companies and can feel good about making a difference. Another benefit is that consumers can choose to support companies that have been awarded certification to ensure a thriving economic system. The certified fisheries rely on consumption to remain profitable.

The MSC makes information easily accessible on their website on seafood products, sustainable seafood awareness, and information regarding certified fisheries. The MSC makes it so simple for a consumer to locate MSC-labeled products on their website at www.msc.org

/where-to-buy. The website can also be used to find a supplier, find a product, and even find a restaurant that serves sustainable seafood products.[54]

The Blue Ocean Institute and the Monterey Bay Aquarium offer accessibility to the public through their extended research on fishing method ratings. This research includes a list of seafood that is rated green, yellow, or red based upon fishing practices. A green rating indicates fishing practices that are environmentally conscious and abundant, a yellow indicates a good alternative, and a red means the species is in danger or is caught under fishing practices that are harming ocean habitats. Collaboration with the Blue Ocean Institute, Monterey Bay Aquarium, and the Marine Stewardship Council has led to Whole Foods Market eliminating the sales of red-rated seafood in all stores. On Earth Day, April 22, 2012, Whole Foods Markets stopped selling red-rated seafood. Whole Foods Market already offers MSC-labeled seafood products to their consumers and is increasing efforts by promoting environmentally conscious seafood purchasing practices.[55]

Conclusion

The MSC Ecolabel is a globally recognized label for seafood that ensures traceability throughout every step of the supply chain. The seafood traces back to the well-managed, certified, and sustainable fishery that caught it. The MSC Ecolabel encourages fisheries to make a positive impact; while consumers can purchase seafood that guarantees that the fish come from a world-class, environmentally responsible fishery.

7.4 Forest Stewardship Council

America is a beautiful country. From the forests of the Pacific Northwest to the oceans of Maine, the country's scenery couldn't be more breathtaking. The forests are the lungs of the earth's natural system to produce fresh air and remove carbon dioxide from the atmosphere. The forests are essential to all life on the planet.

Introduction

The Forest Stewardship Council (FSC) establishes high standards in responsible and sustainable forestry practices. FSC's sustainable forestry practices are focused on the TBL, and include practices that protect forest health and the ecosystem from harmful production methods. The Forest Stewardship Council created a reward system rather than punishments to promote responsible forestry practices that are based on society, economy, and the environment.

FSC wants to make a positive impact for the world's forests through responsible forestry management. Forests are essential resources for many natural resources, such as fresh air, clean water, and provide raw materials for timber and paper. FSC wants to do their part to make sure forests and their natural resources are managed properly to benefit people and the planet.

The FSC certification assessment is completed by an independent third party that is accredited through FSC. The participants who receive certification are able to share that value with the end consumer. Consumers can trust that their product was tracked throughout the entire process and can feel good knowing that the wood came from a certified forest. Rising consumer demand for certified wood and products will continue to drive an increase in certified forests.

Background

The FSC was founded through the efforts of business representatives, social groups, and environmental organizations to improve forest management worldwide. FSC's origins were founded at the U.N. Conference on Sustainable Development in 1992. From 1990 to 1993, 10 countries participated in fostering support to develop a worldwide certification system to cover all forest types, independent of ownership or location, which includes natural forests as well as plantations. In March of 1992, in Washington D.C., the Interim FSC Board of Directors was established. In October 1993, in Toronto, Canada, the FSC Founding Assembly convened, where 130 participants from 26 countries attended. The founders included timber users, traders, environmentalists, and human rights organizations. The founding assembly agreed that there was a need to establish a system that would be based on a global consensus defining responsible forest management.[56]

FSC is a non-governmental organization that sets stringent standards for responsible management of the forests worldwide in response to concerns of global deforestation.[57] Since that time, FSC sets high standards in forest management, labeling of products, and certifications. There are over 800 members in the Forest Stewardship Council internationally.[58] FSC is now nationally represented in over 50 countries and has a membership within the following well-respected organizations: International Social and Environmental Accreditation and Labeling Alliance (ISEAL) and International Union for Conservation of Nature (IUCN).

FSC was originally established because of concern regarding forest destruction and irresponsible forest management. In many countries, forests are destroyed in order to build and make room for a vastly increasing population. In some areas around the world, timber is produced illegally and human rights and forests are not being protected. This is seen as an environmental issue because forests provide such important natural resources to sustain life. The forests maintain and restore clean water and fresh air that are vital to healthy ecosystems. FSC is devoted to protecting the forests.[59]

Robert J. Hrubes, PhD, Senior Vice President for Scientific Certification Systems, is proud to have been an FSC Founding Assembly member from 1993–1998. During that timeframe, he was a forestry consultant and worked for the U.S. Forest Service, which coupled his love for the forest and his occupation. Dr. Hrubes is quite honored to have been involved in forming an important collaborative to manage the forests internationally.

He states that FSC created a system based on collaboration and partnerships. He knew there had to be a way to responsibly manage the forests. He knew focusing on certification and reward systems, instead of punishments, would build trust between business, conservationists, and forest managers.

Dr. Hrubes has spent the past 12-years certifying forests through Scientific Certification Systems (SCS). SCS is an independent certifying body that was formed in 1984, and conducts assessment for certifications under FSC.[60]

FSC Overview

FSC Vision

The vision for the world's forests is to meet the needs of the present without sacrificing future generations through social, ecological, and economic rights.[61]

FSC Mission

The Forest Stewardship Council's mission is to promote holistic management of worldwide forests.

Table 6: FSC Mission

Environmentally appropriate:	Forest management assures the harvest of wood products ensures biodiversity.
Socially beneficial:	Forest management provides long-term benefits and also incentives for locals to maintain the management plan for the forest.
Economically viable:	Forest management ensures that forest operations are profitable but not at the expense of the ecosystem or community.[62]

Note: these three standards are referred to as a "sustainably managed forest" for the remainder of this section.

Certification Process and Procedures

FSC Principles and Criteria Overview

In order for a company or individual to receive a FSC certification, they must meet all 10 principles plus 56 associated criteria. The FSC principles and criteria are the basis for forest management standards. A full version of the principles and associated criteria can be found at www.fsc.org.

The 10 Principles are as follows:

Principle 1: Follow all appropriate laws and international treaties.
Principle 2: Established and un-challenged land possession and use rights.
Principle 3: Acknowledgement and respect of indigenous people.
Principle 4: Support or improvement of long-term social and economic well-being of forest workers and local society. Respect of worker's rights in conformance with International Labor Organization (ILO) conventions.
Principle 5: Equal use and sharing of benefits obtained from the forest.
Principle 6: Decrease environmental impact of logging operations and continual maintenance of the ecological processes and integrity of the forest.
Principle 7: Relevant and consistent updates to management plans.
Principle 8: Relevant supervision and auditing processes to assess current state of the forest, management, and the impact on triple bottom line.
Principle 9: Continual upkeep of High Conservation Value Forests (HCVFs) regarding environmental and social values.
Principle 10: Promote sustainable practices within forests.[63]

There are three core activities that support the 10 FSC principles and criteria to be implemented in forests worldwide through FSC certification:[64]

1. Standards Setting
2. Trademark Assurance
3. Accreditation Program

1. Standards Setting

FSC standards strive for open participation by being available to anyone. Standards are developed at the FSC International Center where a team of experts review and improve these procedures by the General Assembly, FSC Board of Directors, and FSC Members. These standards are set based on consultations with the major stakeholders of FSC. FSC Standards ally with the requirements of the ISEAL Code of Good Practice for Setting Social and Environmental Standards. ISEAL is globally recognized for developing social and environmental standard systems. The Forest Stewardship Council is the only certification system to be aligned with ISEAL's standards.[65] To learn more about ISEAL's standards, visit www.isealalliance.org.

2. Trademark Assurance

The FSC trademark guarantees that a product has come from a well-managed and responsible source. Only companies, owners, managers, etc. who have obtained authorization can use the FSC trademarks.[66]

3. Accredited Certification Bodies for FSC Certification

FSC does not issue certifications to ensure transparency. An accredited independent certifying body issues certification. The independent auditors must first achieve accreditation through FSC in order to issue labels and certifications. A full list of accredited certification bodies can be found at www.fsc.org/certifiers.[67]

Certifications

There are two types of certifications: 1) Forest Management (FM) Certification; and 2) Chain of Custody.

1. Forest Management (FM) Certification

Forest managers or owners can be certified as a way for sustainable management to be recognized. This certification is voluntary. In order to become forest management certified, one must be inspected for their forest management by a certification body (as mentioned above) to check that it passes the FSC Principles and Criteria of forest management. FSC accredited certification bodies issue certifications after an audit is conducted of the company's forest management operation. If forest management meets FSC principles and criteria, the certification is awarded.

2. Chain of Custody Certification

FSC certifications begin with the forest. From there, every legal owner of parts or products sourced directly from the certified forest must hold a Chain of Custody Certification, otherwise the value is lost. Chain of Custody applies to any manufacturer or company making, altering, exchanging, re-labeling, or re-packaging FSC-certified products. This certification is for operations that manufacture, process, or trade in forest products. This certification tracks FSC-certified material through the entire production process: from the forest to the customer including all stages of processing.[68]

The forest manager must also obtain the FSC Chain of Custody Certification.[69] Whether it be an independent logger, wholesaler, or bulker, the Chain of Custody Certification is necessary in order for the wood to be tracked along FSC's standards to maintain integrity. Transportation companies do *not* need to hold Chain of Custody Certification.[70]

The FSC label provides the consumer with a social and environmental purchase decision. Whole Foods Market, in May 2009, achieved this certification that enabled them to be the first retailer to issue FSC-certified paper bags at its checkout counters. Michael Besancon, of Whole Foods Market Southern Pacific Region, was thrilled to continue to improve the reduction of their environmental impact by closing the loop with paper bags that use 100% post-consumer materials. The decision that Whole Foods made to become FSC-certified set an example to its competitors, as well as differentiated them, and now they can proudly inform their customers about the Forest Stewardship Council.[71]

Another example of the value created by obtaining a FSC Chain of Custody Certification is the story of Oliver Jeffers. Oliver Jeffers is an illustrator who printed an FSC-certified children's book called *The Great Paper Caper* in November of 2009. This book was the first FSC-certified book in China.[72]

Different Types of Chain of Custody Certification
There are three Chain of Custody certifications available:

1. **Small Enterprises**
   Smaller enterprises may create or merge into a group of operations and apply for the group Chain of Custody certification to ensure accessibility for smaller enterprises.
2. **Larger companies**
   Businesses with several locations can choose to apply for multi-site Chain of Custody certification. This is designed to be more efficient for larger companies, as it is more economically friendly to obtain than seeking a separate certification for each site within the company.
3. **FSC Project Certification**
   This is specifically designed for building projects. This certification is given if projects are using FSC-certified material or post-consumer reclaimed wood material for which third party certification and/or approval for the use of FSC trademarks is desired. Project certification requires a minimum of 50% of the cost or volume of all the wood products to be FSC-certified and/or post-consumer.

Quadco Printing, Inc. in Chico, California has been Chain of Custody certified through the Forest Stewardship Council since 2010. Owner, Richard Braak, formed Quadco Printing in 1976, and has offered high quality printing services to consumers ever since. Quadco Printing has many sustainable practices within the organization and knew that the next step would be to earn Chain of Custody certification through the Forest Stewardship Council. Quadco Printing has implemented many sustainable practices, such as uses soy-based inks, recycles 95% of waste, purchases bio-degradable cleaning products that have recyclable packaging material, and encourages consumers to utilize digital ordering and proofing to reduce paper and automate processes.

To continue to reduce its environmental footprint, Quadco decided to achieve FSC Chain of Custody certification. A printing company in Sacramento, CA had just received FSC certification and helped lead the way for owner Richard Braak to pursue the certification as well.

The FSC Chain of Custody certification cost Quadco Printing $4,000.00 to earn and the process took three months. There is also an annual fee that Quadco pays to hold the certification along with an annual audit of the facility and job orders.

The initial certification required job training for all employees. Employees learned to segregate FSC job reports in order for those jobs to be traced back to the original location of the forest. An auditor visits annually to check these reports in order to maintain FSC's integrity.

Mr. Braak explains that while FSC paper is more expensive, it has created a competitive advantage and brought value to Quadco Printing. Staying ahead of consumer trends is a priority for the owner, he knew it was time to earn the Chain of Custody certification. FSC paper is experiencing growing demand from consumers as awareness continues to build. Companies such as Sierra Nevada Brewing Co. and Lundberg Family Farms request print jobs only with FSC-certified paper. Quadco Printing, Inc. is far ahead of their competitors in offering these services and is a leader in sustainable printing services.[73]

Other FSC Labels

FSC Controlled Wood—Mixed Sources

Even though the FSC market share is growing, there are still some shortages in the supply of FSC-certified material. In order for manufacturers to provide FSC products, FSC has developed the "FSC Mixed Sources" label which enables these companies to mix FSC-certified materials with non-certified materials.

The non-certified material must meet the FSC Controlled Wood Standards that makes sure that the companies and traders associated with the material avoid unacceptable products.[74] Unacceptable products are specified below:

- Illegally gathered wood
- Wood gathered that violates relevant rights
- Wood that is gathered in forests in which High Conservation Values are in danger or are threatened through management practices
- Wood gathered from conversion of forests
- Wood gathered from locations where genetically-modified trees are grown.

Five Step Process of FSC Certification

Certification through the Forest Stewardship Council can be achieved through five steps. The steps are the same for both Forest Management (FM) and Chain of Custody certification.

Table 7: Five Step Process of FSC Certification

The five steps toward certification are as follows:	
Step 1:	Contact one or multiple FSC-accredited certification bodies to give an initial estimate regarding cost and time needed. The certification body will ask for basic information about operations and will give information about the requirements for certification being pursued.
Step 2:	Decide which certification body to work with and sign an agreement with them.
Step 3:	An audit will take place to assess the company's operations.
Step 4:	The assessment is completed to consider if standards are met to attain certification.
Step 5:	If the certification body decides the company is in compliance with FSC criteria then a certificate will be issued. If not, the company can take corrective action and request a final audit at that time.

FSC certifications are valid for five years. Each year the third party certifier will conduct an annual surveillance audit to ensure the company continues to meet standards.[75]

Costs

The costs for the certification vary depending on the size of the operation as well as the range of products and services being used or offered.[76]

Costs for an FSC certification are divided into: cost for an enhancement of sustainability, costs for auditors (which are controlled by third parties), and secondary costs. There is an annual fee in addition to earning FSC certification. According to a study by the Southern Center for Sustainable Forests, an auditing firm visits and reports average costs at $1.28 per acre to certify forests for FSC.[77] More information regarding costs can be found on the Accreditation Services International website.

Certifying the forest is based on costs for labor time of the certifying body, travel, supplies needed, and complexity and location of the forest. FSC has developed different cost models based on the size of the forest. To find out more information regarding these models, visit www.fsc.org/smallholders.[78]

Humboldt Redwood Company
Humboldt Redwood Company was created in July of 2008, taking over ownership from the former Pacific Lumber Company. The Fisher family took ownership of the forest while it was facing bankruptcy and disrespect from surrounding communities.[79] Under the new ownership, and within less than two years, Pacific Lumber became Humboldt Redwood Company (HRC) was awarded certification through the Forest Stewardship Council. Humboldt Redwood Company applied for certification and was audited by two accredited certifiers: Scientific Certification Systems and SmartWood. (Full reports of the certification process are available at www.hrcllc.com.) Becoming certified in December of 2009, was a game changer for Humboldt Redwood Company's entire framework in managing the forest.[80]

Becoming certified was critical to the takeover and future success of the new owners. The new owners had to earn the respect of the community as well, as the previous owners had a poor reputation. Humboldt Redwood Company undertook immense management changes as they implemented forest management practices to sustain the future for species within the forest. Humboldt Redwood Company's story is an excellent example of how environmental stewardship can be achieved, and how certification can build trust between partners and the community. Humboldt Redwood Company is continuously improving efforts to conserve the forest through responsible forest management practices.

7.5 Summary

1,000 Forest Management certifications and over 15,000 Chain of Custody certifications have been awarded.[81]

FSC certification is a competitive advantage and a collaborative effort to protect the world's forests. The entire value chain benefits from companies that strive to provide products that are sustainable. For the end consumer, the buyer can feel confident knowing office supply paper, direct mail promotional materials, and packaging all come from companies that value responsibility to the environment, society, and economy. Start checking your direct mail pieces for the FSC label from major brands, such as Best Buy, Office Depot, and Staples. Both Home Depot and Lowe's sell FSC-certified wood, and the entire value chain is making a difference by supporting forestries that sustainably manage their land.

SAMPLE QUESTIONS

Questions from Fair Trade

1. Fair Trade USA's mission is to stabilize the world economy.

    A. True
    B. False

2. Fair Trade USA's vision is to empower poverty stricken communities to prosper in the global economy to enrich their lives.

    A. True
    B. False

3. Fair Trade USA mainly focuses on coffee farmers.

    A. True
    B. False

Questions from USDA Organic

4. USDA Organic is third party certification for how food is raised or grown.

    A. True
    B. False

5. Which of the following would not be considered a standard for the USDA Organic certifications?

    A. Sewage sludge
    B. Antibiotics
    C. Prohibited pesticides
    D. Synthetic fertilizer

6. What is the certifying body's name for the USDA Organic certification?

    A. USDA
    B. Farm Bureau
    C. National Organic Program
    D. Natural Organic Standards Board

Questions from Marine Stewardship Council

7. Marine Stewardship Council's vision is to conserve ocean life and seafood supplies for current and future generations.

    A. True
    B. False

8. There are 3 ways to use the MSC logo if authorized. Which is not one of them?

   A. Fishery
   B. Fishing boats
   C. Chain of Custody
   D. Marketing materials

9. Traceability ensures the customer can obtain data on the origins of the fish.

   A. True
   B. False

Questions from Forest Stewardship Council

10. The United Nations founded the Forest Stewardship Council.

    A. True
    B. False

11. FSC's certification was an alternate solution to global mandates to stop rainforest destruction.

    A. True
    B. False

12. FSC issues certifications directly.

    A. True
    B. False

Answers: 1B, 2A, 3B, 4A, 5B, 6C, 7A, 8B, 9A, 10B, 11B, 12B

ENDNOTES

[1] *Sales of Fair Trade Certified Products up 75 Percent in 2011.* (2012). Retrieved on April 12, 2012 from: http://www.fairtradeusa.org/press-room/press_release/sales-fair-trade-certified-products-75-percent-2011

[2] *Sell Products.* (2010). Retrieved on April 7, 2012 from: http://www.fairtradeusa.org/certification/get-certified

[3] *Vision statement.* (2010). Retrieved on April 7, 2012 from: http://www.fairtradeusa.org/about-fair-trade-usa/mission

[4] *Mission.* (2010). Retrieved on April 7, 2012 from: http://www.fairtradeusa.org/about-fair-trade-usa/mission

[5] *Our Values.* (2010). Retrieved on April 7, 2012 from: http://www.fairtradeusa.org/about-fair-trade-usa/mission

[6] *Co-op Link.* (2011). Retrieved on April 12, 2012 from: http://fairtradeusa.org/sites/default/files/Co-op%20Link.pdf

[7] *Make a Difference with Fair Trade Flowers.* (2011). Retrieved on April 12, 2012 from: http://fairtradeusa.org/get-involved/blog/make-difference-fair-trade-flowers

[8] *What is Fair Trade?* (2010). Retrieved on April 7, 2012 from: http://www.fairtradeusa.org/what-is-fair-trade

[9] *History.* (2010). Retrieved on April 7, 2012 from: http://www.fairtradeusa.org/what-is-fair-trade/history

[10] *Environmental Standards.* (n.d.). Retrieved on April 12, 2012 from: http://fairtradeusa.org/sites/default/files/Environmental%20Standards_Fair%20Trade%20USA.pdf

[11] *Environmental Standards.* (n.d.). Retrieved on April 12, 2012 from: http://fairtradeusa.org/sites/default/files/Environmental%20Standards_Fair%20Trade%20USA.pdf

[12] *Certification and your business.* (2010). Retrieved on April 7, 2012 from: http://www.fairtradeusa.org/certification

[13] *Vanguard for Women's Empowerment.* (2012). Retrieved on April 12, 2012 from: http://fairtradeusa.org/get-involved/blog/quality-coffee-sustainable-futures

[14] *National Organic Standards Board.* (2011). Retrieved on April 3, 2012 from: http://www.ams.usda.gov/AMSv1.0/ams.fetchTemplateData.do?template=TemplateQ&navID=NationalOrganicProgram&leftNav=NationalOrganicProgram&page=NOSBHome&description=NOSB&acct=nosb

[15] *Former NOSB Members.* (2012). Retrieved on April 3, 2012 from: http://www.ams.usda.gov/AMSv1.0/ams.fetchTemplateData.do?template=TemplateG&navID=NationalOrganicProgram&leftNav=NationalOrganicProgram&page=NOSBFormerMembers&description=NOSB%20Former%20Members&acct=nop

[16] *National Organic Program.* (2011). Retrieved on April 3, 2012 from: http://www.ams.usda.gov/AMSv1.0/ams.fetchTemplateData.do?template=TemplateN&navID=OrganicStandardslinkNOSBHome&rightNav1=OrganicStandardslinkNOSBHome&topNav=&leftNav=NationalOrganicProgram&page=NOPOrganicStandards&resultType=&acct=nopgeninfo

[17] *Instruction. General Accreditation Policies and Procedures.* (2011). Retrieved on April 3, 2012 from: http://www.ams.usda.gov/AMSv1.0/getfile?dDocName=STELPRDC5087104

[18] *FAQ: Becoming a Certifying Agent.* (2011). Retrieved on April 3, 2012 from: http://www.ams.usda.gov/AMSv1.0/ams.fetchTemplateData.do?template=TemplateN&navID=NOPFAQsHowAccredited&topNav=&leftNav=NationalOrganicProgram&page=NOPFAQsHowAccredited&description=FAQ:%20%20Becoming%20a%20Certifying%20Agent&acct=nopgeninfo

[19] *Sea into the Future.* Retrieved on June 29, 2011 from: http://www.msc.org/documents/msc-brochures/Sea-into-the%20future.pdf/view

[20] *Our Solution.* Retrieved on July 2, 2011 from: http://www.msc.org/healthy-oceans/our-solution

[21] *MSC in Numbers.* Retrieved on April 18, 2012 from: http://www.msc.org/business-support/key-facts-about-msc

[22] *Marine Stewardship Council.* Retrieved on July 1, 2011 from: http://www.igd.com/index.asp?id=1&fid=1&sid=5&tid=155&foid=77&cid=800

[23] *Net Benefits: The First Ten Years of MSC Certified Sustainable Fisheries.* (2009). Retrieved on June 29, 2011 from: http://www.msc.org/documents/fisheries-factsheets/net-benefits-report/Net-Benefits-report.pdf

[24] *Marine Stewardship Council Third Party Certifications.* Retrieved on July 1, 2011 from: http://www.msc.org/about-us/standards/third-party-certification

[25] *Net Benefits: The First Ten Years of MSC Certified Sustainable Fisheries.* (2009). Retrieved on June 29, 2011 from: http://www.msc.org/documents/fisheries-factsheets/net-benefits-report/Net-Benefits-report.pdf

[26] *Vision and Mission.* Retrieved on June 30, 2011 from: http://www.msc.org/about-us/vision-mission

[27] DeCesare, M. (April 16, 2012). Personal interview.

[28] *Fish and Kids.* Retrieved on July 3, 2011 from: http://www.fishandkids.org/

29 *Sustainable Seafood Day.* Retrieved on July 3, 2011 from: http://www.msc.org/cook-eat-enjoy/ssd

30 *Walmart's Commitment to Sustainable Seafood PDF.* Retrieved on March 29, 2011 from: http://www
.walmartstores.com/sustainability/10607.aspx?p=9173

31 *Sustainable Seafood.* Retrieved on March 29, 2011 from: http://www.walmartstores.com/sustainability/10607
.aspx?p=9173

32 *MSC Environmental Standard for Sustainable Fishing.* Retrieved on June 28, 2011 from: http://www.msc.org
/about-us/standards/standards/msc-environmental-standard

33 *Eligible Fisheries.* Retrieved on July 1, 2011 from: http://www.msc.org/get-certified/fisheries/eligible-fisheries

34 *Third Party Certification.* Retrieved on July 1, 2011 from: http://www.msc.org/about-us/standards/
third-party-certification

35 *Sustainable Seafood Certification.* Retrieved on March 19, 2012 from: http://www.scscertified.com/fff
/fisheries.php

36 *Standards and Methodologies.* Retrieved on June 28, 2011 from: http://www.msc.org

37 *Standards and Methodologies.* Retrieved on June 28, 2011 from: http://www.msc.org

38 *Standards and Methodologies.* Retrieved on June 28, 2011 from: http://www.msc.org

39 *Standards and Methodologies.* Retrieved on June 28, 2011 from: http://www.msc.org

40 *Know the Basics.* Retrieved on 07-01-11 from: http://www.msc.org/get-certified/fisheries/assessment-process
/know-the-basics

41 *Know the Basics.* Retrieved on July 1, 2011 from: http://www.msc.org/get-certified/fisheries/assessment-process
/know-the-basics

42 *How Much Does it Cost?* Retrieved on July 1, 2011 from: http://www.msc.org/get-certified/fisheries
/assessment-process/know-the-basics

43 *After Certification-MSC.* Retrieved on July 6, 2011 from: http://www.msc.org/get-certified/fisheries
/after-certification

44 *How Can I Get Chain of Custody Certification?* Retrieved on June 22, 2011 from: http://www.msc.org
/get-certified/supply-chain/how-can-i-get-chain-of-custody-certification

45 *How Can I Get Chain of Custody Certification?* Retrieved on June 22, 2011 from: http://www.msc.org
/get-certified/supply-chain/how-can-i-get-chain-of-custody-certification

46 *Group Certification.* Retrieved on June 22, 2011 from: http://www.msc.org/get-certified/supply-chain
/group-certification

47 *MSC Chain of Custody Case Study – Bamboo Sushi.* (2009). Retrieved on July 2, 2011 from: http://www.msc
.org/documents/get-certified/get-certified-chain-of-custody/get-certified-restaurants
/MSC-BambooSushi-lo.pdf/view

48 *How to Get a Copy of the MSC Ecolabel.* Retrieved on June 25, 2011 from: http://www.msc.org/get-certified
/use-the-msc-ecolabel/permission

49 *How to Get a Copy of the MSC Ecolabel.* Retrieved on June 25, 2011 from: http://www.msc.org/get-certified
/use-the-msc-ecolabel/permission

50 *Costs.* Retrieved on June 25, 2011 from: http://www.msc.org/get-certified/use-the-msc-ecolabel/costs

51 *Benefits of MSC Certification.* Retrieved on July 1, 2011 from: http://www.msc.org/get-certified/fisheries
/benefits-of-msc-certification

52 *Western Australia Rock Lobster.* Retrieved on July 2, 2011 from: http://www.msc.org/documents
/fisheries-factsheets/net-benefits-report/Western-Australia-rock-lobster.pdf

53 *US North Pacific Halibut.* Retrieved on July 2, 2011 from: http://www.msc.org/documents
/fisheries-factsheets/net-benefits-report/US-North-Pacific-halibut.pdf

54 *Traceability in the Supply Chain.* Retrieved on July 2, 2011 from: http://www.msc.org/about-us/credibility
/traceability-in-the-supply-chain

55 *Whole Foods Market to Stop Selling Red-Rated Seafood.* (2012). Retrieved on April 6, 2012 from: http://
media.wholefoodsmarket.com/news/whole-foods-market-to-stop-selling-red-rated-seafood

56 *History of FSC.* Retrieved on June 2, 2011 from: http://www.fsc.org/history.html

57 *About FSC.* Retrieved on June 4, 2011 from: http://www.fsc.org/aboutfsc.html

58 *Frequently Asked Questions.* Retrieved on June 6, 2011 from: http://www.fsc.org/faq.html?&no_cache=1

59 *Frequently Asked Questions.* Retrieved on June 6, 2011 from: http://www.fsc.org/faq.html?&no_cache=1

60 *Hrubes, R.* March 7, 2012. Personal Interview.

61 *Our Vision.* Retrieved on June 1, 2012 from: http://www.fsc.org/vision-mission.12.htm

62 *Our Vision and Mission.* Retrieved on June 4, 2011 from: http://www.fsc.org/vision_mission.html

63 *FSC Principles and Criteria.* Retrieved on June 4, 2011 from: http://www.fsc.org/pc.html

[64] *FSC Certification.* Retrieved on June 16, 2011 from: http://www.fsc.org/certification.html

[65] *Policy and Standard Setting.* Retrieved on June 2, 2011 from: http://www.fsc.org/893.html

[66] *Protecting FSC Trademarks.* Retrieved on June 7, 2011 from: http://www.fsc.org/trademarkassurance.html

[67] *FSC Accreditation Program.* Retrieved on June 5, 201 from: http://www.fsc.org/accreditation.html

[68] *Chain of Custody (CoC) Certification.* Retrieved on June 5, 2011 from: http://www.fsc.org/chainofcustody.html

[69] *Chain of Custody (CoC) Certification.* Retrieved on June 5, 2011 from: http://www.fsc.org/chainofcustody.html

[70] *Hrubes, R.* March 7, 2012. Personal Interview.

[71] *Whole Foods Market Offers FSC Certified Bags at Checkouts.* (2009). Retrieved on June 7, 2011 from: http://www.fsc.org/news.html?&no_cache=1&tx_ttnews(tt_news)=132&cHash=294e7c3703

[72] *FSC Annual Report 2009.* Retrieved on June 6, 2011 from: http://www.fsc.org/fileadmin/web-data/public/annual_report_2009/index.html

[73] *Braak, R.* (March 15, 2012). Personal Interview.

[74] *FSC Controlled Wood.* Retrieved on June 3, 2011 from: http://www.fsc.org/cw.html

[75] *5 Steps Toward FSC Certification.* Retrieved on June 3, 2011 from: http://www.fsc.org/5-steps-certification.html

[76] *Chain of Custody (CoC) Certification.* Retrieved on June 5, 2011 from: http://www.fsc.org/chainofcustody.html

[77] *Implementing Forest Certification in North Carolina.* Retrieved on June 25, 2011 from: http://sofew.cfr.msstate.edu/papers/0502cubbage.pdf

[78] *Forest Management (FM) Certification.* Retrieved on June 1, 2011 from: http://www.fsc.org/fmcertification.html

[79] *Hrubes, R.* (March 7, 2012). Personal Interview.

[80] *Humboldt Redwood Company, LLC.* Retrieved on June 19, 2012 from: http://www.mrc.com/pdf/HRC-Approach-2011.pdf

Chapter 8

Communications and Sustainability Reporting

8.1 Sustainability Management Metrics—Triple Bottom Line Focus

Recall in Chapter 2's Environmental Metrics section that key performance indicators (KPIs) can be measured, tracked, and communicated both internally and externally. It is also important to develop KPIs from a holistic lens. Developing KPIs, measuring performance, and then communicating results can be extremely rewarding for employees as they can clearly see how their impacts make a significant difference.

Communicating sustainability management can be reported in any of the following ways:

- Internally within the organization
- Informally to an external audience
- Formally to an external audience

William Blackburn's sustainability metrics are an excellent guide for organizations of any size. The following metrics are a compilation from *The Sustainability Handbook: The Complete Management Guide to Achieving Social, Economic, and Environmental Responsibility.*[1] Quantifying TBL impacts is an important managerial responsibility to measure KPIs. These metrics quantify metrics and can be used to communicate results.

Table 1: Sustainability Metrics

Category of Activity	Unit of Performance	Ratio or Per Unit
General Metrics		
Compliance	✓ Number of fines paid ✓ Number of inspections ✓ Number of violation notices	✓ Amount of fines paid ✓ Percent of inspections resulting in violation notice(s)
Liabilities	✓ Number of unresolved lawsuits	✓ Amount or payments
Operations	✓ Business units committed to SMS	✓ Average percentage of implemented projects ✓ Average identifying and practicing SMS

Audits	✓ Number of audits by department ✓ Minor and major items	✓ Percentage of audited departments ✓ Percent of facilities conducting internal audits ✓ Average time for corrective action
Budget	✓ Capital and operational costs for implementing SMS	✓ Amount of expenses incurred ✓ Future planned expenses
Suppliers	✓ Funds spent with local merchants ✓ Number of local suppliers ✓ Number of suppliers from disadvantaged groups ✓ Number of suppliers undergone sustainability training ✓ Number of rejected suppliers that do not align with strategic imperatives ✓ Funds spent on certified or third party inspected suppliers	✓ Percent of purchases from local suppliers ✓ Percent of purchases from disadvantaged groups ✓ Percent of suppliers attending training ✓ Percent of funds spent from certified or inspected suppliers
External Stakeholders	✓ Survey results ✓ Number of complaints	✓ Percent change year-to-year of survey results ✓ Percent complaints resolved
Investments	✓ Number of investments in responsible organizations ✓ Number of investments rejected due to lack of alignment	✓ Percentage of portfolio invested in responsible organizations
Training	✓ Number of employees trained on SMS ✓ Number of management team trained on SMS	✓ Percent training completed ✓ Percent ongoing development completed
Awards	✓ Number of awards	✓ Percent awarded from applications
Economic Realm		
Financial Statements	✓ Income statement ✓ Balance sheet	✓ Percent growth due to sustainability initiatives
Health and Safety	✓ Number of injuries and illnesses ✓ Number of days lost to injuries ✓ Number of serious injuries and reported to workers compensation ✓ Number of vehicular accidents ✓ Number of fires or explosions ✓ Number of safety training classes ✓ Number of suggestions from employees	✓ Per 100 FTE for contractors and employees ✓ Average lost days ✓ Average sick days claimed ✓ Percent of employees undergoing safety training ✓ Percent of sites with safety programs
Social Realm		
Philanthropy	✓ Number of company-wide donations ✓ Number per region ✓ Number of in-kind donations ✓ Number of grants awarded	✓ Percent of pre-tax donations

Community Partners	✓ Number of paid employee volunteers ✓ Number of unpaid employee volunteers ✓ Number of hours volunteered ✓ Number of outreach projects	✓ Percent of employees participating in service
Pay and Benefits	✓ Total salary costs ✓ Total benefits paid ✓ Number of employees participating in voluntary benefits	✓ Average salary per employee role ✓ Ratio of CEO pay to lowest paid ✓ Average salary for temporary staff ✓ Percent of workforce without benefits
Employees	✓ Number of employees ✓ Number of contracted workers ✓ Number of days of training ✓ Training cost ✓ Employee satisfaction survey results ✓ Number of job applicants with sustainability experience or education	✓ Average training days and cost per FTE ✓ Employee turnover rate ✓ Training expense percent of sales ✓ Retention rate ✓ Percent employee satisfaction from implementing SMS
Human Rights	✓ Number of rejections of suppliers, investments due to questionable practices ✓ Number of workers broken down by young age groups: 14, 16, 18	✓ Percent suppliers and investments investigated for human rights violations ✓ Percent workforce trained on human rights issues
Diversity	✓ Number of workers from diverse groups ✓ Number of discriminatory litigation	✓ Percent diversity to entire workforce ✓ Percent of local hires in management
Ethics	✓ Number of signed code of ethics ✓ Number of bribes or unethical behavior reported ✓ Number of ethics complaints by employees	✓ Percent employees who have signed code of ethics/conduct ✓ Amount paid for violations
Environmental Realm		
Energy	✓ Joules consumed ✓ Gasoline or fuel consumed ✓ Natural gas consumed ✓ Coal consumed ✓ Cost of energy ✓ Number of employees with alternative commuting modes ✓ Number of employees in ride-share ✓ Expense reduction from conservation	✓ Percent energy recycled or reused ✓ Energy used per sq. meter ✓ Percentage produced from renewable energy source ✓ Average fuel economy fleet ✓ Average commuting distance per employee ✓ Average employee participating in other than single commuter mode

Solid and Hazardous Waste	✓ Tons of hazardous and non-hazardous waste ✓ Tons of recycled materials ✓ Tons of waste disposed ✓ Value of materials disposed ✓ Disposal cost ✓ Revenue from recycling programs	✓ Percentage waste reused or recycled ✓ Percent incinerated ✓ Percent to landfill ✓ Waste generated by department ✓ Percent waste projects completed
Carbon Footprint	✓ CO_2E reduced ✓ Cost savings from mitigation ✓ Metric tons of ozone ✓ Number of registries reported to	✓ Emissions per unit
Hazardous Cleanup	✓ Oil, fuel, chemical spills cleaned up ✓ Costs of cleanup	✓ Percent of accidents/violations ✓ Concentration of pollutants in soil
Water	✓ Amount of water used ✓ Number of contaminations to water system ✓ Savings realized from conservation	✓ Percent usage by department ✓ Annual percentage change in volume ✓ Percent of total usage in finished good ✓ Percent of tested samples contaminated
Waste Water	✓ Volume of discharge ✓ Volume reused or reclaimed ✓ Cost savings from reduce, reuse, recycle	✓ Amount discharged per department ✓ Amount discharged per employee ✓ Percent volume reused or recycled
Natural resources and biodiversity that are owned or leased	✓ Amount of land for operations ✓ Acres with diverse ecosystem ✓ Number of sites with cultural heritage conflicts ✓ Acres of land improved ✓ Number of protected lands	✓ Percent sites completed biodiversity assessment ✓ Percent land impacted by operations ✓ Percent land in open ✓ Volume of fertilizer or herbicide applied to land

Measuring progress will bring value to the organization in countless ways, a few of which include:[2]

- Metrics provide comparative information for use over time,
- Metrics prove to workforce that goals can be achieved,
- Accounting holistic measurements satisfies different intrinsic values,
- Use metrics to know when goals are achieved and the next milestone should begin,
- Collect data for certifications,
- Collect data for reporting, and
- Collect data for communicating achievements and challenges.

Compiling these metrics will enable the organization to rate performance, hold employees accountable, and celebrate success. It will also identify new programs that can be implemented for continuous improvement. Once metrics have been quantified and compiled, the results can be communicated internally and externally.

8.2 Internal Communication

Change management takes time. Incremental target goals and communicating results are great ways to keep the workforce motivated. It is important to phase in incremental goals so employees are not overwhelmed. The result is that employees will feel good about making these changes. Communicating metrics and progress are catalysts to change management.

The organization is responsible for rewarding great new ideas and successful implementation and evaluation of projects. To achieve a culture of responsibility, employees can be rewarded for taking initiatives and meeting expectations in any of the following ways:

- Public recognition, such as awards ceremonies, celebrations, certificates of accomplishment
- Integrating expectations into formal job duties and responsibilities
- Performance appraisal that document successful completion of projects
- Incentives, such as ride-share or employee travel rewards and bonuses for outstanding achievements
- Intrinsic value, such as a sense of accomplishment and job satisfaction

Organizations communicate progress to internal stakeholders in many ways:

- Newsletters
- Emails, instant messages, or intranet announcements
- Signage throughout the facility
- Announcements at meetings
- Managerial progress reports
- Board of Directors reports

Communicating often will ensure that motivation does not wane after short-term goals are accomplished. Low-hanging fruit is easy to accomplish, but continuous improvement should be a long-term goal. Knowing how to reach strategic imperatives far off in the future will also help to align business systems around the strategy.

8.3 Informal External Communication

Communicating progress is much more difficult with external stakeholders due to the wide array of outreach programs and partnerships the organization is involved with.

Building brand reputation takes a long time. In seconds, an organization can tarnish its image. It is difficult to regain the trust of stakeholders. Beyond Petroleum (BP), has spent generations in research and development and was a respected leader in sustainability management. BP was a pioneer in developing strategic sustainability management systems, programs, process improvement, innovation, research, and development. Most stakeholders immediately forgot BP's sustainability focus when the 2010 oil spill occurred in the Gulf of Mexico, an accident that also involved contractors. Even with the proportion of the tragedy, BP still did the right thing by not abandoning its responsibility and embracing the help of multitudes of organizations to clean up the spill. Their long-standing reputation as a sustainable organization also helped to bridge the gap to reach out to partners to help manage the cleanup.

Another leader that oftentimes overcomes public outcry is Nike. Nike has been a true leader in managing supplier relationships for generations. Since they are a large organization that takes responsibility, they are often subjected to NGO attacks on their image due to impacts made upstream in the supply chain. Attacking a large and well respected organization like Nike brings public attention to social or environmental issues, such as labor conditions, fair wages, environmental degradation, and irresponsible practices. Attackers also know that Nike will take charge and work with suppliers to improve conditions. Large sustainable organizations carry an additional burden. They are oftentimes the catalyst for economic, social, or environmental change. Therefore, communicating with stakeholders is an imperative for sustainable organizations.

Targeting stakeholder groups should also be a part of the strategic plan. The best in class sustainable organizations deploy some of the following tactics to accomplish broad communications:

- Two-way communication
  - Partnerships with NGOs and associations
  - C-suite to C-suite where executives share information
  - Value chain coalitions or associations
  - Competitor coalitions
  - Partnerships with universities and schools
  - Partnerships with government and business
  - Customer taskforces for direct research
  - Information readily available about goals and progress on company websites
  - Social media to communicate directly with stakeholders
  - Open blogs with sustainability executives
  - Public relations and speaking engagements at conferences
  - Supporting economic development training programs in communities
  - Supporting communities to build knowledge, skills, and abilities
- One-way communication
  - Simple, verifiable, and clear communication of KPIs
  - Informal sustainability reports on company websites
  - Formal sustainability reports either integrated with financial statements or issued as a separate report
  - Advertisements and media announcements

Managing communications is not only for large businesses. Investors and consumers want to spend their money with responsible organizations. Managing the organization's message about the strategic direction will reduce the risk of a tarnished brand image.

8.4 Formal External Communication

The next section will focus on one-way communication—reporting intrinsic and extrinsic value in formal reports.

Sustainability Reporting

Sustainability reporting is a formal communication avenue to inform internal and external stakeholders of sustainability management successes and challenges. Most organizations that publish sustainability reports are large corporations. Medium and small business, government entities, and non-profits can issue sustainability reports, yet many organizations choose to include the information on websites. There is not a requirement to include a sustainability report alongside financial statements for stockholders, yet there are multiple benefits in compiling information and providing stakeholders with an inside look into the organization.

Some of the benefits of communicating progress to stakeholders include:

- Well-respected brand value
- Respect and loyalty from consumers
- Ability to benchmark other competitors or share ideas
- Sharing results and methodologies within the industry
- Collaboration efforts increase
- Sharing lessons learned

Sustainability reporting is a time consuming effort, but certainly an achievement an organization can be proud of accomplishing.

As reporting sustainability management is not a requirement, or a compliance issue, there are many methodologies available on the market today. Some of the most prevalent reports are:

- Global Reporting Initiative: https://www.globalreporting.org/Pages/default.aspx;
- SA 8000, Social Accountability International: http://www.sa-intl.org/index .cfm?fuseaction=Page.ViewPage&PageID=1095;
- Global Citizenship 360, Future 500: http://www.future500.org/; and
- BS 8900 British Standards: http://shop.bsigroup.com/ProductDetail /?pid=000000000030118956.

Most organizations begin by compiling data to form a base year to compare year-over year-results in the future.

8.5 Global Reporting Initiative

The next section will discuss sustainability reporting and the details that should be included. Quantifying metrics is the first step before considering publishing a formal report. Compiled metrics provide verifiable details to share with stakeholders.

A widely used reporting methodology, but is not globally accepted, is the Global Reporting Initiative (GRI) guideline.

History of GRI

The non-profit organizations CERES and the Tellus Institute created the Global Reporting Initiative (GRI) in 1997. It was created as a system for accountability in regard to the environmental conduct of organizations. The first version of GRI was released in 2000, and the second version in 2002. Currently, there are over 1,000 organizations that report using the GRI guidelines.[3] G3 was published in 2006, and in March 2011, GRI released G3.1.[4]

Sustainability Reporting Guidelines

The purpose of sustainability reporting is to measure and disclose progress toward sustainable development. Sustainability reports are communication devices tailored to stakeholders. The report can be used by the organization for benchmarking performance, demonstrating influence over development, and comparing progress over time.[5]

GRI is a guideline for organizations to report on the Triple Bottom Line. There are three key categories: 1) indicator protocols, 2) sector supplements, and 3) technical protocols. Indicators are definitions. Sector supplements are additional guidelines for different commercial industries; this should be used in addition to the main GRI guideline. The technical protocol provides guidance on how to create the sustainability report.[6]

A complete GRI sustainability report needs to have three characteristics:

- Relevant content
- High quality
- A defined boundary

The content of the report should be relevant to portraying the critical aspects of an organization's sustainable development. Information that could influence stakeholder decisions should also be included in the report. A sustainability report should be complete, materially relevant, include a sustainable context, and be tailored to stakeholders. Quality reports are: balanced, comparable to previous years, contain accurate information, released on a regular schedule, clear, understandable, and reliable. The boundary of the report should include information about entities that the organization has direct control or influence over.[7] The extent of reporting for each entity depends on potential impacts of the information.

GRI contains a set of standard content that every report needs to include. The three required aspects encompass strategy and profile, management approach, and performance indicators. Strategy and profile focuses on summarizing the organization's overall goals and makeup. The management approach is based on performance in specific activities. Finally, the performance indicators focus on the TBL measures of an organization.[8]

GRI Application Levels

GRI created a ranking system. Application levels represent how much material the organization includes based on the core or additional categories. The available levels or rankings are C, B, and A. An A plus (+) ranking is also available for reports that have been reviewed by GRI or other third parties.[9] After completing a report, the reporting organization self-declares an application level and submits the report to GRI. This is based on self-assessment of how well the GRI guidelines were met by the report. Application levels create many benefits:

- Enables reporting organizations and stakeholders to know to what extent the GRI guidelines are met
- Recommends path and goals for improvements on reporting
- Provides a starting position for beginners and recognition for advanced reporting organizations[10]

Indicator Protocols—Triple Bottom Line

The next section will be a brief overview of the core indicators to report and additional suggested indicators, which organizations can also include in reports to receive a higher application level. The guidelines focus on the three realms of TBL that are abbreviated by the GRI indicator:

1. Economic (EC);
2. Environment (EN); and
3. Social (LA, HR, SO, PR).

1. Economic (EC)

Economic performance is usually reported on financial statements. However, these documents typically fail to represent the organization's economic contributions toward sustainability management. A GRI report can be published in conjunction with, or separate from, the organization's financial documents.[11] Economic aspects concentrate on reporting the following economic indicators; this is not an all-encompassing list:

a. *Economic Performance*
   Economic wealth created by an organization. The ability to create wealth reflects the health of an organization and its ability to invest in sustainable development such as employee benefit plans and/or financial assistance received from different governments. Financial impacts from global warming that have been identified should also be reported.

b. *Market Presence*
   Market presence reflects an organization's position in the market and local communities. Key data to report in this section should reflect the organization's position within plus any economic contribution to local communities. An organization should also report a comparison of its entry-level wage compared to local minimum wages and policies for hiring and promoting locals into senior management positions.

c. *Indirect Economic Impacts*
   Indirect impacts are other ways an organization contributes economically to society. This can be done through investments in infrastructure.

2. Environment (EN)[12]

Environmental indicators focus on inputs, outputs, and impacts of an organization. Environmental impacts of an organization are important to measure and understand. The following is not an all-encompassing list.

a. *Materials*
   Material consumption is a direct indicator of an organization's effort toward sustainability. Conservation of materials also affects the bottom line of an organization. An organization should disclose its use of raw materials, process materials, semi-manufactured parts, and packaging material. In addition the report should indicate what percent of the materials come from non-renewable, renewable, and recycled sources.

b. *Energy*

An organization needs to disclose direct and indirect energy consumption by source. Initiatives to conserve energy consumption and provide energy efficient products and services including reductions achieved should also be included

c. *Water*

The report should include water use by source, any source affected by withdrawal, and volume of water recycled and reused.

d. *Biodiversity*

Biodiversity is a measure of life in a certain area. The reporting organization should include the location of any operation in or near areas of high biodiversity and the impacts its activities have on these areas. Additionally, actions taken by the organization to protect habitats and reduce impacts on biodiversity should be reported.

e. *Emissions, Effluents, and Waste*

The largest source of negative environmental impact comes from emissions, effluents, and waste. The report should include total direct and indirect greenhouse gases, ozone, and other types of gas emissions along with reductions achieved. (Direct emissions include emissions from manufacturing, fleets, reimbursed travel, livestock, which are all sources in the direct control of the owner. Indirect emissions are due to usage of purchasing a product or from electricity generation.) Effluents, a discharge of waste, either of liquid, solid, or gas, should be recorded by type, total discharge, quality, and destination. Waste disposal should be recorded by type and disposal method. Any hazardous waste should be recorded separately by the organization.

f. *Products and Services*

The organization needs to report any initiatives to reduce any environmental impacts of its products or services. End-of-life statistics should also be recorded, including the percent of product packaging reclaimed by the organization.

g. *Compliance*

Any fines an organization has received for non-compliance of environmental laws and regulations should be recorded.

h. *Transport*

Impacts from transporting products and goods should be reported for emissions.

i. *Overall*

To summarize the overall environmental efforts, it is important to report expenses and investments in detail.

3. Social (LA, HR, SO, PR)

Social impacts are the third leg of TBL reporting. The following indicators are an overview of GRI and are not a complete list.

a. Labor Practices and Decent Work (LA)[13]

Fair and decent work is an important aspect of both social and economic development. The goal of fair labor practices is social equity or fairness. Communication between an organization and employees is also important.[14] Labor practices and decent work consists of the following:

Employment

Employment numbers are a direct indication of an organization's impact on society and local communities. Statistics that should be included in the report include total workforce, turnover, full-time benefits, parental leave, and retention rates. Age group, gender, and location should also be categorized.

Labor/Management Relations

Report the number of employees covered by collective bargaining agreements. An organization should also report on the minimum notice period for significant operational changes, whether specified in a bargaining agreement or not.

Occupational Health and Safety

The health and safety of employees is a top priority for any organization. This section should include statistics on employee injury, death, absenteeism, missed days, and diseases. Education, training, formal agreements, and committees on safety should also be included.

Training and Education

Providing training and education to employees provides direct benefits to the organization, employees, and society. This should be recorded through hours of training per year, skill management, lifelong learning, and performance reviews. Information on training should be broken down by gender.

Diversity and Equal Opportunity

Diversity is a reflection of an organization's human capital. Information on diversity should include a breakdown of employees by gender, age group, minority, and other relevant categories.

Equal Remuneration for Women and Men

An organization should treat men and women equally. This section should disclose a comparison of wages and benefits that are received by men and women in the organization.

b. Human Rights (HR)[15]

Stakeholders expect organizations to practice responsibility and protection of human rights. An organization needs to disclose the impact it has on human rights, to include both positive and negative impacts. This section goes beyond the organization's impact on its employees and focuses more on society as a whole. The topic of human rights is made up of the following:

- *Investment and Procurement Practices*
  One way an organization can ensure the protection of human rights is by integrating it into investment and procurement practices. Information on this subject should include business partners who have undergone human rights screening and employees trained on the subject.

  Reports should include the following human rights indicators:

  - Areas of risk where violations may occur
  - Incidents and their results
  - Actions taken to eliminate violations in society

  The report should also include details on:

  - Non-discrimination
  - Freedom of Association and Collective Bargaining
  - Child Labor
  - Forced and Compulsory Labor

- *Security Practices*
  In areas of high risk for human rights violation, security can be a major concern. It is important that an organization's hired security is aware of its human rights policies. The number of security personnel hired and trained needs to be reported.

- *Indigenous Rights*
  No organization should violate the rights of indigenous people. The reporting organization should report on any incidents and the outcomes.

- *Assessment*
  To protect human rights all operations of an organization need to be assessed. An organization should include the number of countries it operates in and the percent of those operations that have gone through human rights assessments.

- *Remediation*
  Formal mechanisms can help to resolve human rights violations that arise. The report should include what mechanisms were used and the number of grievances reported and resolved in the reporting period.

c. Society (SO)[16]

This section addresses the social interactions both within the market as well as with other institutions:

- *Local Communities*
  Interactions with local communities are an important aspect of an organization's sustainable development. An organization should list all community involvement, engagement and development plans, and programs it employs. Special attention should be paid to operations with the possibility for negative impacts on a community and the steps taken to reduce or eliminate this impact.

- *Corruption*
  Corruption can have a large negative impact on an organization and its image. The organization's operations that have been given corruption assessments and employees trained in anti-corruption practices should be reported. Additionally, the report should include any incidents of corruption and how they were resolved.

- *Public Policy*
  Organizations can influence communities through public and political involvement. This section of the report should identify what issues of public policy an organization is involved with and any positions or lobbies the organization is part of.

- *Anti-Competitive Behavior*
  Anti-competitiveness, anti-trust, and monopolist practices go against the best interests of society and economy. An organization should report if there were any incidents relating to this subject and the outcome.

- *Compliance*
  Non-compliance with laws and regulations can be costly for an organization. Any fines related to non-compliance should be recorded including monetary and non-monetary sanctions.

d. Product Responsibility (PR)[17]

Products and services have a large impact on all aspects of the triple bottom line. On the social side, an organization must ensure its products and services do not harm customers, users, or society. An organization should also provide customers with adequate information about its products and services. Product responsibility consists of several criteria:

- *Customer Health and Safety*
  Protecting consumers is a duty every organization owes to society. An organization should identify and report measures taken to improve the safety of its products and services across different stages of its life cycle. Incidents of non-compliance with product or service laws and regulations should also be mentioned.

- *Product and Service Labeling*
  Consumers should be able to make informed decisions about a product or service before buying and using them. Proper labeling can enable consumers to do just that. The report should include the required labeling of products and services, issues of non-compliance and customer service practices[18] (IPS Product Responsibility, 2011).

- *Marketing Communications*
  Along with clear and transparent labeling, an organization's marketing communications should be responsible. All marketing and advertising should ensure compliance with laws and regulations.

- *Customer Privacy*
  Customer privacy is a very important topic, especially due to Internet technology. Protecting customer information and privacy is a risk and should be a top priority of an organization. An organization needs to report any cases of complaints about infringement of customer privacy and leaks of customer information.

- *Compliance*
  Any additional monetary fines relating to non-compliance with laws and regulations of products and services should be recorded in this section.

8.6 Summary

Communication is a necessity for change management. Communicating internally and externally will ensure that sustainability is not just a senior management imperative or a fad; it will build the desired workplace culture. You will gain the respect of external stakeholders by sharing your progress and reporting challenges. Transparency is more important than ever as greenwashing and scare tactics have created skeptics. Be honest, be accurate, and also be realistic with the details that you share. Then you will continue to attract the best employees, retain a faithful consumer market, improve brand image that enhances profitability, engage with suppliers that share similar values, and create a closed loop system of partners who are innovating solutions.

8.7 Experiential Exercises

I. Sustainability Reports

Organizations that already formally report sustainability are well on their journey to sustainability management.

A. Research the Dow Jones Sustainability Index. Review the sustainability reports of your competitors or favorite companies.
B. What details will enhance your own reporting?

For organizations that are interested in preparing a sustainability report, ask yourself the following questions to prepare the planning process:

A. What methodology works best for reporting your initiatives?
B. Do you have the human resources to complete a detailed report?
C. How long must you collect data before you can report?
D. How will you deliver reports to investors or other stakeholders?

II. Communication

Internal

Celebrating wins will continuously motivate the workforce. Sending updates, successes, challenges will contribute to systemic change. What technology uses can improve suggestions, sharing ideas, collaborating, and brainstorming for employees?

External

Financial statements and sustainability reports are one-way communication tools. How can you engage customers, suppliers, investors, and bankers in two-way communication? Social media, blogging, and website comments can achieve great results in understanding what the customer wants and needs. Most importantly, making sustainability fun and engaging for stakeholders is very effective. What are some of the ways your organization can elicit feedback and respond to stakeholders in an interactive way?

SAMPLE QUESTIONS

1. Which one of the following is not one of the methods used for sustainability reporting?

   A. Informal external reporting
   B. Formal external reporting
   C. Informal internal reporting
   D. Formal internal reporting

2. Which of the following is not a "general metric" used by William Blackburn's reporting methodology?

   A. Compliance
   B. Audits
   C. Liabilities
   D. Human rights

3. William Blackburn's unit of performance for "liabilities" is to report resolved lawsuits.

   A. True
   B. False

4. Change management is easy and quick in most cases.

   A. True
   B. False

5. How should managers ensure they do not overwhelm employees with too many new sustainability initiatives?

   A. Training
   B. Establish incremental target goals
   C. Create policies
   D. Empowerment

6. Which of the following isn't a suggested tool for internal communication?

   A. Newsletters
   B. Social media
   C. Announcements
   D. Managerial progress reports

7. The phrase "low-hanging fruit" means what?

   A. Target goals
   B. Medium range goals
   C. Easily attainable goals
   D. Short term goals

8. The purpose of issuing a formal sustainability report is to comply with regulations.

   A. True
   B. False

9. The Global Reporting Initiative is a globally accepted sustainability reporting guideline.

   A. True
   B. False

10. Any fines received for non-compliance should be reported under Environmental indicators.

    A. True
    B. False

ENDNOTES

[1] Blackburn, W. (2007). *The sustainability handbook: The complete management guide to achieving social, economic, and environmental responsibility.* Washington D.C.: Environmental Law Institute.

[2] Epstein, M. (2008). *Making sustainability work: Best practices in managing and measuring corporate social, environmental, and economic impacts.* Sheffield, UK: Greenleaf Publishing Limited.

[3] Hill, K. (2007). *Sustainability Reporting 10 Years On.* Global Reporting Initiative. Retrieved June 14, 2011 from: http://www.globalreporting.org/NR/rdonlyres/430EBB4E-9AAD-4CA1-9478-FBE7862F5C23/0/Sustainability_Reporting_10years.pdf

[4] *The G3 Guidelines.* n.d. Global Reporting Initiative. Retrieved on June 14, 2011 from: http://www.globalreporting.org/ReportingFramework/G3Guidelines/

[5] *The G3 Guidelines.* n.d. Global Reporting Initiative. Retrieved on June 14, 2011 from: http://www.globalreporting.org/ReportingFramework/G3Guidelines/

[6] *Technical Protocol Applying the Report Content Principles.* (2011). Global Reporting Initiative. Retrieved on June 2, 2011 from: http://www.globalreporting.org/NR/rdonlyres/53984807-9E9B-4B9F-B5E8-77667F35CC83/0/G31GuidelinesinclTechnicalProtocolFinal.pdf. (pp. 179–195).

[7] *Sustainability Reporting Guidelines.* (2011). Global Reporting Initiative. Retrieved on June 2, 2011 from: http://www.globalreporting.org/NR/rdonlyres/53984807-9E9B-4B9F-B5E8-77667F35CC83/0/G31GuidelinesinclTechnicalProtocolFinal.pdf. (pp. 1–51).

[8] *Sustainability Reporting Guidelines.* (2011). Global Reporting Initiative. Retrieved on June 2, 2011 from: http://www.globalreporting.org/NR/rdonlyres/53984807-9E9B-4B9F-B5E8-77667F35CC83/0/G31GuidelinesinclTechnicalProtocolFinal.pdf. (pp. 1–51).

[9] *GRI Application Levels.* (2011). Global Reporting Initiative. Retrieved on June 2, 2011 from: http://www.globalreporting.org/NR/rdonlyres/53984807-9E9B-4B9F-B5E8-77667F35CC83/0/G31GuidelinesinclTechnicalProtocolFinal.pdf. (pp. 52–56).

[10] *GRI Application Levels.* (2011). Global Reporting Initiative. Retrieved on June 2, 2011 from: http://www.globalreporting.org/NR/rdonlyres/53984807-9E9B-4B9F-B5E8-77667F35CC83/0/G31GuidelinesinclTechnicalProtocolFinal.pdf. (pp. 52–56).

[11] *Indicator Protocols Set Economic (EC).* (2011). Global Reporting Initiative. Retrieved on June 2, 2011 from: http://www.globalreporting.org/NR/rdonlyres/53984807-9E9B-4B9F-B5E8-77667F35CC83/0/G31GuidelinesinclTechnicalProtocolFinal.pdf. (pp. 57–71).

[12] *Indicator Protocols Set Environment (EN).* (2011). Global Reporting Initiative. Retrieved on June 2, 2011 from: http://www.globalreporting.org/NR/rdonlyres/53984807-9E9B-4B9F-B5E8-77667F35CC83/0/G31GuidelinesinclTechnicalProtocolFinal.pdf. (pp. 72–111).

[13] *Indicator Protocols Set Labor Practices and Decent Work (LA).* (2011). Global Reporting Initiative. Retrieved on June 2, 2011 from: http://www.globalreporting.org/NR/rdonlyres/53984807-9E9B-4B9F-B5E8-77667F35CC83/0/G31GuidelinesinclTechnicalProtocolFinal.pdf. (pp. 112–134).

[14] *Indicator Protocols Set Labor Practices and Decent Work (LA).* (2011), March. Global Reporting Initiative. Retrieved on June 2, 2011 from: http://www.globalreporting.org/NR/rdonlyres/53984807-9E9B-4B9F-B5E8-77667F35CC83/0/G31GuidelinesinclTechnicalProtocolFinal.pdf. (pp. 112–134).

[15] *Indicator Protocols Set Human Rights (HR).* (2011). Global Reporting Initiative. Retrieved on June 2, 2011 from: http://www.globalreporting.org/NR/rdonlyres/53984807-9E9B-4B9F-B5E8-77667F35CC83/0/G31GuidelinesinclTechnicalProtocolFinal.pdf. (pp. 135–149).

[16] *Indicator Protocols Set Society (SO).* (2011). Global Reporting Initiative. Retrieved on June 2, 2011 from: http://www.globalreporting.org/NR/rdonlyres/53984807-9E9B-4B9F-B5E8-77667F35CC83/0/G31GuidelinesinclTechnicalProtocolFinal.pdf. (pp. 150–165).

[17] *Indicator Protocols Set Product Responsibility (PR).* (2011). Global Reporting Initiative. Retrieved on June 2, 2011 from: http://www.globalreporting.org/NR/rdonlyres/53984807-9E9B-4B9F-B5E8-77667F35CC83/0/G31GuidelinesinclTechnicalProtocolFinal.pdf. (pp. 166–178).

[18] *Indicator Protocols Set Product Responsibility (PR).* 2011, March. Global Reporting Initiative. Retrieved on June 2, 2011 from: http://www.globalreporting.org/NR/rdonlyres/53984807-9E9B-4B9F-B5E8-77667F35CC83/0/G31GuidelinesinclTechnicalProtocolFinal.pdf. (pp. 166–178).

Conclusion

Doing the right thing takes more effort than taking the easy way out. Organizations that manage for sustainability are evolving the field of management to meet the needs of the future. Pioneers have proven that you can be profitable because of social responsibility, economic responsibility, and environmental stewardship.

Why should sustainability become a strategic imperative? Social trends in stakeholder expectations and the limits of finite resources are driving the need to manage for sustainability. The carrying capacity of the planet is finite. Many resources are being consumed faster than can be replenished. Managing natural resources makes perfect sense, as well as continuing to drive social responsibility. Organizations are responding to growing consumer expectations that retailers should be held accountable and be held responsible for all actions that occur throughout the supply chain. Emerging social trends of high expectations of business will continue to increase pressure to integrate sustainability management into strategy.

To sum up the change management process, sustainability management is a three-tiered approach that focuses on: 1) internal control, 2) supply chain partnerships, and 3) partnerships within the external environment.

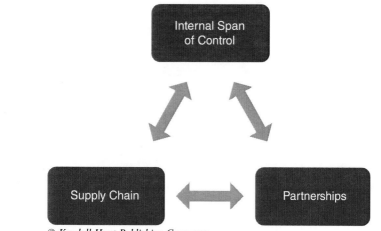

© Kendall Hunt Publishing Company

The journey of sustainability management begins with understanding risks and opportunities, as well as the impacts made on the economy, society, and the environment. Organizational values and ethics are important to identify before the journey can begin.

The journey of sustainability management will take time and change management tactics must be a daily focus. Follow the pathway below to continuously improve efforts to holistically manage for the environment, society, and economy:

1. Develop and communicate a clear strategic vision.
2. Collaborate with suppliers to create a supply chain strategy and code of conduct.

3. Identify partners to collaborate on finding solutions who may be competitors, experts, government, NGOs, and business professionals, etc. Remember no one can solve these large issues alone.
4. Evaluate life cycle analysis to identify the organization's largest risks.
5. Evaluate the system dynamics of sources (materials) and sinks (waste and byproducts) of internal consumption of energy, water, waste, pollution, and solid waste.
6. Utilize systems thinking to identify the largest negative impacts to reimagine and redesign the system.
7. Provide the organization with the case for engaging sustainability management—show the value of taking action on the bottom line of profitability or whatever matters most to the organization.
8. Obtain senior management level commitment to viable and feasible plans and proposals.
9. Create a strategic Sustainability Management System policy and if necessary, create subset policies for Environmental Management Systems and Environmentally Preferable Purchasing.
10. Form cross-functional teams to understand how resources are used today.
11. Cross-functional teams evaluate how to achieve internal efficiencies and develop tactical plans with clear targets of short-, medium-, and long-term goals.
12. Identify technology needs to manage the change.
13. Train employees on how to implement, measure, track, and celebrate success. Train front-line staff on why it is important for each individual to manage for sustainability. Making the case for a personal investment inspires motivation and dedication. Each employee is making a direct impact by making a difference. Knowledge will empower.
14. Motivate the workforce and have a plan to communicate and celebrate achievements.
15. Compile data and metrics for internal and external reporting to communicate efforts.
16. Prepare and deliver reports in a method that is effective.
17. Continue to move forward in reaching or exceeding target goals.

Sustainability management is the natural evolution of continuously improving the management discipline. The evolution of modern management theories asks organizations to go beyond compliance, integrate quality management, practice ethics and values, and be socially responsible. Today, mastering environmental impacts is the next stage in the evolution of management. Each organization and each professional positively and negatively impacts the natural environment in a profound way. Throughout the journey of sustainability management, know that each person makes a positive difference in many compelling ways.

© *Kendall Hunt Publishing Company*

Responsibility and stewardship is a choice. Every person reading this book is making a profound journey to learn, listen, and lead.